SUPERBIKES

STREET RACERS: DESIGN AND TECHNOLOGY

ALAN DOWDS

THUNDER BAY
P·R·E·S·S

San Diego, California

Thunder Bay Press
An imprint of the Advantage Publishers Group
5880 Oberlin Drive, San Diego, CA 92121-4794
www.thunderbaybooks.com

ISBN-13: 978-1-59223-777-7
ISBN-10: 1-59223-777-0

Library of Congress Cataloging-in-Publication Data

Dowds, Alan.
  Superbikes : street racers : design and technology / Alan Dowds.
      p. cm.
  Includes bibliographical references and index.
  ISBN 978-1-59223-777-7 (alk. paper)
  1. Motorcycles, Racing. I. Title.
  TL442.D69 2007
  629.227'1--dc22
                                    2007004498

Editorial and design by
Amber Books Ltd
Bradley's Close
74–77 White Lion Street
London N1 9PF
United Kingdom
www.amberbooks.co.uk

Printed in Singapore

1 2 3 4 5 11 10 09 08 07

Contents

Superbikes: History and Development

The world of motorcycling must seem strange to those used to cars. Whereas the majority of four-wheeled vehicles are designed and built for practicality, with a small majority aimed at the performance market, the two-wheeled world is almost the exact opposite. The most popular designs from all the large manufacturers are purely sporting, performance machines. Sports bikes – or superbikes – are utterly central to biking in a way that the esoteric breed of supercars could never be to the car world. Indeed, in pure performance terms – acceleration, top speeds, braking and circuit performance – most modern motorbikes operate at a level far above all but the most extreme motor cars.

The 999 was the first Ducati to adopt advanced digital electronics from the automotive world. Together with its punchy V-twin motor and race-developed chassis, it made a formidable package.

The modern superbike world is dominated by the four large Japanese manufacturers. Honda, Kawasaki, Suzuki and Yamaha produce the vast majority of all motorbikes built and sold today, from the tiny 50cc (3 cu in) commuters that drive the developing world, to the fire-breathing MotoGP machines which compete for the road racing world championship. But there are several important niche players in the market too. European motorcycle production is led by Italy – Ducati and Aprilia (owned by scooter giant Piaggio) are the largest, with MV Agusta, Cagiva, Moto Guzzi, Benelli, Moto Morini and Bimota also flying the Italian *tricolore* to greater or lesser degrees. Germany has BMW, Sachs and MZ, Austria has KTM, and Britain has Triumph. The U.S. has one large scale player – Harley-Davidson, with its Buell sportsbike arm – and countries like China and India have large domestic motorcycle industries producing small utilitarian machines for home consumption.

Post-war Bikes

At the end of World War II, the situation was very different. The Japanese, Italian, and German motorcycle industries were as ravaged as the rest of those countries' economies. Britain was the acknowledged champion of motorcycle building, with several large firms producing machines. Companies like BSA, Triumph and Norton powered their way out of the fifties, when few people could afford motor cars, and a sidecar-equipped motorcycle was luxury family travel.

But as post-war austerity diminished in the 1960s, the British industry was caught out by a lack of innovation and investment. The increased availability of cheap family cars attacked the utilitarian market. Suddenly, bikes from Japan – formerly little more than a joke – were catching up in terms of performance, technology and even race wins in world championships.

So by the time Honda revealed its landmark 1969 CB750, the writing was on the wall for the UK bike industry. Its death throes lasted another decade or so, by which time the Japanese had a stranglehold on motorcycle design and production which they've kept ever since.

The CB750 offered performance and reliability British manufacturers could only dream of. Its four-cylinder engine was light years ahead of the typical British twin, the chassis boasted advanced innovations like disc brakes, and its styling was similarly awe-inspiring. It was the shape of things to come.

Building Foundations

Japanese bike design spent most of the 1970s trying to establish its foundations. Designers and engineers tried all sorts of engine and chassis innovations and layouts, from large capacity two-strokes, Wankel rotary engines and turbocharged four-strokes through drum brakes, inboard disc brakes, anti-dive brakes and

Triumph's 675 Daytona Triple took on the dominant Japanese inline-fours in the 600cc (36 cu in) class, and won. Its 675cc (41 cu in) engine, light weight and sophisticated design made it an instant classic.

various frame and suspension systems. But by the end of that decade, a discernible design trend began to emerge. Air-cooled four cylinder engines, mounted across a welded steel tube frame, with telescopic front forks, disc brakes and swingarm rear suspension defined the so-called 'Universal Japanese Motorcycle', or UJM. This design – typified in Honda's CB range, Suzuki's GS models and Kawasaki's Z bikes – combined good levels of engine power with decent handling. Those engines generally had two valves per cylinder, with double overhead camshafts, driven by chains, and a bank of four carburettors. A wet multiplate clutch drove a five-or six-speed sequential gearbox, while final drive to the rear wheel was by chain, or shaft in touring models. Power outputs approached 37kW (50bhp) for a 550cc (33.5 cu in) design like the Kawasaki Z550, or 67kW (90bhp) for a 1,000cc (61 cu in) design like the Suzuki GS1000.

However, even these modest (by modern standards) power outputs were at the edges of what these bike's chassis could handle. The standard chassis design consisted of a 'double cradle'-type steel tube frame, a double-sided steel tube swingarm with a shock

absorber each side, and a pair of telescopic forks at the front. When ridden hard, these heavy, flexible layouts and basic suspension damping systems tended to wallow in fast corners and weave at high-speed. Aluminium cast wheels carried crossply tyres and solid disc brakes, neither of which worked well in the wet.

It wasn't until the 1980s that chassis design began to catch up. Early innovations like aluminium swingarms made frames lighter and stiffer, both essential factors for good handling. Advances in disc brake materials – both pads and discs – improved wet weather performance, while rear suspension systems adopted single-shock layouts, with rising-rate mechanisms to allow better wheel control. These interim models, epitomized by Kawasaki's early GPz range, formed a bridge between the 1970s dinosaurs and the early modern superbikes.

For fans of exotic, designer motorcycling, machines like the limited edition MV Agusta F4 1000 Senna cleverly combine art and engineering into gorgeous, potent two-wheeled missiles.

The Modern Superbike

Kawasaki's 1984 GPZ900R is generally accepted as the first modern superbike. Perhaps its biggest leap forward was in its engine, which moved to both a 16-valve cylinder head, and water cooling. Neither of these were new technologies: Suzuki's GS range had used 16-valve air-cooled engines, while Yamaha's two-stroke RD range had used liquid cooling for some time. But put together, these changes allowed the inline-four cylinder engine to rev higher, producing a true 74.5kW (100bhp), enough for a genuine 240km/h (150mph).

The rest of the bike was as innovative. The frame was still a steel tube affair, but it used the engine as a 'stressed member' to add stiffness. The rear swingarm was a stiff aluminium design, operating a single monoshock via Kawasaki's 'Uni-Trak' rising-rate system of linkages. Twin front brake discs carried single-piston sliding calipers, and also incorporated an anti-dive system to prevent excessive fork movement under braking. Finally, an aerodynamic full plastic fairing helped protect the rider from the elements, while allowing the GPZ to achieve sustained high speeds. The GPZ900R's excellence was proven in the legendarily tough Isle of Man TT races in 1984, where the bike took the top two places in the production race. That year also saw the launch of Suzuki's GSX-R range, a range of 'race replica' bikes using aluminium frames and oil-cooled engines to achieve light weight and high power outputs.

The Handling Gap

Throughout the 1980s, power outputs increased from all the Japanese manufacturer's engines, But their chassis technology wasn't advancing as quickly. Switching to aluminium frames started to cut weight while adding much-needed stiffness to the chassis, and suspension units became more sophisticated, incorporating adjustable damping to suit different riding styles. Brakes were more powerful, using multi-piston calipers on larger and larger discs, while tyre design also took a great leap forward with the first radial Michelin design appearing in the late 1980s. Radials run much cooler than crossply or bias-belt designs, and this allows the use of softer compounds with longer life, giving much improved grip.

But it was all taking time, and late 1980s Japanese superbikes like Kawasaki's ZX-10, Honda's CBR1000F or Suzuki's GSX-R1100 still had more power than their chassis could handle. The best of them – Yamaha's FZR1000 – was an excellent machine, with decent handling, but those competing models were overweight, saggy and vague when their considerable engine power was fully utilized.

The discrepancy between the massive horsepower outputs of Japanese engines and the mediocre handling of Japanese chassis created a significant niche market in chassis upgrades. This came in two forms – small aftermarket firms like Harris and Spondon in the UK built bespoke frame kits that accepted Japanese engines, and uprated running gear. Frame kits like the Harris Magnum range used large-bore, handbuilt aluminium tube frames which were a magnitude of stiffness above the standard factory parts. When a Suzuki GSX-R1100 engine was fitted into a Magnum frame, and high-performance suspension, wheels and brakes fitted, the result was astounding.

The second way to rectify wayward Japanese handling was provided by Italian firm Bimota. This small Rimini-based factory sourced engines from Suzuki, Kawasaki, Yamaha and Honda through the 1970s and 1980s, and installed them in its own incredibly high-specification bikes. Bimota pioneered various types of aluminium beam frames, the use of carbon-fibre composites and other exotic materials, as well as radical suspension and brake designs. The

Yamaha's FJR1300 married up engineering from the firm's 'R' range of superbikes to a long-distance, touring brief. The result was a superfast, comfortable distance machine with real performance.

resulting bikes were as beautiful as they were expensive, and were frequently described as automotive art.

The mainstream Italian motorcycle industry wasn't having such a good time. Famous names like Moto Morini, Benelli and MV Agusta faltered and disappeared, unable to compete with Japanese engineering, while dinosaurs like Moto Guzzi lurched from one financial crisis to another, suffering from a terminal lack of investment and a legacy of uncompetitive, 50s-era technology.

Ducati, led by charismatic Italian industrialist Claudio Castiglioni, fared better. The Bolognan firm became part of Castiglioni's Cagiva group in 1983, and by the late 1980s was producing high-performance race-ready motorcycles. Thanks to the genius of engineers Fabio Taglioni and Massimo Bordi, the firm developed four-valve-per-cylinder water-cooled V-twin engines of superlative performance, installed in fine-handling steel tube trellis frames. Using Ducati's now-trademark 'desmodromic' valve actuation (where a camshaft positively closes as well as opens the valves), the first design was a 748cc (45 cu in) capacity, quickly developing into the 851cc (512 cu in) Superbike of 1986. Legendary racer Marco Lucchinelli showed its capability in Superbike racing – a class that Ducati would virtually dominate over the next two decades.

Future Shock

Then in 1992, Honda shocked the world again. Unveiled at that year's trade shows was a bike utterly unlike anything seen before. It looked like an exotic 400cc (24 cu in) Japanese-only racing machine, or perhaps a clay concept model of some unthinkable future shock version of a motorcycle. Even the name seemed unreal – FireBlade.

And even as Honda press flunkies confirmed that, yes, this was a production model, and yes, these numbers written on the display plinth were real, the biking world stood pinching itself. Here was a 900cc (55 cu in) machine that weighed just one kilo more than Honda's own CBR600F middleweight sportsbike. Propelled by a claimed 190kW (118bhp) from an impossibly compact 16-valve, water-cooled four-cylinder engine, it was held together by a chassis of previously unheard-of levels of stiffness and lightness. Journalists were told about its cartridge front forks,

Austrian firm KTM built upon its offroad competition roots with a range of road machines that began to appear in the late 1990s, headed by the naked Super Duke machine shown here.

Aprilia had long played second fiddle to Ducati in the Italian bike industry, but this began to change in the early 21st century, thanks to the success of bikes like the RSV Mille, as well as a takeover by Piaggio.

drilled front brake discs, and top-fairing holes to improve turning speed in a daze that only disappeared at the world riding launch in Australia.

And it was in Australia, at the Philip Island GP circuit, that the truth finally sunk in. Honda's claims weren't the product of wildly ambitious PR spin, or artful exaggeration – they were the annunciation of a whole new generation of motorcycle performance. The 'Blade (as it quickly became known) was built around a new concept, which the Japanese firm called 'Total Control'. Rather than continue up a performance cul-de-sac of increasing engine power, with chassis technology trying to keep up, and mass remaining at the quarter-tonne mark, the FireBlade's designer, Tadao Baba, had attempted to make a lighter, more controllable machine. Centralizing what little mass there was, using tried and tested technologies and, most importantly, designing powertrain and chassis as one, rather than as two systems which were bolted together late in the development cycle, resulted in a new performance motorcycle paradigm. The FireBlade was very short, so it had the nimble handling of a smaller machine, allowing it to change direction very quickly, and the 190kW (118bhp) produced by the 893cc inline-four engine gave the light 185kg (408lb) Honda incredible acceleration. Wide radial sports tyres and race-spec brakes gave superbike-level grip and stopping power, and that sharp race fairing added style as well as aerodynamic prowess at high speeds.

First launched in 1999, Suzuki's Hayabusa redefined open-class superbikes, becoming an instant classic. Its package of massive power in a usable chassis appealed to a wide range of riders.

Over the next five years, Baba and his magnum opus ruled the open class superbike class, virtually unchallenged. It seemed like no other manufacturer had even guessed at this new direction of lighter, smaller, more extreme sportsbikes. Kawasaki launched a ZX-9R in 1994 which had massive horsepower, but weighed 30kg (66lb) too much. Suzuki's GSX-R1100 had reached its nadir in 1989, with the ill-handling K model, but by the mid-1990s it was a real anachronism, getting heavier and more dated with every model update.

Yamaha's FZR1000 EXUP was the nearest the FireBlade had to a close competitor, and when the firm announced a replacement model in 1995, hopes were high that the FireBlade would finally have a fight on its hands. The Thunderace – as it was called – certainly had the dramatic name to take on the FireBlade, and it had the power too, with a claimed 108kW (145bhp). However, it still carried a 15kg (33lb) weight penalty, and despite its modern design and aerodynamic bodywork, it remained a distant second behind the Honda.

Yamaha was determined though, and by 1997, it was a smug set of PR men standing on its stand at the EICMA show in Milan. The small shape outlined under the tuning-fork-logoed satin sheet could have been a new 600cc (36 cu in) sportster – hell, it could have been a new 400cc (24 cu in) bike. In fact, it was a full-bore 1,000cc (61 cu in) sports machine, dubbed the R1. Like the FireBlade half a decade before, the R1 was the bike of the year, the name on every biker's lips. Again, light weight seemed to be the key to the

design. That's pretty logical, since the lighter you can make something, the easier it is to make it go, stop and change direction really fast. But a closer look revealed a host of detail design philosophies aimed at improving the control the rider had over the bike. A new 'stacked' engine/gearbox design arranged the crankshaft and the two gearbox input/output shafts into a triangular layout when viewed from the side. Sitting the clutch and input shaft higher up, behind the cylinders, moved the gearbox output shaft with the final drive sprocket further forward, closer to the crank. This made the engine more compact, while moving weight forward, and also allowing a longer swinging arm, all of which improved stability and weight distribution.

Into the first years of the 21st century, Suzuki's GSX-R1000 (2001) and Kawasaki's ZX-10R (2004) appeared, cranking up the power and control levels of the class. The resulting quartet of Japanese flagship sportsters were incredibly close in terms of performance by 2006 – and what performance! Suzuki's 2005 GSX-R1000 produces nearly 134kW (180bhp), while weighing less than 166kg (366lb) dry, and has fully-adjustable front and rear suspension, incredibly strong brakes and extremely grippy sports tyres. This road bike has performance that would embarrass many top-class racing superbikes of just a few years before.

Continuous Improvement

The various sportsbike alternatives have followed a similar pattern of improvement. The middleweight class – mostly made up of 600cc (36 cu in) inline-fours –is an incredibly important market in most countries, and development here has aped the litre-class, with more power, less mass and higher specification suspension, braking and control systems. By 2006, Yamaha's YZF-R6 topped the pile, with computer-controlled 'fly-by-wire' throttle, high/low speed compression damping adjustment, and a stratospheric claimed 17,500rpm redline on its super-short-stroke 89kW (120bhp) engine. A long way from the first 600cc (36 cu in) sportsbike, Kawasaki's GPZ600R of 1985 with its 56kW (75bhp) and 200kg (440lb).

Outside Japan, pure sports machines from Italy, Germany and even the UK continue to snap at the heels of the big four. Generally offering a slightly different riding experience, bikes like Ducati's 999 range, Aprilia's RSV or the BMW R1200S may not have the outright performance to match the best from Japan, but they offer character, styling and heritage, as well as more character-filled, 'soulful' performance. Indeed, in the case of Triumph's 675 Daytona, the non-Japanese machine soundly beats the opposition in sheer performance terms, as well as in the style and class stakes.

Massive Leaps

It's not just sportsbikes that have benefited from these massive leaps in performance. Touring and sport-touring machines have similarly ratcheted up engine power and chassis sophistication, while improving rider and passenger comfort and luggage capacity. Riders who like to cross continents in search of their motorcycling 'fix' are incredibly well-served, whether they want a high-speed 'hypersports' bike like Kawasaki's ZZR1400 or a slower, yet more comfortable Grand Tourer like Honda's Pan European. And for the truly decadent, the 'megatourer' class defined by BMW's K1200LT and Honda's Gold Wing redefine moto luxury, offering heated seats and grips, stereo systems, satellite navigation and more luggage capacity than some supercars. That's as well as providing genuinely thrilling sporty performance.

And even less grand machines – basic, naked roadsters designed for simple motorcycling pleasure –

have benefited from modern design. Indeed, the fashion for naked models increased greatly in the late 1990s and early 21st century. Riders appreciated the benefits of a naked bike in terms of limited top speed (to avoid increasing police crackdowns on speeding) and more relaxed riding position. Around town, a naked bike made much more sense than a 'heads-down' supersports bike, and with light, powerful bikes like Aprilia's Tuono and BMW's K1200R, there was no sacrificing performance either.

In this book, we have tried to place the most important modern superbikes in context. We outline their history, development and market positioning, and place them (loosely) into six classes: small superbikes up to 400cc (24 cu in), middleweights, naked bikes, Italian exotic sportsbikes, open-class sportsters and tourers.

Where possible, the specifications are those of the latest model at time of writing (late 2006), and we have stuck to manufacturers' claimed figures for weight and power. Top speed figures are (necessarily) an approximation; achieved maximum velocities on motorcycles are incredibly dependent on rider size and skill, as well as weather conditions. The available figures would not give a fair comparison.

Even Harley-Davidson sometimes moves with the time. Its 2001 launch of the V-Rod saw the first water-cooled production Harley V-twin, and the company's first genuine high-performance model.

Mini Superbikes:
small-capacity sportsbikes

The world of the 'mini superbike' is essentially broken down into two or three types. The smallest bike that can really be considered a sporty bike, or superbike, is the 125cc (7.6 cu in) class. A good sports 125 offers lively performance in a super-lightweight package, and is also the capacity limit to which novice riders are restricted in European markets.

The next rung up the capacity ladder is the 250cc (15 cu in) class. This is an historically important class, although it has become less popular since emissions rules have stymied the development of the dirtier two-stroke engines commonly used in the class. Two-stroke engines can produce much more power than a four-stroke design of similar capacity, and are also lighter, since they don't have complex cylinder heads.

There have been high-performance 250cc (15 cu in) four-stroke designs, and they have included some of the smallest bike engines ever built. Bikes like Honda's CBR250RR had four tiny 62cc (3.8 cu in) cylinders, with four miniscule valves per cylinder, and had to rev to incredible speeds to produce sufficient horsepower. The CBR250RR revved to around 19,000rpm. These bikes were mostly restricted to the Japanese home market, where local licensing laws restricted many riders to small-capacity bikes.

Teenage dreams: a top-spec 125cc (7.6 cu in) naked sportsbike like Cagiva's Raptor offers the same fun and thrills as much larger machines. And for many young novice riders, bikes like this are the perfect choice.

Japanese laws also made 400cc (24.5 cu in) bikes very popular in the 1980s and 1990s. For many riders, this was the biggest bike they could ever ride without submitting to difficult testing procedures. So firms produced 400cc (24.5 cu in) versions of their superbikes, often with extremely high-spec chassis and engine components. Unlike the 250s, however, these machine produced sufficient power at reasonable revs, and were popular in coutries where laws didn't resstrict riders to 400cc (24.5 cu in). Bikes like Honda's RVF400 and Kawasaki's ZXR400 were officially imported to the UK, where their 48kW (65bhp) engines, light weight and small size made them popular with women riders and novices.

The Japanese licensing laws changed in the mid-1990s, and hit the 250 and 400 bikes hard. Riders could choose 600cc-(36 cu in)-plus bikes, which offered much more performance, for little extra cash. Larger bikes were also beginning to lose weight and size, and could offer handling to equal the mini superbikes. These factors, together with the death of road-going two-strokes, largely spelt the end of the 125cc-(7.6 cu in)-plus small superbike market in the 21st century.

Aprilia RS125 (+125 Tuono)

The RS125 has a very high-tech dashboard, with a large analogue rev counter, LCD speedometer display, built-in lap timer, fuel reserve indicator and battery voltage display.

Pillion accommodation is pretty minimal, and the small power output of the RS means it's best kept as a solo machine. If a passenger is carried, however, the rear suspension-spring preload can be adjusted to suit.

The rear aluminium swingarm is curved upward to allow space for the large exhaust. This 'expansion chamber' exhaust is essential for good power production from a two-stroke engine.

The fuel tank doesn't need to be very big on such a small, economical machine. So the RS only holds 14l (3 gal.).

The RS125 has a very distinctive aerodynamic fairing design, which resembles Aprilia's 1000cc (61cu in) RSV Mille superbike.

The sleek, minimalist tail unit echoes the aerodynamic design of Aprilia's own 125GP racing machines, which have enjoyed so much success on track.

The 125cc (7.6cu in) class has been important for Aprilia for as long as the Italian firm has been making motorcycles. The first sports 125 was the ST125 of 1982, and the Noale-based company has placed great emphasis on its ⅛l (7.6cu in) road bikes ever since. That basic steel-framed 125 was followed by the AF125 of 1988, a very high-specification 125, with a twin-spar steel frame, full race fairing and a 170km/h (105mph) top speed. The designs of bikes like the Futura and the Europa of 1991 were refined further, with aluminium frames, electric start and new, reed-valve engines.

But it was the RS125, which first appeared in 1992, that really took Aprilia's 125 sportsbike class to new levels. Alessandro Gramigni had won the 125GP world championship on an Aprilia the previous year, and

here was a machine that looked just like the successful Grand Prix racebikes, with similar chassis and engine design. The frame was made from lightweight aluminium and used the same twin-spar design

Aprilia RS125 (+125 Tuono)

Top speed:	169km/h (102mph)
Engine type:	124.8cc (7.6cu in), l/c single cylinder two-stroke
Maximum power:	34bhp (27kW) @10,500 rpm
Frame type:	twin-spar aluminium
Tyre sizes:	front 110/70 17, rear 150/60 17
Final drive:	chain
Gearbox:	six-speed
Weight:	126kg (278lb)

Like any other top-spec sportsbike, the RS125 has upside-down front forks and four-piston brake caliper. The 2006 RS125 used a radial-mount caliper, underlining the serious nature of the little RS.

pioneered on the firm's world championship winning bike of the year before. Suspension was again visually similar to the parts used on racebikes, with upside-down front forks, an asymmetrical rear swingarm and an adjustable rear monoshock suspension unit. The brakes were also very high specification – a 320mm (12.5in) front disk with a four-piston caliper gave great stopping power, especially considering the RS125's light 115kg (254lb) weight.

The RS engine was a compact, lightweight 124.8cc (7.6cu in) design, with a bore and stroke of 54x54.5mm (13.7x13.8in). Its so-called reed valve induction design, which used flexible 'reed' flap valves, prevented the engine's intake charge from being blown back out of the inlet, giving a wider spread of power.

This chassis and engine package was matched to a smart aerodynamic fairing, with a racy riding position, low handlebars and high footrests.

The RS125 received minor updates over the next several years, including a new fairing to match the RS250. It was on an Aprilia that Valentino Rossi won the 1997 125cc (7.6cu in) title (his first championship), and a Rossi replica machine was produced in 1999.

But it wasn't until 2006 that Aprilia gave the RS a full redesign. This time, the firm reshaped the bike to resemble its RSV 1000 superbike, instead of the discontinued RS250, and the new RS certainly looked like a much bigger bike. Its bodywork – with new dual headlights and angular looks – echoed the lines of the RSV, and the chassis components were also upgraded to suit. The upside-down front forks proudly wore a radial-mount four-piston Brembo caliper, and even the wheels had the same multi-spoked cast-aluminium design that was used on the 1000cc bike (61cu in).

The engine remained the same tried-and-tested unit. It is built for Aprilia by the Austrian firm Rotax, and in restricted form, produces 15bhp (12kW), to comply with European laws for those learning to drive. The engine can be de-restricted though, and in full power form makes more than 34bhp (27kW). The full power model has a fully operational 'exhaust valve' in the engine. This uses a movable valve, controlled by an electric motor, to alter the exhaust port shape between a low- and high-speed position. The low speed position gives good torque at low engine speeds, while the high-rpm position allows the engine to produce its top bhp (kW). This valve, along with carburation, exhaust and ignition changes allows the 15bhp (12kW) restricted engine to more than double its power output.

The transmission has six speeds and a wet clutch, with chain final drive to the rear wheel.

The RS125 gave excellent performance for its class. Top speed is more than 160km/h (100mph), and on a track or tight twisty back road, its short 1345mm (53in) wheelbase, grippy sports tyres, strong brakes and excellent ground clearance all make it an incredibly thrilling lightweight machine to ride.

The stripped-down RS is dominated by the massive exhaust pipe and its 'expansion chamber' front section. This and the ram-air intake scoop are essential to produce maximum power.

Aprilia RS250

The RS250 was also available in a GP-replica 'Chesterfield' paint scheme, celebrating Max Biaggi's three 250cc (15cu in) GP championships for Aprilia in 1994, 1995 and 1996.

The RS250, like all two-strokes, uses a total-loss lubrication system, and stores its engine lubrication oil in a small tank under the seat. Fuel capacity is 19.5l (5gal).

Although it looks like there is no pillion accommodation, the RS250 has a removable seat pad, and small pillion foot pegs. As with all small sportsbikes though, carrying a passenger is best avoided.

The twin 'stinger'-type silencers are tucked in and mounted high to improve ground clearance. High-performance carbon or titanium race parts are often fitted to improve power and styling.

Two-stroke engines need an exhaust pipe for each cylinder to work effectively. So the RS250 has two complexly curved expansion-chamber pipes, squeezed in below the 90° V-twin engine.

For Aprilia, 250cc (15cu in) bikes are highly significant: it was the 250GP class that gave the Noale-based firm seven world-championship wins between 1994 and 2003. The rules allow a machine to weigh a minimum of 100kg (220lb) in the 250GP class so, in the modern era, this championship has been contested by two-stroke twin-cylinder engines, in incredibly lightweight chassis packages. Aprilia's RSW250GP racing bike has taken on the finest Japanese race machinery and won, time after time, but producing a road version of this

fire-breathing, highly-tuned disc-valve would prove prohibitively expensive for the small firm.

Instead, Aprilia turned to Japan for a road-going powerplant. Suzuki's RGV250 was widely regarded as the best 250cc (15cu in) road-bike package in the early 1990s, and it was this unit that Aprilia sourced for its

Tiny weight, incredibly radical steering geometry and enormous ground clearance mark the RS250 out as a cornering machine. On a twisty racetrack it can outrun many much more powerful machines.

Tuck in behind the 'bubble' windscreen, keep the tachometer dial reading over 9000rpm and the little RS250 can give you one of the purest, most extreme motorcycling experiences around.

RS250, launched in 1994. Using a 90° V-twin layout, the Suzuki engine was one of the most advanced road two-strokes ever built, with reed-valve induction, electronically controlled 34mm (1.3in) Mikuni carburettors and a three-stage guillotine-type power-valve system. This used sliding aluminium 'blinds' to raise and lower the effective exhaust port height, optimizing power production at various revs. Large expansion-chamber type exhausts were installed, tucked in under the engine, which necessitated a shaped, 'gull-arm' type swingarm to provide cornering clearance. The result of all this technology was a very high power output of 62bhp (46kW).

Aprilia took the Suzuki engine, fitted 'Aprilia'-branded engine covers, and added its own exhaust and intake systems. Aprilia's improved modifications meant the RS250 produced 70bhp (56kW)@10,500rpm, which was even more power than the RGV.

This engine was then fitted to Aprilia's own chassis package. The resemblance to the firm's 250GP racebike was immediately clear, and the little RS combined a very high chassis specification with attractive, modern styling. The chassis design was based around a curvaceous aluminium-beam frame, made from welded sheets and cast-pivot sections, and carries race-specification suspension components. Up front is a pair of 41mm (1.6in) Showa upside-down front forks,

with full damping and preload adjustment, while the rear suspension uses a fully adjustable monoshock unit, operated by a fabricated asymmetric swingarm. This shaped arm, similar to the example on the RGV250, is essential to allow the large-capacity exhaust expansion chambers to be tucked in under the bike and give good ground clearance for cornering. Front brakes are fit for a full-bore 1000cc (61cu in) superbike, with twin 298mm (11.75in) drilled disks and four-piston calipers. Massively powerful, they can take an unwary novice rider by surprise with their astonishing braking. The final part of the chassis package is a pair of lightweight cast-aluminium wheels, shod with grippy radial sports tyres.

The RS is a tiny, tiny machine, with high footrests and low bars. There's no electric starter, because the necessary motor, battery and charging system would add too much weight, so you have to prod the high, light kickstarter to provoke the RS into action.

All small-capacity two-stroke engines have a peaky power delivery, and although the RS250 is one of the best, it still feels very weak low down, especially for riders used to larger machines. The cleverly designed exhaust and intake systems do their best, but the rider really has to keep the engine over about 8000rpm for strong progress. And since peak power is produced just 2500rpm later, there's a very narrow window of useful performance. Constant gear changes are essential to keep the engine in this peak power band. This, combined with the small, sharp-steering chassis makes the RS a poor choice for longer journeys.

It makes an excellent track bike, and once away from public roads, the RS makes perfect sense. The sharp steering, powerful brakes, light handling and razor-edged power delivery all help the RS embarrass much more powerful machinery on a twisty track.

Aprilia RS250

Top speed:	205km/h (128mph)
Engine type:	249cc (15cu in), l/c 90° V-twin two-stroke
Maximum power:	70bhp (56kW)@10,500rpm
Frame type:	twin-spar aluminium
Tyre sizes:	front 110/70 17, rear 150/60 17
Final drive:	chain
Gearbox:	six-speed
Weight:	140kg (224lb)

The Suzuki RGV250, which donated its engine to the RS250, was a pretty bike – but Aprilia's Italian flair took it to a new level: the curvaceous rear swingarm brilliantly combined function and form.

Cagiva Mito

To de-restrict a 15bhp (12kW) Mito, the dealer either modifies the standard exhaust by removing a restricting cone or pipe, or else fits a racing-exhaust pipe. The carburettor jets and airbox also have to be modified.

Most Mitos are sold in restricted form, to comply with government power restrictions for novice riders. Restricted bikes produce 15bhp (12kW), but can be converted to full power by a dealer once the rider has qualified.

Although the Mito looks very like the Ducati 916 at first glance, its single front brake disk, aluminium frame and double-sided rear swingarm are the quickest ways of telling it from the big bike.

Cagiva also produced a 50cc (3.05cu in) version of the Mito. This had a similar design, but with a 49.5cc (3cu in) engine, suitable for (well-heeled) 16-year-olds to ride in the UK.

As well as its trademark red, the Mito was also offered in yellow and race-replica paint schemes, such as the 'Lucky Explorer' and Eddie Lawson GP replicas.

Perhaps the best trick a small-capacity superbike can manage is to convince the casual observer that it is in fact a much larger, faster, more powerful machine. Few small bikes manage this as well as Cagiva's Mito (meaning 'myth' in Italian), which manages to look virtually identical to Ducati's 916, one of the most evocative Italian bikes ever made.

This is no accident. Indeed Ducati and Cagiva were part of the same company when the 916 was being developed. Massimo Tamburini was the designer of the 916, and so his evocative moto vision was also

Cagiva also produced a naked version of the Mito – the Planet, later renamed the Raptor 125, to tie-in more closely with the firm's 650 and 1000cc (39 and 61 cu in) range of naked roadsters.

Cagiva Mito	
Top speed:	160km/h (100mph)
Engine type:	124.6cc (7.6cu in), l/c single cylinder two-stroke
Maximum power:	34bhp (25kW)@10,500rpm
Frame type:	aluminium twin spar
Tyre sizes:	front 110/70 17, rear 150/60 17
Final drive:	chain
Gearbox:	six-speed
Weight:	129kg (285lb)

A racing exhaust could help the Mito produce up to 27kW (37bhp) – an incredible 220kW/litre (5bhp/cu in) specific power output. But this came at the cost of drastically reduced engine life.

unrestricted form. Two-stroke engines can produce so much power because they have a combustion pulse every time the piston reaches the top of its stroke, instead of every second time the piston reaches the top, as on a four-stroke engine. The Cagiva engine used a reed-valve induction system to give a broader spread of power, and an exhaust-power valve further enhanced efficiency.

Early models used a seven-speed gearbox to allow the rider to make the most of the narrow usable rev range of the highly tuned engine. However, later models were able to use a six-speed box.

The chassis is also typical of its class, being built around a stiff, light aluminium frame, with high-quality suspension and braking components from the same suppliers as found on 'proper' open-class superbikes. That means a pair of Marzocchi 40mm (1.5in) upside-down front forks, with a Sachs monoshock at the rear, adjustable for spring preload. A four-piston Brembo caliper bites onto a single 320mm (12.5in) disc at the front, with a small single-piston caliper for the rear brake. Wide, grippy Michelin Pilot Sport tires and light aluminium wheels complete the rolling chassis specification.

The Mito demands the rider's total concentration, because the highly specific power output of the Mito means the engine is on the highly tuned side, so it has a somewhat narrow usable rev range. Outside of this band, the engine makes much less power, and the rider must continually juggle gears to ensure the engine stays in the band. This is thrilling on a race track or a twisty back road, but can be wearing on longer trips, where the Mito's committed riding position also counts against it.

Cagiva used the Mito engine and chassis as the basis for two naked models – the Planet 125 and the Raptor. The Planet had a natty roadster design, with a chromed exhaust and upright riding position. It was a good choice for urban commuting and for fun in town. Cagiva updated the Planet with its Raptor family styling in 2004, with different paint, logos and bodywork parts. Like the Planet, the Raptor 125 made an extremely stylish city bike, although the engine was still somewhat peaky.

Cagiva also produced a track-only variant of the Mito, the SP 525. Homologated for Sports Production race classes, the 525 produced an extra 4bhp (3kW), thanks to revised exhaust and intake systems, and a redesigned crankshaft. The chassis specification was also enhanced, with lighter, stronger, forged-aluminium wheels, more adjustable suspension units and a single-seat race fairing.

transferred onto the smaller canvas of a 125cc (7.6cu in) machine. That vision starts at the front end of the bike with the twin slit headlights, back along the slim yet curvaceous fuel tank and the blood-red flanks of the fairing. The rear end is similar, apart from being unable to boast a pair of booming V-twin silencers under the seat, or a beautiful, if heavy and expensive, single-sided swingarm. Instead, the Mito has a smart gull-arm style swingarm, making room for an efficient expansion chamber-type exhaust to tuck in below the engine.

Under the outer panels, the Mito is a typical 125cc (7.6cu in) race-replica design. A single-cylinder two-stroke engine puts out an impressive 31bhp (23kW) in

Honda CBR125R

Although most CBR riders are novices, and unable to carry a passenger, the CBR still has a neat pillion grab rail, dual seat and pillion pegs.

In the UK, legendary ex-Grands Prix racer Ron Haslam used the CBR125R at his Honda Haslam Race School. Novices and younger riders could begin learning on the 125 before graduating to the CBR600RR and CBR1000RR Fireblade.

The CBR125R replaced Honda's previous race-replica 125, the two-stroke NSR125RR, which was discontinued in 2003.

The CBR125R's front fairing has a similar 'line-beam' headlight design to Honda's CBR1000RR Fireblade. The nosecone itself and the paint scheme also deliberately echo the bigger bike.

Based on the CBR150, the CBR125 engine is simple yet well built. Its water-cooled single-cylinder design is reliable and smooth, but it's down on power compared with some of its two-stroke competitors.

Honda's CBR125R is an unusual entry in the 125cc (7.6cu in) sportsbike class. That's because it uses a rather low-powered, 'tame' four-stroke single-cylinder engine, instead of the screaming, high-powered two-stroke designs offered by firms like Aprilia and Cagiva. Partly this is because Honda has always had a corporate aversion to two-stroke engines, only using that dirtier, less efficient design when forced to, for example, in 500cc (30cu in) GP racing. But the CBR125 design is also a pragmatic one: in most markets where 125cc bikes (7.6cu in) are sold, particularly in Europe, they are used by people learning to drive, who are also subjected to a power restriction. A novice rider in the UK cannot ride a bike with an engine capacity greater than 125cc (7.6cu in) or that produces more than 15bhp (12kW). So a learner on an Aprilia RS125 has to ride a restricted version,

Honda also offered the CBR125 in a 'Repsol' replica paintscheme, allowing young riders to emulate such MotoGP heroes as Nicky Hayden, Dani Pedrosa and Valentino Rossi.

that is artificially 'strangled' so it only makes 15bhp (12kW) – the same as the CBR125. Once the novice is fully qualified, they can have the Aprilia de-restricted to produce its 32bhp (27kW). However, at that point, most riders prefer to move up the capacity scale and ride a larger, more powerful machine.

So Honda's CBR125 merely acknowledges the fact that the vast majority of its riders will only ever use 15bhp (12kW). This isn't necessarily a disadvantage though. Since the CBR's small, efficient four-stroke engine was designed from the start to produce 13bhp (9.6kW), its power curve, carburation and drivetrain are all performing within their ideal parameters. Some machines that were designed to produce 30bhp (24kW), then artificially 'strangled' to 15bhp (12kW), have somewhat poor power delivery as a consequence.

The bike itself is a development of the CBR150, designed for South-East Asian markets, and the CBR125 is made in Thailand like the 150. The engine is a two-valve, single overhead-camshaft liquid-cooled design, with a single carburettor. The transmission has six-gears and a wet clutch, with chain final drive. It's an economical design, and is capable of high mileages with minimal maintenance, which is down to its intended market in less developed countries, where servicing can be infrequent. The liquid cooling allows finer internal tolerances than on a cheaper, air-cooled motor, and also helps reduce noise. This refinement is further enhanced by the electric starter system, and a balancer shaft, which reduces the vibrations inherent in a single cylinder engine.

Like the powertrain, the CBR125 chassis has a pretty high specification for what is a novice machine. The styling deliberately echoes the firm's full-bore sportsbikes, with a full race fairing, dual headlights and upswept exhaust silencer. The steel frame and

Although 'only' a 125, the CBR's dashboard has all the dials and gauges found on many much larger machines, including a fuel gauge and engine temperature gauge.

swingarm resemble the aluminium parts on the CBR600RR and CBR1000RR, the wheels have lightweight cast-aluminium parts with sports tyres, and there are disk brakes front and rear. Suspension is basic, but adequate, consisting of a pair of 31mm (1.2in) front forks, and a single rear shock, all suited to handling the CBR's light dry mass of 115kg (254lb).

Riding the littlest CBR is huge fun, even for an advanced rider used to much more horsepower. Getting the most from the small, gutsy engine is easy, with a smooth, uncomplicated power delivery. The riding position is comfortable, and the dashboard is extremely well appointed, with fuel gauge, tachometer, speedometer and engine-temperature gauge. The gearchange is smooth, and both front and rear brakes offer powerful stopping ability. The suspension is, as you'd expect, a little harsh and basic, but works well for the CBR's performance parameters.

Perhaps the best part of the CBR125R isn't immediately visible on the spec sheet though. Thanks to its Thai-based manufacture, and shared development costs with the CBR150, Honda was able to sell the CBR125R at a very competitive price. It cost just more than £2,300 ($3,800) in the UK when launched, which was £1,700 ($2,800) less than Cagiva's Mito.

Honda CBR125R

Top speed:	121km/h (75mph)
Engine type:	124.7cc (7.6cu in), a/c single, 2-valve, SOHC
Maximum power:	13bhp (9.6kW)@10,000rpm
Frame type:	twin-spar steel
Tyre sizes:	front 80/90 17, rear 90/90 17
Final drive:	chain
Gearbox:	six-speed
Weight:	115kg (253lb)

Honda RVF400 NC35 (+NC30)

The RVF400 and VFR400 are small, compact machines, making them unsuitable for very tall or large riders.

The RVF's trademark design uses this aluminium single-sided rear swingarm, borrowed from endurance racing. It's heavier than a conventional design, but looks superb, and makes wheel changes easier.

The focussed race replica design of the RVF means pillion accommodation is vestigial at best.

The silencer is mounted on the left to give a clear view of the multispoked rear wheel. It's a one-piece design, making after-market silencer replacement difficult. Most replacement race exhausts are full systems.

Honda built a very compact and tough engine for its smallest V-four. The camshafts – four in total – are driven by a series of gears, rather than the usual chain. This is more expensive to produce, but more reliable, accurate and longer lasting.

Of all the Japanese firms, it was probably Honda that put the most effort into its small-capacity superbikes in the late 1980s and into the 1990s. It had no fewer than three ranges of mini sportsbikes, covering the full range of race categories and road-biased sportsbikes. There was the NSR range of 250cc (15cu in) two-stroke designs, which used incredibly exotic V-twin engines, in chassis that were unbelievably close to GP machines, and with bleeding-edge styling and performance. The NSR range included models with dry clutches, 'smart-card' ignition systems, exhaust power valves and all kinds of suspension and braking innovations. Almost as exotic was the CBR range of in-line four-cylinder bikes, which came in 250 and 400cc (15 and 24cu in) capacities. The CBR400RR range offered a more road-biased riding experience, with gorgeous chassis components like 'gull-arm' swingarms and fabricated aluminium frames.

But it was Honda's V-four 400cc (24cu in) bikes that were arguably the most evocative, the strongest performers, and the most successful models.

Honda had moved to V-four engine designs in the early 1980s, with its VF750 and VF1000 models. The first 400 was the VF400 of 1982, and this model developed over the next few years into a half-faired sportsbike, with unusual 'inboard' front brake discs. The VF400s were decent performers, but were replaced by the VFR400 in 1986. The first VFR, the NC21, had much improved performance from a gear-

A simple three-dial layout befits the racing heritage of the VFR and RVF400. The speedometer and warning light panel is easily removed leaving the tacho and temperature gauge required for race use.

Honda RVF400 NC35 (+NC30)

Top speed:	135mph (216kph)
Engine type:	399cc, l/c V-four, 16-valve, DOHC
Maximum power:	66bhp (48kW)@13,000rpm
Frame type:	twin spar aluminium
Tyre sizes:	front 120/60 17, rear 150/60 17
Final drive:	chain
Gearbox:	six-speed
Weight:	165kg (363lb)

driven camshaft engine design, a full fairing, aluminium frame and monoshock rear suspension, with a conventional swingarm and front forks. It produced around 60bhp (45kW), and had twin-piston front brake calipers. The NC21 was replaced by the similar NC24 in 1988, but it was the NC30 of 1989 that really moved the VFR400 on. This little gem of a machine had similar engine performance to the previous models, but an all-new chassis. Designed to ape the bigger, super-exotic 750cc (46cu in) RC30, the NC30 had a single-sided rear swingarm, new four-piston brakes, and a four-into-one exhaust with a silencer mounted on the left side. The fairing was sharper and echoed the firm's endurance racing bikes, with a pair of small round headlights in the nosecone replacing the earlier single square headlight. Engine power was up to 60bhp (45kW), the dry weight was 170kg (375lb), and there was a racing seat unit, with a small passenger pad. Suspension was fully adjustable for circuit set-up, and the neat multi-spoked cast wheels wore sports tyres.

The NC30 was so popular that Honda exported it to the UK from 1989 to 1991. But the high specification and expensive build quality of the bike meant it sold for almost the same price as more powerful 600 and 1000cc (37 and 61cu in) bikes, and most riders chose the bigger bikes.

The final version of the V-four 400, the NC35 RVF400 appeared in 1994, and like the NC30, it looked very similar to its 750cc (46cu in) sibling, the RC45 RVF750. Although it had a similar specification to the NC30, it had been updated in most areas. The engine had different carburettors, and a ram air-intake system, and peak power was up around 5bhp (4kW) to 66bhp (49kW). The chassis had a new frame design, that was fitted with new upside-down front forks, and

a revised rear suspension system. Both front and rear suspension was fully adjustable, and the RVF had a 43cm (17in) rear wheel rather than the 46cm (18in) part on the VFR400.

For their size, both the NC30 and NC35 offered amazing performance. The V-four engine design gave a much stronger, torquier feel, much like a larger bike. The chassis was stiff, compact and agile. The standard suspension was a little soft, but still gave handling typical of bigger, more 'serious' machines.

Like their 750cc (46cu in) siblings, both the VFR and RVF400s enjoyed much race success, both on short tracks and on longer road-based circuits, such as the Isle of Man TT race.

The RVF's compact fuel tank holds just 15 litres (4 gal.), which could be a handicap for the RVF in long-distance endurance races. The older VFR400 had a larger 18-litre (4.75gal.) capacity.

Go on! The rider has had to work hard to achieve this wheelie – the VFR's tall gearing, modest power output and forward weight bias means lifting the front wheel takes lots of effort.

Kawasaki ZXR400

The ZXR400 was one of Kawasaki's most enduring models, staying in production virtually unchanged for nearly 15 years. Over the years it appeared in various colours, including the corporate green/white/blue scheme, metallic blue and a purple/black livery.

Twin headlights, a full race fairing, high-set footpegs and low, clip-on handlebars follow the design of Kawasaki's ZXR-7 endurance racebikes.

Kawasaki fitted a full four-into-one sports exhaust. This design gives the best peak power output, and the 65bhp (48kW) ZXR was always among the most powerful of all the 400cc (24cu in) class.

Like the bigger 750, the ZXR400's suspension is very firm front and rear, and can be uncomfortable on bumpy roads. However, it gives excellent performance on smooth racetracks.

The conventional 399cc (24cu in), 16-valve inline four-cylinder engine has double overhead camshafts, four CV carburettors and liquid cooling. It produces around 65bhp (48kW).

Like all the Japanese firms, Kawasaki wanted to capitalize on the success of the bigger racebikes in its home market. Licensing laws meant very few riders could ride bikes like the firm's exotic ZXR750, so a 400cc (24cu in) version was needed.

Kawasaki had a long line of modern 400cc (24cu in) sportsbikes. There was a 400 version of its GPX range, identical to the GPX600, apart from the engine. This was followed by a much racier bike, the ZX-4 of 1988. This was a very high-spec model for the time, with a twin-spar aluminium frame, aluminium swingarm, and a 59bhp (44kW) inline-four cylinder engine.

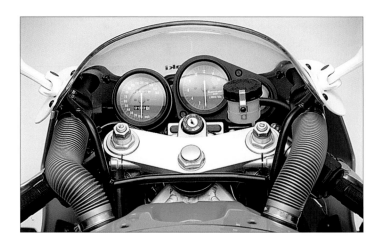

The ZXR's strong engine, good handling and comparatively cheap purchase price made it a firm favourite among 'privateer' racers who are generally self-funded.

The race-styled instruments had a separate speedo which could be removed easily for competition. Note the twin 'Hoover' tubes feeding cooling air to the engine area under the fuel tank.

To improve handling, the ZXR's beefy aluminum frame, with separate rear subframe and aluminum swingarm, has a compact engine mounted well forward.

A race-type full fairing was fitted, and the running gear was also track-ready.

But the next year's ZXR400 was the pinnacle of Kawasaki's 400cc (24cu in) mini superbike range. The first H1 version was released in 1989, and had moved the styling on again from the ZX-4. It now looked just like a small-scale version of the ZX-7 endurance racing bikes, which Kawasaki teams were running world-wide. The front fairing had a pair of small round headlights, just like the racebikes, and above the lights were a pair of air intakes. These led back to a pair of ribbed hoses that disappeared into the fuel tank, just in front of the rider. These ducts were designed to feed cooling air to the top of the cylinder head to help reduce the engine's operating temperatures (even though the engine was liquid-cooled).

The engine itself was developed from the GPX and ZX motors, and was a fairly conventional unit. It had

four cylinders, with twin overhead camshafts, four valves per cylinder, and four carburettors. The transmission was a six-speed unit, and the final drive was by chain. Peak power was up to around 62bhp (46kW) and was produced at around 12,000rpm.

Kawasaki also developed a new chassis for the ZXR. The layout was similar, with an aluminium twin-spar frame, and a fabricated aluminium swingarm with a monoshock, but the front forks were changed to upside-down parts, and the brakes were also upgraded to more powerful four-piston calipers. The one-piece dual seat of the ZX was swapped for a more racy two-piece race seat, and the chassis had a more forward bias, to improve handling.

The first H1 model was replaced by a similar H2 model for 1990. Then, for 1991, an overhauled L1 model was released. This had a similar modernizing update to the ZXR750 range, with sharper bodywork, up-to-date styling and improved performance.

The biggest change to the styling was the move to a single headlight unit from twin lamps, and new graphics and colours. Under the new fairing, minor engine modifications raised the power output again, this time to 65bhp (48kW) at 13,000rpm.

Like all Kawasakis, the little ZXR400 had a very strong motor for its size, with a torquey power delivery. The handling was more stable than many small bikes, thanks to its front-biased chassis. The ZXR was less expensive to purchase, maintain and run, and was also easier to tune than either the comparatively exotic Honda V-four machines, or the Yamaha FZR range.

Kawasaki chose to import the ZXR400 into the UK, where it was available, unchanged, from 1991 to 2004.

Kawasaki ZXR400

Top speed:	224km/h (140mph)
Engine type:	398cc (24cu in), l/c inline-four, 16-valve, DOHC
Maximum power:	65bhp (48kW) @13,000rpm
Frame type:	twin spar aluminium
Tyre sizes:	front 120/60 17, rear 160/60 17
Final drive:	chain
Gearbox:	six-speed
Weight:	159kg (350lb)

Kawasaki ER-6

Kawasaki also produced a faired version of the ER-6, called the ER-6f. It was identical to the naked version, but had a full fairing, new instruments and altered riding position.

The parallel twin engine was specially developed for the ER-6n. It's a modern design, with fuel injection, eight valves, water cooling and twin cams. The same engine was later used in the Kawasaki Versys adventure-sport bike.

The frame is made from inexpensive-to-manufacture steel tubing, with a stiff, perimeter design. It's matched to the paintscheme, giving a modern feel to the styling.

Rear suspension uses a simple, direct monoshock linkage instead of more complex rising-rate linkages used on more sporting bikes. The shock is offset to make more space under the seat for electrical and other components.

The offset shock also means the seat is fairly low, sitting just 785mm (31in) from the ground. This, with the narrow chassis, makes the ER-6 more suited to smaller riders.

The early part of the twenty-first century had seen Kawasaki revive its fortunes in the sportsbike world. New models like the ZX-636R, ZX-10R and Z1000 all competed for top position in their markets, thanks to improved design, technology and performance.

So by 2005, Kawasaki was ready to apply these improvements elsewhere in its product range. The novice/budget middleweight-roadster market is an important one, and was largely dominated by Suzuki's SV650 – a neat, small V-twin with a sporty chassis and low purchase price. Kawasaki's ER-5 was some way off the SV, so the designers went back to the drawing board to create a fresh, new-generation bike, and the result appeared in June 2005. The ER-6n immediately

The faired version of the ER-6, the ER-6f makes a smart little budget tourer, perfect for a medium-distance commute or even occasional two-up touring holidays.

attracted attention due to its radical design, especially the bulbous headlight, tint-matched perimeter-tube frame and the unusual offset rear monoshock suspension unit. And while the ER was clearly still a budget bike, it had a host of premium components, including 'petal'-type brake discs, which save weight over conventional items, optional ABS anti-lock brakes, and a neat dashboard, with large analogue tachometer and LCD speedometer.

The ER's engine was also impressive. Rather than simply revise the dated ER-5 design, the powerplant engineers had started from scratch, and built an all-new motor. The basic layout – a parallel twin – has both cylinders side by side mounted across the frame. This is a rather unusual layout, but it is both compact and narrow, and Kawasaki has used it several times over the years. The '180°' layout means the pistons are moving up and down out of phase (one piston is at the

This is the ER-6f dashboard, with a larger, dual-dial layout. The naked bike has a smaller combined LCD speedo and analogue tachometer display.

Despite its budget nature, the ER-6 range has excellent brakes, including petal discs and an optional ABS system. The calipers are twin-piston parts, which aren't as powerful as four-piston designs.

top when the other is at the bottom of its stroke), and a gear-driven balancer shaft cancels out the inherent vibrations of such a layout.

Brought up to date with fuel injection, compact four-valve cylinder heads and modern materials, the little motor produced a very credible 71bhp (52kW), with good low-down torque characteristics, putting it on a par with the SV650 class leader. A six-speed gearbox and light cable clutch allowed the rider to get the most from the free-revving engine, and the Keihin dual-valve fuel injection gives smooth, flawless fuelling. A fashionable underslung muffler helps keep mass centralized and low, improving handling, while curved stainless steel downpipes are carefully shaped to improve power delivery. A catalyst in the exhaust helps reduce harmful emissions, and allow the ER-6n to pass tough Euro III emissions rules.

Riding the ER shows that Kawasaki had applied the lessons learned by its sportsbike designers. It's a fun, lively little bike, which has enough performance to satisfy more advanced riders, yet remains accessible enough for novices and commuters looking for a practical, basic entry-level machine. Controls are light and easy to use, and the willing engine spins up easily, with good low-down power and a decent top end too.

The handling is stable and predictable, the brakes are progressive, and the sport-touring tires give enough grip for committed riding. Although the suspension looks somewhat basic, with only preload adjustment on the rear shock, it's a big improvement over the budget parts found on the older ER-5. The fact that the

ER-6n looks good, is economical and boasts above-average equipment levels merely adds to its appeal.

Kawasaki chose to expand the ER range in 2006, when it released a fully faired version. This bike, the ER-6f (for 'faired') had a much wider level of ability – the extra wind and weather protection meant it was suited to longer, faster journeys. Along with a range of accessories, the little ER-6f could make a very capable light tourer or distance commuter. Then, in late 2006, Kawasaki released yet another variant based on the ER, the Versys. This machine had a more 'adventure-sport' biased design, with longer travel suspension and hints of offroad styling. Performance was similar to the base ER models, but the Versys was more suited to use on rougher roads.

Kawasaki ER-6

Top speed:	205km/h (128mph)
Engine type:	649cc (39cu in), l/c parallel twin DOHC 8v
Maximum power:	71bhp (52kW) @8500rpm
Frame type:	tubular-steel perimeter
Tyre sizes:	front 120/70 17, rear 160/60 17
Final drive:	chain
Gearbox:	six-speed
Weight:	174kg (383lb)

Middleweight Maestros: 600–750cc

To many riders, a middleweight machine is the ideal solution – whether they are looking for ultimate track performance, or simply everyday usability. For performance fans, a modern 600cc (37 cu in) four-cylinder sportsbike can produce almost 89kW (120bhp), while weighing in at less than 160kg (350lb), and boasting chassis and engine technology every bit as advanced as more expensive, larger capacity machines.

These high-revving supersports models give a superbly thrilling experience on the track and road without the intimidating peak horsepower of 1,000cc (61 cu in) bikes. They are also generally cheaper to run – they cost less to buy, insurance is cheaper, and they are easier on consumable parts like tyres, chains and brakes.

The 600cc (37 cu in) supersports class is the one most closely contested by all the big manufacturers, and in many markets it's the most important sportsbike sector. It's also an important class in worldwide production-based racing: the World Supersport and British Supersport championships are contested on four-cylinder machines of 600cc (37 cu in), 675cc (41 cu in) triples (in Britain only), or 750cc (46 cu in) twins. Many manufacturers support these classes heavily, running factory-sponsored teams, working on the 'Win on Sunday, Sell on Monday' principle. Honda's CBR600RR is the most successful current supersports machine,

Kawasaki's ZX-636R was one of the finest 600-class sportsbikes produced. Its slightly larger engine capacity gave strong midrange performance, while the chassis offered excellent track and road handling. It had limited success in racing, however.

having won every World Supersport championship since it was launched in 2003.

Middleweight roadsters also make a lot of sense for less performance-obsessed riders. This sector was pretty much invented by Suzuki's GSF600 Bandit, first launched in 1995. Based on a reliable, well-proven oil-cooled engine in a classic roadster chassis, its combination of performance, price and looks made it an instant success, and showed the way for other manufacturers. The latest lightweight roadsters like Honda's CB600F Hornet or the Suzuki GSR600 provide a fun, practical way for many riders to enter the bigger bike market after passing their test. Naked bikes like this also provide a 'blank canvas' for owners to personalize their mounts with screens, bellypans, exhaust cans and chromed or anodized fasteners.

Not all middleweight machines are four-cylinder designs, however. BMW's F800S twin, launched in 2005, is a superb everyday commuting machine, perfect for city riding and cross-town journeys. But it's also flexible enough to take on a touring holiday with optional luggage fitted, or even for an occasional high-speed trackday blast.

BMW F800S/ST

The F800 was available in S and ST versions. The ST was more suited for touring, with a luggage rack, larger fairing and higher bars, while the S had sportier tyres and a smaller nosecone.

BMW developed its first parallel twin engine with Rotax, which also produces its 650cc (40cu in) single-cylinder engines. The 798cc (49cu in) design is extremely modern, with fuel injection, advanced cylinder-head design and a novel 'reciprocating bar' balance system.

BMW promoted the F800 as a fun, high-performance machine by giving one to its sponsored stunt rider, World Stunt Champion Christian Pfieffer.

The F800 uses conventional telescopic forks and monoshock rear suspension. BMW's usual Paralever and Telelever suspension systems would be too heavy for the smaller F800 range.

When BMW launched the F800S in 2005, it was one of the most conventional designs that the Bavarian firm had ever produced. Eschewing its trademark unusual suspension systems, shaft drive and unconventional engine layouts, BMW engineers instead revealed a middleweight machine of an almost conservative nature. A water-cooled, eight-valve parallel twin engine is housed in a twin spar-cast aluminium frame, with conventional telescopic front forks, and a monoshock rear suspension system.

But that's not to say the F800S isn't innovative. In fact, the closer you look at it, the more you see clever, elegant engineering solutions within that seemingly conformist layout. Perhaps the most interesting feature of the F800 engine (produced for BMW by Austrian firm Bombardier-Rotax) is its balancing system. Parallel twin engines are naturally unbalanced – they either have both pistons travelling up and down together (a 360° layout), or have one piston at the top of its travel while the other is at the bottom (a 180° design). Conventional approaches to this problem have used geared or chain-driven balance shafts, which use off-centre weights to oppose the unbalanced forces of the moving pistons. These set-ups, however, take up space and sap power, creating engines that are bigger yet less efficient at the same time.

BMW F800S

Top speed:	200km/h (125mph)
Engine type:	798cc (49cu in), l/c 360° parallel twin, 8-valve, DOHC
Maximum power:	85bhp (63kW) @8000rpm
Frame type:	twin spar aluminium
Tyre sizes:	front 120/70 17, rear 180/55 17
Final drive:	Kevlar belt
Gearbox:	six-speed
Weight:	182kg (401lb)

This CAD image shows the F800's basic engine and chassis layout. Note how the rear swingarm pivots on the back of the engine crankcases rather than on the aluminum twin spar frame.

The F800S makes a fun, practical first sportsbike. Its light handling is perfect for riding on mountain back roads, yet it's comfortable enough for day-to-day use as a commuter and light tourer.

BMW's system is much more elegant. A balance bar pivots at the rear of the engine, and is connected to the crankshaft by a central, slave conrod. As the crankshaft turns, it moves this carefully weighted bar up and down. This movement opposes the piston movements, cancelling out the unbalanced forces, producing a smoother engine.

The engine cylinder head is based on the firm's K1200 superbike, with a compact four-valve layout, chain-driven twin camshafts and cam-driven waterpump. BMW's BMS-K engine-management system controls an advanced fuel injection and ignition system, with two 46mm (2in) throttle bodies. An oxygen sensor and catalyst in the exhaust helps reduce harmful emissions, allowing the F800 to comply with strict Euro-3 regulations.

The chassis is less interesting, but still cleverly designed. The fuel tank has been located below the seat, with a filler cap on the rear panel. This keeps the weight of the fuel low down in the chassis, improving handling, and also allows more room above the engine for an optimized airbox and intake system. A cast-aluminium rear swingarm has a beautifully sculpted design, with a single-sided layout and belt final drive. This rubber/Kevlar belt needs much less maintenance than a chain, and gives a smoother ride, thanks to its inherent shock-absorbing qualities. The cast-aluminium wheels are a lightweight design, and sticky Continental Attack tyres give good road-riding grip.

BMW offers an optional ABS system for the F800, which uses a computerized ECU to analyze the speed at which each wheel is turning. If the computer senses a wheel locking under braking, due to ice or a slippery surface, it momentarily releases brake pressure to that wheel, allowing the bike to regain grip before re-applying the brake.

Riding the F800S reveals a satisfying, torquey power delivery from the engine. Its 360° firing order gives a distinctive sound, not unlike BMW's trademark flat-twin Boxer engines. It's not a particularly powerful engine, producing around 85bhp (63kW), but the punchy nature of the power gives strong acceleration from low down in the rev range.

The chassis is similarly impressive, despite its unexceptional specification. Steering is light and responsive, and the suspension offers smooth damping and good control over bumpy surfaces. The brakes are powerful and progressive, while controls and instruments are light and clear (despite BMW's quirky turn signal controls).

BMW also offers the F800S in a more touring-orientated ST version. This model has a slightly larger top fairing, higher handlebars, different wheels, built-in luggage rack and more mileage-biased tyres.

The F800's final belt drive is smooth, quiet, and maintenance free. The kevlar-reinforced toothed belt needs no lubrication or adjustment, and typically lasts over 40,000 km (25,000 miles).

Honda CB600F Hornet

Production of the Hornet was centered in Honda's Italian factory at Atessa in Italy. This put production near the Hornet's primary markets – Italy and Europe, while saving on import duties. The engines, however, were still produced in Japan.

The large high-mounted silencer and wide 180-section rear tyre gave the Hornet a very stylish back end. The front tyre was a wide 130-section 40.6cm (16in) size.

Honda borrowed the inline-four cylinder engine from its 1997 CBR600F sportsbike and fitted it to the Hornet. Minor changes improved low-down and midrange torque.

To cut costs for this budget machine, Honda used a rather basic steel-tube backbone frame, box-section swingarm and twin-piston brake calipers. These components gave adequate performance, but added little to the style or quality of the design.

Honda also produced a 900 Hornet, using the CBR900RR FireBlade engine. It looked very similar to the 600, and used the same frame, but wasn't a great sales success.

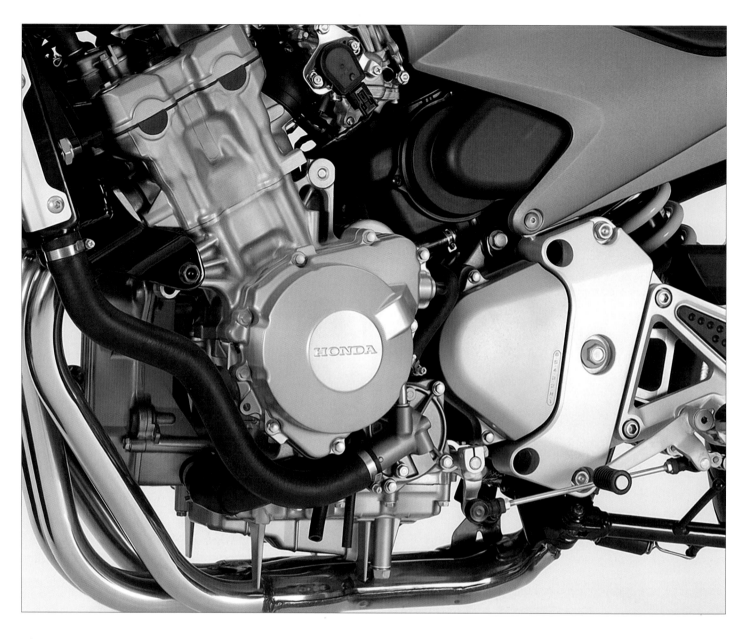

The first Honda Hornet was a 250cc (15cu in) roadster, sold in the Japanese home market. Like the insect it was named after, the 250 Hornet was small, buzzy and extremely agile. It was powered by a detuned version of the (also Japan-only) CBR250RR engine, a clockwork-like inline-four of tiny dimensions, and sky-high rev limits. The little Hornet was a big hit in Japan, where its funky styling, wide rear tyre and high-mount exhaust silencer were all right on target for the legendarily fashionable Japanese bikers.

The rest of the world was desperate for its own version though. License limits made 250s very popular in Japan, but the European market needed a larger-capacity machine. Honda took the engine from the 1997 version of its CBR600F sportsbike, made minor modifications, and shoehorned it into the 250 Hornet chassis. The frame and wheels stayed the same, with small changes, but the suspension and brakes were upgraded to cope with the increased performance.

The Hornet 600 engine was taken from Honda's CBR600 sportsbike – one of the most successful bikes ever. The retuned engine had less peak power, but more usable power lower down the rev range.

Honda CB600F Hornet 665

Top speed:	217km/h (135mph)
Engine type:	599cc (36.5cu in), l/c inline-four, 16-valve DOHC
Maximum power:	96bhp (71kW) @12,000rpm
Frame type:	steel-tube spine
Tyre sizes:	front 120/70 17, rear 180/55 17
Final drive:	chain
Gearbox:	six-speed
Weight:	178kg (392lb)

So when the 600 Hornet was launched in late 1997, it was a prime example of the naked middleweight roadster. That class had been invented by Suzuki's GSF600 Bandit, but the Hornet was a new breed. Like its close competitor, Yamaha's Fazer, the Hornet had a modern sportsbike engine in a simple, cheap chassis. Subtle changes to the engine intake and exhaust systems, and internal modifications reduced the engine's peak power output from the CBR600's 105 bhp (79kW) to nearer 95bhp (71kW). This lower power was more suited to a naked bike, where the high speeds attained by more powerful bikes are less practical.

Honda had aimed the Hornet at the burgeoning novice market, as well as more advanced riders, and this led to some criticism of the bike's brakes. Initial test reports suggested they lacked initial bite and power, particularly in comparison with Yamaha's Fazer (which had outstanding sportsbike brakes). Honda claimed that the soft initial braking was intended to suit new riders, who may have been alarmed by sharp, powerful brakes.

This, together with a premium price initially dented the Hornet's showroom appeal (the Hornet cost £300 [nearly $500] more than the Fazer when both appeared in the UK in 1998). However, it soon recovered sales to become one of Honda's most successful roadster models. Owners liked the good looks, solid build quality and brisk performance of the CB600, and several countries ran one-make race series, often

Early Hornets had simple, dual analogue instruments, with classic white faces. Later models switched to LCD/dial instruments with much more rider information.

supported by Honda, underlining the Hornet's surprising track potential.

The Hornet has had several updates since its launch. The first revised model appeared in 2000, with a 43cm (17in) front wheel instead of the original 40.6cm (16in) part. It also received improved brake pads and hoses, giving stronger braking power, and minor engine changes improved pickup. The 2000 model year also saw the launch of the CB600F S, which had a small nosecone fairing. This added practicality to the Hornet, giving more comfort on longer rides. Nonetheless, many Hornet fans preferred the style of the naked bike.

Early Hornets had a poor range, due to the 16l (4gal) fuel capacity, so starting in 2003, Honda increased the capacity to 17l (4.5gal). 2003 also saw a host of other updates to the Hornet, with a new silencer, different bodywork, revised instruments and smaller indicators.

By 2005, Honda was expected to fit fuel injection to the still-carburetted Hornet – if only to comply with forthcoming Euro III emissions limits. But the 2005 update stuck with carburettors, which used a 'fuel-cut' system to allow the use of a catalytic convertor. This reduces harmful emissions to the same level as fuel-injected bikes. In addition, the front suspension was given a new 41mm (16in) upside-down front fork. This improved feedback and performance, and gave the Hornet a handling edge over its competitors.

Honda saved money by using a directly operated rear suspension system, rather than a progressive linkage system used on more sporting bikes. The suspension was basic, but effective.

Honda CBR600RR

The aluminium rear swingarm is heavily braced to give high stiffness for minimal weight. It uses a similar suspension system to Honda's RCV211V MotoGP bike.

Sebastien Charpentier, the French World Supersport racer, won the WSS championship on his CBR600RR in 2005 and 2006. Australian Karl Muggeridge won the 2004 championship on one, as did his compatriot, Chris Vermeulen, in 2003.

The 2007 CBR600RR incorporated an updated version of the electronic steering damper fitted to the Honda Fireblade. This lighter, smaller version increased the damping effort as speed increased.

A pair of ram air-intakes below the narrow headlights feed air to the CBR's large airbox under the tank cover.

Each cylinder has two fuel injectors. One injector is mounted close to the cylinder, and operates at low revs, and one is mounted above the intake, in the upper airbox, and also operates at high revs. This gives good fuelling at both low and high engine speeds.

Honda's massively successful CBR600F range was in some ways paradoxical. On the road, for thousands of riders, it was a practical, flexible bike, as suited to long-distance two-up touring or daily-grind commuting as it was to sports riding. Meanwhile, when race teams took the inline four-cylinder 599cc (36.5cu in) bike into the sports arena, it regularly swept the board at national and world-level supersport racing. Although it had an unfashionably practical design, its basic set-up was so good that it could still beat even the most focussed 600cc (36.5cu in) designs on the racetrack.

By 2002 though, bikes like Yamaha's R6 and Suzuki's GSX-R600 had put the CBR600F under pressure on track. So for the 2003 model year, Honda finally revealed the CBR600RR. For several years there had been stories going around that Honda had been working on the concept of a 'mini-FireBlade', with a 600cc (37cu in) version of the legendary 900. But what was unveiled was a much more track-biased machine, and the CBR600RR looked more like Honda's RC211V V5 MotoGP bike. A sharp twin-headlight fairing led back to a taut aluminium-beam frame, with a massive, stiff rear swingarm laid bare by an audacious single underseat exhaust silencer. Underneath the plastic was an all-new powerplant, revving to an impressive 15,000rpm, helped by an advanced dual-injector fuel injection system. Ram-air ducts in the fairing fed cool, dense air to the sealed airbox, and a six-speed gearbox transmitted the power to the rear tyre.

The chassis was simple, but effective. The front suspension used conventional, fully adjustable forks,

Honda CBR600RR

Top speed:	265km/h (165mph)
Engine type:	599cc (36.5cu in), l/c inline-four, 16-valve DOHC
Maximum power:	115bhp (86kW) @13,000rpm
Frame type:	aluminium twin spar
Tyre sizes:	front 120/70 17, rear 180/55 17
Final drive:	chain
Gearbox:	six-speed
Weight:	163kg (359lb)

while a fully adjustable monoshock controlled the rear swingarm. The powerful brakes had twin four-piston calipers at the front. With a committed, forward-biased riding position and Bridgestone sports tyres, the chassis gave dynamic yet stable handling and steering.

On the track, where the engine spends its time revving in the upper part of the range, and the slightly cramped riding position isn't an issue, the RR was truly awesome. But on the road, it was bested by its more flexible, road-biased competitors, such as Kawasaki's ZX-636R. The Kawasaki's larger engine capacity and spacious chassis made it more relaxing on the road, where gear selection and engine revs didn't have to be so precise.

But for 2005, Honda slightly revamped the RR, with seemingly minor engine and chassis modifications.

Underneath the aerodynamic bodywork, the CBR600RR is a no-nonsense sportsbike. Note the large dual ram-air intakes.

While track riding brings out the best in the 600RR, it's still a perfectly competent, fun road bike.

The front suspension changed to an upside-down fork, with radial-mounted four-piston brake calipers. The fairing was made slightly narrower and more sleek, while detail changes were made inside the engine. Different-shaped inlet ports and a new combustion-chamber design seemed like insignificant changes, but the result totally altered the somewhat revvy nature of the RR engine, giving it a much stronger midrange, and massively improving rideability.

These modifications helped race teams, and the new front fork and brakes in particular added performance and enabled the CBR to keep a step ahead of the competition. And that's where the CBR600RR had been since its launch. It won the World Supersport championship in its 2003 maiden season, and went on to win again in 2004 and 2005.

The second-generation CBR600RR was first shown by Honda in September 2006. This machine, launched for the 2007 model year, was a radical update, with focus placed on its small size and low mass. The

Honda mounted the four-cylinder engine low and forward, giving a distinct front bias to the bike.

engine was all new. It had around 118bhp (88kW) and was incredibly compact. Clever design made it smaller than the firm's CBR250 engine, and 2kg (4.4lb) lighter than the previous motor. This, plus a lighter frame, allowed Honda to claim a dry mass of 155kg (342lb), which was 8kg (17lb) less than before. New bodywork incorporated a central ram-air intake system. The bike also had an inlet and exhaust-fume control valve for the first time, which further improved power delivery.

Honda CBR600F

The CBR600F boasted a pillion grab handle and spacious dual seat, as well as a more upright riding position, with low footpegs and high bars. This made it the best 600 in its class for touring.

The CBR was well built, reliable and highly durable, and a machine that lived up to Honda's excellent reputation.

The CBR600F engine was powerful and gave outstanding power delivery. It was also used in a modified version in the CB600F Hornet. Carburettors were used until 2001, when a PGM-FI fuel injection system was fitted. Both set-ups offered smooth fuelling.

Unusually for a 600 sportsbike, the CBR600F has a centrestand, useful for rear wheel and chain maintenance. Most manufacturers only fit a sidestand to sportsbikes, to cut weight and increase ground clearance.

Honda resisted fitting an aluminium frame to its CBR until 1998. Previous models had used a rather low-tech (but perfectly serviceable) welded steel-tube design.

If you had to choose one bike as the archetypal Japanese middleweight sportsbike of the late twentieth century, the CBR600F would surely be it. First launched in 1987, it has been steadily refined and updated over the years.

While the original CBR600FH of 1987 is very far from the final version of 2006, there's a very clear family resemblance, and the general layout is similar. The original design used a water-cooled, inline-four engine, with a 16-valve, DOHC head, six gears and four CV carburettors. Modern for its time, the engine made around 85bhp (63kW), and was fitted into a cheap yet sturdy steel frame, hidden under all-enveloping plastic bodywork. Performance was strong, yet the CBR600 had a practical, 'real-world' bias that continued throughout the model's lifespan. Honda

Compared with the more track-biased CBR600RR, the comfortable F-model is better suited to two-up touring. It's a relaxing ride too, with a softer engine and more compliant suspension.

fitted a centerstand to make maintenance easier, but at the cost of extra weight and reduced ground clearance. The CBR also boasted good pillion accommodation, and this, together with a relaxed riding position, and protective fairing, made it more suited to touring and commuting than competitors like the Yamaha FZR600.

Over the next decade and a half, the CBR performed a veritable miracle, staying ahead of its Japanese competitors overall, while seemingly sacrificing ultimate performance for all-round capability. The competition continued to move towards racetrack performance – Suzuki's GSX-R600 and Yamaha's R6 were extremely focussed machines, with sharp steering chassis and high-revving engines. Yet the CBR not only maintained its sales success in showrooms, it also managed to stay near the top of comparative press tests, and maintained a strong racing pedigree, winning many supersport races and championships.

The CBR's minor updates appeared roughly every two years, with significant improvements in

Although the CBR600F is a less focussed sportsbike, it still has a very high specification. Forks are fully adjustable, and twin Nissin four-piston brakes offer powerful stopping.

A comprehensive dash is clear and easy to read: Honda's HISS immobilizer system makes casual theft nigh-on impossible. The bike won't start without the correct chip-enabled key.

suspension and chassis performance. But major updates in 1991 saw a new, 100bhp (74.5kW) engine and smaller, lighter chassis, 1995 brought a ram air-intake system, 1997 added 5bhp (4kW) and a more aggressive body shape. An aluminium frame finally appeared in 1999, and the final, fuel-injected version was first seen in 2001. This marked the pinnacle of the CBR600F, and it had performance figures that put it on a par with the competition. Dry weight was 170kg (375lb), peak power was 109bhp (81kW) @12,500rpm and maximum torque of 65Nm (48lb ft) was produced at 10,500rpm. The F model was packed with technology too. The cockpit was an all-electronic digital design, with a dial-type stepper motor tachometer, LCD speedometer and fuel gauge as well

as an engine rev-light, which illuminates when the engine revs reach the red line. A standard immobilizer used a coded chip inside the key to prevent unauthorized starting, and the fuel injection system used two pairs of 38mm (1.5in) throttle bodies. The chassis was further refined from the original 1999 aluminium-framed design, with stronger frame castings, lighter wheels and reduced mass in brake calipers and suspension components.

2001 also saw the launch of the CBR600F Sport, a stop-gap model intended to improve Honda's racing chances against new models from Suzuki and Yamaha. The Sport model was essentially the same as the basic CBR, with some minor chassis modifications – the centrestand disappeared, and a two-piece seat appeared. More importantly though, were the internal engine changes – lighter crankshaft, stronger valve springs and lowered final gearing. Although these made little difference to road riders, they enabled race teams to get more power on track.

The Sport was a stop-gap, because Honda had the CBR600RR, an all-new race-ready CBR, in the wings. But when the new, MotoGP-styled RR appeared, Honda kept the F model on its books, giving CBR fans a choice of the all-out track tool, or the almost-as-fast but much more civilized F model. In road-riding circumstances, many riders will be as fast on the 600F as on the latest Yamaha R6, despite that bike's MotoGP styling, fly-by-wire engine and 161kg (355lb) dry weight. And they'll certainly find themselves travelling in a more comfortable, relaxed fashion.

Honda CBR600F

Top speed:	265km/h (165mph)
Engine type:	599cc (36.5cu in), l/c inline four, 16-valve, DOHC
Maximum power:	108bhp(80.5kW)@12,500rpm
Frame type:	aluminium twin spar
Tyre sizes:	front 120/70 17, rear 180/55 17
Final drive:	chain
Gearbox:	six-speed
Weight:	170kg (375lb)

Kawasaki ZX-636R (+ZX-6RR)

Early ZX-6R designs had the ram air-intake under the headlights, but later versions moved the intake between the twin headlights. This central position is where the airflow generates maximum pressure, improving power.

'Petal'-type front brake discs have sections cut out of the edge of the disc, which makes it lighter, while maintaining its strength. A lighter front wheel and disc assembly reduces gyroscopic forces, allowing easier steering.

Kawasaki uses an unusual 120/65 section front tyre, instead of the 120/70 size normally used by most other sportsbikes. This means a shorter, slightly stiffer sidewall, intended to improve feeling from the tyre.

The ZX-6R has a combined LCD/analogue dashboard, with a large tachometer and digital speedometer.

The underseat location of the exhaust silencer moves its mass closer to the centreline of the bike, improving agility. However, it does move that mass high up and to the rear, which may reduce sporty handling.

The 600 supersports class has always been one of Kawasaki's most important. It was that firm's GPZ600R that launched the modern middleweight sportsbike when it first appeared in 1985. Its inline-four, liquid-cooled engine in a sporty chassis set the pattern for the next two decades of supersport development.

The first 599cc (36.5cu in) ZX-6R was launched in 1995 as a high-performance, supersports alternative to the firm's softer ZZ-R600 sports tourer. The ZX-6R 'Ninja' had an aggressive edge missing from the ZZ-R – the fairing was sharper and sleeker, the riding position was more focussed, and both the engine and chassis were aimed at providing exciting, sporty riding. The layout was roughly similar to the ZZ-R, but the ZX was an all-new bike. The engine had a shorter stroke and wider bore, higher rev ceiling and more power, while the entire bike weighed 13kg (29lb) less than the ZZ-R.

Kawasaki developed the ZX over the rest of the 1990s, with more power, less weight and improved

Kawasaki ZX-636R (+ZX-6RR)

Top speed:	265km/h (165mph)
Engine type:	636cc (39cu in), l/c inline-four, 16-valve, DOHC
Maximum power:	130bhp (96kW)@14,000rpm
Frame type:	aluminium twin spar
Tyre sizes:	front 120/65 17, rear 180/55 17
Final drive:	chain
Gearbox:	six-speed
Weight:	164kg (361lb)

One of Japan's finest front ends. Four-piston radial-mount Tokico calipers bite on a pair of 300mm (12in) petal-type drilled discs to give superb stopping power.

From 2005 the ZX-6R was fitted with a slipper-type clutch. This used a series of ramps and springs to release the clutch's grip under savage downchanges.

handling. But the firm lost its way slightly near the end of the century, and by 2001, the Ninja was some way off its competitors. Kawasaki had to do something radical, so for 2002, it performed a rather neat trick. It cheated. Engineers took the standard 599cc (36.5cu in) ZX engine, replaced the iron bores with aluminum-plated cylinders, and had enough room to fit bigger bore pistons. The engine capacity was increased to 636cc (39cu in), gaving the engine a real advantage over its competitors.

The first ZX-636 used a chassis very similar to the 599cc (36.5cu in) bike, but by 2003, the firm had entirely revamped it. The ZX-636B1 of that year was almost unrecognizable compared with the 2002 bike – pretty much every part was new, from the small race fairing to the track-ready suspension and brakes. Even the venue for the press-riding launch was carefully chosen to accentuate the special performance of the new bike: Kawasaki took journalists to the world-class F1 circuit at Sepang, in Malaysia. On Sepang's long straights, the new fuel-injected engine could show its full potential, while the track's hard braking zones and mix of slow and fast corners really tested the new radial-mounted brakes and suspension. Finally, the Ninja was back on top of the class. The engine performed exhilaratingly, steering was fast, midrange acceleration was strong and braking was incredible.

Kawasaki's 'cheat' only really handicapped the firm in one way: the 636cc (39cu in) engine wasn't eligible for racing. This meant that the firm also had to produce and sell a limited number of 599cc (36.5cu in) 'homologation' bikes to race the Ninja. Dubbed the ZX-6RR, this bike had a slipper clutch, adjustable swingarm pivot position and a single seat.

The supersports class is so competitive that machinery is often updated every two years, so for 2005, the ZX-636R was overhauled once again. The RR bike's slipper clutch was fitted, while the engine received a new cylinder head, bigger valves, more radical camshafts and oval-section throttle bodies. The bodywork was styled to echo the firm's ZX-RR MotoGP bike, and the side-mounted silencer was changed to an underseat design, further improving aerodynamics. The exhaust itself received a butterfly valve in the silencer to improve low-speed running and cut noise. The frame, swingarm, brakes and suspension were also all new.

For 2007, Kawasaki decided to move back to a single 599cc (36.5cu in) capacity, rather than a 599 (36.5) and 636 (39). It released an all-new bike, which featured a revised engine, frame and swingarm, and new, more aerodynamic bodywork. More than ever the bike resembled the ZX-10R, with smaller, projector-type headlights and a central ram-air intake, which was reduced in size, for the engine. The engine was designed to match the power and torque of the 636, and still had a slipper clutch, dual-valve fuel-injection and an underseat exhaust.

Kawasaki Z750

The seat unit is similar to Kawasaki's ZX range of sportsbikes, with a two-piece sports seat, and a light, reliable, compact LED tail lamp. The pillion seat can be replaced by a cover for solo riding.

An unusual 'diamond'-type frame is made from welded-steel tube, and uses the engine as an additional strengthening member. This layout is also similar to the Z1000 design.

The Z750 differs visually from its 1000cc (61cu in) sibling by having a simpler, four-into-one exhaust system, with a stylish oval silencer. The forks, nosecone and brakes are also different.

Kawasaki maintained the high specification of the Z750 by fitting the same LCD digital clocks as used on the ZX-6R and ZX-10R sportsbikes.

The Z750 has a small headlight fairing, which deflects some of the windblast around the rider's shoulders. The faired 'S' version has a much more substantial fairing, making it ideal for riding at speed on highways.

The original Z750 – a classic roadster chassis combined with a strong air-cooled inline-four engine – was a strong performer for Kawasaki in the late 1970s and early 80s. This interpretation of the Z takes its inspiration from those original roadsters, but with a very modern execution.

Kawasaki based this Z750 on the successful Z1000 'streetfighter', first launched in 2003. So for 2004, this smaller-capacity, budget version appeared, intended to shake up the naked-middleweight sector dominated by the likes of Honda's Hornet 600 and Yamaha's FZ-6. The 'streetfighter' name is used for certain naked roadsters, which have high power levels, sharp, aggressive design, and levels of chassis performance near the level of a sportsbike. They're ideal for use in cities, where their upright riding position, high handlebars and strong acceleration work best, but also offer good performance out of town, on country roads.

The Z750 shared styling with the Z1000, but with cheaper chassis components. The complex, pricey four-into-four exhaust system of the Z1000 was replaced with a less expensive, simpler four-into-one silencer, while the upside-down front forks and four-piston calipers of the bigger bike are swapped for cheaper conventional forks and two-piston sliding calipers. Sport-touring tyres with a slightly narrower rear tyre still give the Z750 ample grip for road riding, and a cheaper, rebound/preload adjustable rear shock is a step down from the fully adjustable part on the Z1000. Meanwhile, the 750 motor was developed from the Z1000's design, sharing the same 50.9mm (2in)

stroke, but with a smaller 68.4mm (2.7in) bore. Narrower 34mm (1.3in) fuel-injection throttle bodies are better suited to the smaller engine, and give smooth, predictable power delivery. The 750 also shares the LED tail light and small nosecone of the Z1000, albeit with a slightly different profile, and the high-tech instrument panel is a similar design to that on the ZX-6R and ZX-10R Ninja sportsbikes.

Often, small-capacity versions of a bike can be a little dull. Giving essentially the same motorbike a smaller, weaker engine rarely improves the experience, but with the Z750, Kawasaki managed to pull the trick off. The Z750 is only 3kg (6.6lb) lighter than the 1000, makes 17bhp (13kW) less peak power, and has lower-specification chassis components. Yet despite this, it's just as exciting and fulfilling as its bigger brother. The engine is a lively performer, and has enough performance for more advanced riders, while being eminently suited to novices and less-experienced riders. Equally, the budget chassis is thoroughly suited to both spirited road riding and daily-grind commuting with equal aplomb. The steel diamond-type frame is stiff enough to handle the engine's power, and while the suspension and brakes are budget parts, they have more than acceptable performance for road and even occasional track use.

Although it seems like 'cheating' for Kawasaki to build a 750cc (46cu in) bike to compete in an ostensibly 600cc (36.6cu in) class, the Z750 is priced broadly in line with its competitors, and running costs, such as insurance are also similar. Like its sister bike, the ZX-636R, the Z750's extra cubic capacity

Kawasaki Z750

Top speed:	225km/h (140mph)
Engine type:	748cc (46cu in), l/c inline-four, 16-valve, DOHC
Maximum power:	110bhp (82kW)@11,000rpm
Frame type:	steel-tube diamond
Tyre sizes:	front 120/70 17, rear 180/55 17
Final drive:	chain
Gearbox:	six-speed
Weight:	195kg (430lb)

A compact, integrated LCD display unit combines the central speedometer readout with an LCD tacho display around the outside edge. There is also a practical LCD fuel gauge readout.

gives it a real advantage in terms of torque and outright power over competitor machines, like Honda's Hornet 600 and Yamaha's FZ-6. Gear changes are reduced, and there's ample midrange grunt for safe overtakes on country roads, which lends the Z750 a relaxed feel, even when riding with friends on sportier machinery.

The middleweight roadster category is one where practicality plays a very important role, so Kawasaki launched a faired version of the Z750 in 2005. The Z750S featured a new half-fairing that provided much more weather and wind protection for the rider, making it more suited to longer-distance trips on highways. The two-part seat from the Z750 is replaced with a larger, one-piece dual seat that gives more comfort for rider and pillion, and a pair of grab rails add security for the passenger.

Light, powerful and dynamic, the Z750 put Kawasaki at the top of the middleweight naked market. For all-round sporty riding, its strong engine and competent handling made it a popular choice.

Suzuki GSR600

The GSR600 design is based heavily on the firm's B-King concept bike shown in Tokyo in 2001. The B-King itself was released in 2007, with a GSX1300R Hayabusa engine and uncompromising design.

Instead of a direct replacement for the Bandit 650, Suzuki claimed the GSR was aimed at a different, more sporty sector of the middleweight market.

The GSR engine is a modified version of the 2001 GSX-R600 supersports engine. It was adapted to meet Euro III emissions regulations with different fuel injection and a catalyst-equipped exhaust.

Suzuki fitted a neat, modern instrument panel, with LCD displays for speed, fuel gauge and other readouts, as well as a traditional analogue tachometer.

A modern cast-aluminium frame and swingarm give a stiff chassis, although the budget suspension units mean the GSR has a rather soft, underdamped ride. Bridgestone sports tyres are full sportsbike sized – 120 front, 180 rear.

For a company that arguably invented the class, with its GSF600 Bandit, Suzuki was surprisingly lax when it came to keeping up to date in the naked middleweight world. The mid-1990s appearance of the Bandit sparked huge interest in light, lively 600cc- (36.6cu in-) class motorcycles, and led to the launch of bikes like Honda's Hornet and Yamaha's Fazer. The Bandit was a strong seller for Suzuki throughout the 1990s, but by 2000, its air/oil-cooled engine and basic chassis design lagged far behind its competitors in terms of performance, style and sophistication. Although it was a good seller, thanks to a low price, it looked like a bike of the twentieth century – and Suzuki needed something for the next millennium.

It wasn't until 2005 that Suzuki finally released a modern Bandit: the GSR600. The GSR had an up-to-date water-cooled engine, in an aluminium frame, with sharp, contemporary design and modern running gear.

The GSR's radical styling is straight from the Suzuki concept-bike department's drawingboard. It's clearly influenced by Suzuki's Hayabusa-powered B-King, which was shown off at the 2001 Tokyo Motor Show,

Although it's a naked bike, the GSR is still quite comfortable at high speeds. The rider can tuck in out of the breeze up to around 100mph and the headlight console diverts some windblast upwards.

Suzuki GSR600

Top speed:	217km/h (135mph)
Engine type:	599cc (36.5cu in), l/c inline-four, 16-valve DOHC
Maximum power:	98bhp (73kW)@12,000rpm
Frame type:	aluminium twin spar
Tyre sizes:	front 120/70 17, rear 180/55 17
Final drive:	chain
Gearbox:	six-speed
Weight:	183kg (404lb)

though it lacks some of the more outlandish features of the B-King, not least its supercharged 1300cc (79cu in) engine, fingerprint ignition and GPS system.

What the GSR does have is the B-King's distinctive look – from the angular headlight, shapely frame rails, aggressive front scoop detailing and underseat exhaust system to the enormous aluminium rear swingarm and wide tires.

Suzuki's GSX-R600 engine had been a strong performer in the supersports market, so Suzuki

Despite some criticism of the budget nature of its suspension units, Suzuki's GSR600 is still a very competent introduction to sporty motorcycles for many novices.

engineers began turning the high-revving race-ready engine into a motor more suited to a naked roadster. The priorities move from all-out peak horsepower to a more drivable, torquey power delivery – a naked bike is less able to exploit high-speed high-horsepower riding, and is more likely to need low-down power. City riding, commuting and even the needs of novice riders are all considerations for the designer of the naked middleweight, so the GSR engine has been developed from the base of the second-generation 2004 GSX-R600 engine. Different exhaust, cam and ignition settings have reduced peak power from the 120bhp (89kW) of the GSX-R to nearer 100bhp (74.5kW) and other changes were necessary to comply with Euro III emissions rules.

With sharp, contemporary styling and a supersports-specification engine, something had to give in the budget to allow the GSR to be sold at a competitive price, so the chassis components were compromised. Although the rear swingarm and frame are fashionable, cast-aluminium parts look good and work well, the

suspension units are much more basic. The front forks are 43mm (1.7in) units, with only preload adjustment, and the rear monoshock has adjustable preload and rebound damping. The front brakes have large 310mm (12in) disks, but only conventionally mounted four-piston calipers, and a single 240mm (9.5in) rear disk has a single-piston caliper.

The GSR's running gear offers decent performance for a naked middleweight, although it's some way off a genuine sporting chassis. But it's the engine that is less impressive. The fuelling changes required to meet tighter emissions rules introduced a rather snatchy element to the power delivery, making slow-speed riding trickier. The need to ensure that no unburnt fuel or pollutants comes out of the exhaust means the fuel injection runs very lean. Sudden transitions from off to on throttle can lead to irregular performance. The engine is still rather peaky too, and a GSR rider in a hurry will find regular gear changes are essential to keep the motor in the best rev range for power.

But with some aftermarket tuning – a Dynojet Power Commander fuel injection controller and an exhaust replacement – the GSR grows much more satisfying. Most naked-bike owners customize their bikes, so many will find these changes indispensable anyway.

Suzuki GSX-R600

Inside the engine, Suzuki fitted the K6 model GSX-R600 with a back-torque limiting clutch to reduce wheel hop under fierce downshifts on track. Inlet and exhaust valves are made from titanium.

The underslung silencer design has a large steel muffler box mounted below the engine, which contains a catalytic convertor and an electronically controlled butterfly valve. This keeps weight low and central, and improves aerodynamics over side-mounted or underseat exhausts.

The footrests are adjustable, a different positions. The radial f adjustable for span.

The fuel injection system has 40mm (16in) throttle bodies, with twin butterfly valves and twin injectors for each cylinder. This gives better fuel atomization, reduces emissions and improves drive.

The 2006 model GSX-R600 is virtually identical to the firm's GSX-R750, apart from the engine capacity, paint schemes and the finish on the front fork stanchions.

moved to three
e lever is also

Suzuki's GSX-R range is the longest-running series of race-replica superbikes produced by a Japanese manufacturer. The GSX-R750 first appeared in 1987, and it was soon followed by an 1100 and 400 version. But a GSX-R600 took a long time to appear. The US had one in the mid-1990s, but this was a strange hybrid bike. Instead of an entirely separate model, it was a sleeved-down GSX-R750 designed to suit the American market. The firm's GSX600F, built starting in 1988, was a nominal sportsbike, and hopelessly outclassed from the time it was launched. But by 1996, Suzuki finally had a fully competitive supersports 600.

The first GSX-R600 resembled the GSX-R750, apart from conventional instead of inverted forks, and four-piston brakes instead of six-piston items. It was slightly shorter than the GSX-R750, and had geometry based on the firm's Grand Prix bike. Its aluminium-beam frame with track suspension and full fairing was more racy than street-biased steel-framed 600s like Honda's CBR and Yamaha's YZF. The engine, too, was much more suited to track use, with a high, if peaky, power delivery from its carburetted 16-valve water-cooled engine. Constant gear changes were essentially to keep the engine revs within the peak power range,

Suzuki's GSX-R cockpit provides all the information a sportsbike rider needs – engine revs, gear position and speed. The large white light is a programmable shift light.

otherwise the engine lost some drive, making for a somewhat wearing ride on long journeys. On a track though, where the rider can keep the engine revs high, this is less of a problem.

Suzuki GSX-R600

Top speed:	265km/h (165mph)
Engine type:	599cc (36.5cu in), l/c inline-four, 16-valve DOHC
Maximum power:	125bhp (93kW) @13,500rpm
Frame type:	aluminium twin spar
Tyre sizes:	front 120/70 17, rear 180/55 17
Final drive:	chain
Gearbox:	six-speed
Weight:	161kg (355lb)

Complementing this motor was an impressive handling package, including sharp steering, wide supersport tyres, firm suspension and strong brakes.

For the second model year, the GSX-R600 looked identical, but received various internal changes to improve the power, with some success. But it wasn't until Suzuki totally revised the bike in 2001, dumping the carburettors for fuel injection, that the motor became more relaxed in normal road use. This K1 model was a total revision, along the lines of the 2000-model GSX-R750 K0, and resembled the 750.

The K1 600 engine used the same techniques as on the K0 750 to ensure that it was a lighter, and more compact and powerful machine. It had a dual-valve fuel injection system, which used a secondary butterfly to moderate air/fuel mix into the engine. The secondary valve is controlled by the ECU, which ensures optimum velocity of the air/fuel mix at all engine speeds and throttle openings.

The chassis was, as before, based on the larger bike. But once again, the 750's upside-down forks were exchanged for somewhat less expensive conventional parts, and the swingarm consisted of a lighter, cheaper unbraced part. These alterations, together with the smaller engine, meant the 600 was more than 10kg (22lb) lighter than before. The shorter wheelbase and sporty steering geometry allowed the bike to turn better than ever, while the fully adjustable suspension and Bridgestone tyres provided amazing roadholding.

Two years later, Suzuki gave the K model yet another makeover. The 2004 bike had lightweight titanium engine valves. These allowed the racebikes to rev higher, while intake and exhaust changes gave more power. The chassis was lighter and smaller, with a narrower frame, and new, sleeker, bodywork. Modernizing updates, including a new headlight, LED tail light and digital dashboard also brought the GSX-R's equipment levels right up to date.

For 2006, the GSX-R entered another new phase of its development. The K6 model was a wheels-up redesign, in the same vein as the GSX-R750 of that year. The most obvious change was to the exhaust, which used a large silencer mounted below the engine. This was intended to lower and centralize mass, and meant a total redesign of the engine and frame, to make space for the exhaust. Almost every chassis part was more compact and lighter, and it finally got the same upside-down forks as the 750, although the inner tubes had a chrome finish instead of the dark bronze titanium finish of the bigger bike.

Borrowed from the 2005 GSX-R1000, the 600's sleek tail unit has dual LED tail lights and integrated turn signals. This picture shows the optional pillion seat cover, suited for solo riding.

Suzuki Bandit 650 (+600)

The relaxed power delivery, comfortable riding position and neat half-fairing makes the Bandit 'S' a sound choice for commuting and light touring.

The Bandit uses a fairly conventional rolling chassis. The steel-tube frame is a double-cradle design, which gives good performance at a low price. Standard front forks and a monoshock rear suspension unit are preload-adjustable only.

Suzuki supplied the Bandit with Bridgestone or Michelin tyres. These were more suited to high-mileage road use than sports riding, but for most riders, though, they still offered ample grip.

Instead of using water or air cooling, the 16-valve, inline-four Bandit engine is an oil-cooled design. This uses two separate oil circuits, one for lubrication, the other for cooling. A large oil radiator expels excess heat.

The Bandit's front brakes use a pair of twin-piston calipers and 290mm (11.5in) discs. Suzuki also offered an optional antilock braking system on the Bandit 650 range.

When Suzuki engineers first conceived the idea of the Bandit, they surely never expected it to be such a runaway success. A concoction of parts robbed from other bikes in Suzuki's range, with a no-nonsense, straightforward design and somewhat basic specification, it was the antithesis of the normally complex, expensive superbike-design process.

The first Bandit was a Japanese home-market model, the Bandit 400. Retro-styled machines were very fashionable there in the early 1990s, and bikes like Kawasaki's Zephyr 400 and Honda's CB400 were strong sellers. Suzuki's 1990 entry into this naked roadster 400 market had a simple steel-cradle frame, with an inline-four cylinder engine, monoshock rear suspension, and decent wheels, tyres and brakes.

It was five years before the bigger Bandit appeared, and it received strong praise from press and buyers alike. The styling was very similar to the 400, with

Low tech but effective. The small Bandit's front end used basic components, but the conventional forks and twin-piston sliding calipers worked perfectly well for its target audience.

tint-matched frame rails, a big, shiny engine, chromed exhaust and a round headlight. The engine was taken from the somewhat dull GSX600F sport-tourer, but freshened up with different carburettors and exhaust design. It's a standard 16-valve inline-four design, although it uses oil and air cooling instead of water cooling. A secondary oil-pump circuit circulates the engine oil through channels in the cylinder head, and through a large oil-cooler radiator mounted in front of the engine. Suzuki claimed this was lighter and more efficient than a separate water-cooling system.

A year after the first 'naked' Bandit was launched, Suzuki presented a half-faired version, the GSF600S. The addition of the extra bodywork meant the S could take on longer trips with more comfort, and it made a decent commuter and gentle tourer. It didn't have a very attractive fairing though, and most Bandit fans preferred the simpler style of the naked model.

The Bandit 600 was a huge sales success for Suzuki, thanks to its decent performance, stylish design and great flexibility. The Bandit really was a do-everything bike, able to commute to work every day, go scratching

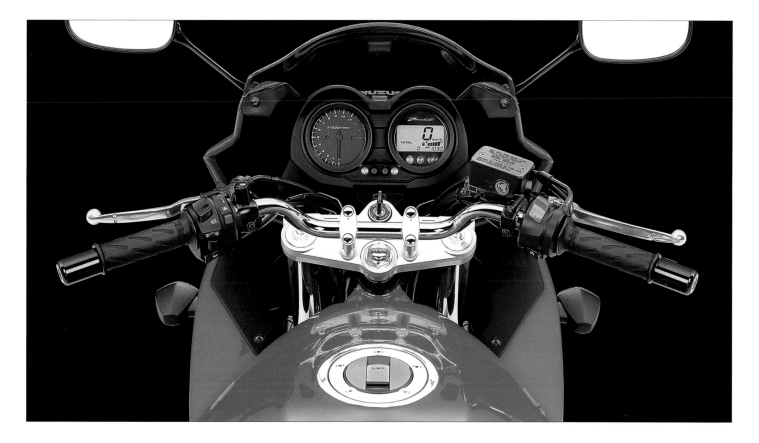

The rider's view from the Bandit 'S' faired version. This later model boasted an LCD speedometer readout, revised fairing and projector headlights. It made a good light tourer and everyday commuter.

around twisty backroads on the weekend, and venture out on longer leisure journeys. More daring owners found that the Bandit was good fun on a track, and even for the odd bit of stunt riding.

The GSF600 remained largely unchanged for the first five years of its life, but by 2000, more advanced rivals had left it somewhat behind. Suzuki gave it a new frame and tweaked the styling, and the engine received new carburettors. Wider, grippier tyres and

different brakes further enhanced the Bandit's handling, but it remained essentially the same inexpensive, fun, practical bike. Yamaha's Fazer 600 and Honda's Hornet 600 both offered much more performance and style, but were more expensive too.

One other important area of Bandit ownership was personalization. The bike's cheap chassis components left much room for improvement, and the simple styling left plenty of space for individuality. As a result, Bandit owners bolted on cosmetic and performance enhancements with gusto. Some parts made a real difference: a good exhaust, brake improvements and suspension upgrades could transform the Bandit's performance from tame to terrific. Other parts, like crash protectors and rear fenders, also made good practical sense.

As each year passed though, it became clear that the Bandit 600 was in dire need of replacement, and was falling further behind its rivals. For 2005, Suzuki gave it one last revamp, in the form of a capacity increase. The Bandit 650 engine had a 656cc (40cu in) capacity, the 57cc (3.4cu in) extra coming from a 2.9mm (.1in) increase in the bore size. This gave stronger midrange, and more torque, although peak power was unchanged. The rest of the bike was almost identical to the 600, with some chassis changes to improve stability. The other major change was the introduction of an advanced, digital antilock braking system.

Suzuki Bandit 650 (+600)

Top speed:	200km/h (125mph)
Engine type:	656cc (40cu in), a/c inline-four, 16-valve DOHC
Maximum power:	77.5bhp (58kW) @10,100rpm
Frame type:	steel-tube cradle
Tyre sizes:	front 120/70 17, rear 160/60 17
Final drive:	chain
Gearbox:	six-speed
Weight:	201kg (443lb)

Triumph Daytona 650 (+TT600)

The Daytona 650 replaced the Daytona 600, pictured here, with a larger 646cc (39cu in) inline-four engine. Apart from the longer stroke engine, the rest of the 650 was virtually identical to the 600.

Triumph's machines have traditionally had excellent brakes. Dual 308mm (12in) discs and four-piston calipers are powerful and progressive for road and circuit use.

Triumph developed the Daytona's chassis mostly on track, so it had excellent handling. The high pegs give superb ground clearance, Bridgestone tyres are grippy and stable, and the suspension is fully adjustable.

The TT600 was criticized for its rounded styling. The more angular bodywork on the Daytona was more popular among sportsbike fans.

Serious fuelling problems with the TT600's Sagem fuel injection system lead Triumph to swap to a Japanese Keihin set-up for the Daytona. The throttle bodies had twin valves to give smooth, predictable power delivery.

In 1991, Triumph began building motorcycles again. The name had disappeared in the 1980s when the original company went bust, but a new firm, run by building tycoon John Bloor, owned the rights to the brand. Bloor's company, based in Hinckley, Leicestershire, began with a 'modular' range of bikes powered by three- and four-cylinder engines, resulting in no small amount of success.

Fast-forward almost ten years, and Triumph launched its first 600-class machine. The TT600 was released in 2000, and like the original Hinckley Triumphs, it appeared to be based on Japanese designs. It had a high-revving inline four-cylinder engine, with advanced fuel injection (a first on a series production 600), full race fairing and a supersports chassis package.

Triumph's first 600, the TT, was roundly criticized for its styling, which was seen as rounded and bland. The shape of the headlight was particularly singled out for opprobrium.

Initial reports were very positive: the little Triumph 600 had an excellent chassis, adjustable suspension, class-leading brakes and its handling on track was superb. At the press launch in France, riders praised its superb ground clearance, well-damped suspension, taut frame and grippy Bridgestone tyres.

But the engine had problems – the fuel injection was woefully inadequate, the motor was down on peak power compared with Japanese competition, and that power was produced in a rather revvy, peaky fashion. At low engine speeds, just off idle, the fuel injection seemed unable to cope, and the engine suffered from poor running, coughing and unpredictable power production at various points in the rev range.

Triumph rushed out a number of fuel-injection updates, and after a year, it even built different camshafts to improve the power. The updates made a difference, and the 2001 TT600 was a much better bike. However, it was still dogged by criticism over its soft-edged styling, and some build-quality issues.

Stripped down, the TT looks much like any other of its class members – i.e. the Japanese four-cylinder machines. That's no surprise – the Triumph was based closely on these market leaders.

But the writing was on the wall for the TT, and it was replaced after just three years by the Daytona 600.

The Daytona retained the excellent characteristics of the TT chassis, (the one area in which that bike really excelled), and added a powerplant that worked well. The new engine was based on the TT design, but with extensive reworking aimed at generating competitive torque and power. Triumph also switched from the TT's Sagem fuel injection to Keihin dual-valve throttle bodies. The much-criticized styling of the TT was also replaced, with a much sharper, more angular look.

Triumph Daytona 650 (+TT600)

Top speed:	257km/h (160mph)
Engine type:	646cc (39cu in), l/c inline-four, 16-valve DOHC
Maximum power:	114bhp (84kW)@12,500rpm
Frame type:	aluminium twin spar
Tyre sizes:	front 120/70 17, rear 180/55 17
Final drive:	chain
Gearbox:	six-speed
Weight:	165kg (364lb)

A pair of geometric headlights, with a small ram air-intake between them, gave the Daytona an instantly recognizable 'face'.

On the road, the Daytona 600 was a sound performer. It was slightly behind the very best of the competition, but in such a competitive class, this is less important than it may seem. The chassis characteristics, especially the brakes and the steering, were superlative, both on road and on the track. New instruments, good mirrors and a decently sized windshield made life easier on longer trips, and while the engine was still a little down on power, torque and refinement, it was much closer than the TT.

But, again, Triumph had a trick up its sleeve for the 2005 model year. The lesson of Kawasaki's ZX-636R had clearly been learned by Triumph engineers – that firm had taken its lacklustre 599cc (36.6cu in) design, and simply added 37cc (2.25cu in) capacity to boost torque and power. Triumph did the same thing to the Daytona, taking the 599cc (36.6cu in) motor up to 646cc (39cu in). The extra cc came from a longer piston stroke – a different crankshaft has a 44.5mm (1.75in) stroke, up 3.2mm (.125in) from the 41.3mm (1.6in) 600 stroke. The extra torque of the larger motor made a real difference, and the 650 became Triumph's most competitive four-cylinder bike.

Some people saw the capacity change as a 'cheat' on Triumph's part, but the 599cc (36.5cu in) capacity is only really important in terms of racing classes, and because Triumph had little involvement there, it could discount this disadvantage.

Triumph 675 Daytona Triple

A high-tech dashboard includes a bright blue LED shift light, LCD digital display and a large analogue tachometer.

To keep up its reputation for excellent brakes, Triumph chose radial mount front calipers normally used on a race bike – Yamaha's TZ250. The caliper pistons are also specially treated with a low-friction aerospace coating to further improve power and feel.

The seat is rather high on the 675, making it initially disconcerting for shorter riders, although its narrow profile helps. The riding position is focussed and can feel cramped for larger riders on long trips.

The Daytona is an extremely light bike, and track preparation makes it even lighter. Replacing the stock catalyst-equipped exhaust with a race item and removing other road equipment can cut dry weight below 155kg (342lb).

Underlining the sporting focus of the 675 Daytona, Triumph fitted no-compromise track-ready tyres. Pirelli SuperCorsa Pros give amazing grip and sharp track handling.

Triumph's 2005 Daytona 650 was a sound machine, but engineers inside the firm were already working on something else. Triumph's three-cylinder engines had traditionally been its best designs, the unusual layout giving some of the best of both worlds between a twin- and four-cylinder design. Triple-cylinder engines have a different sound and 'feel' than other layouts, and the best ones, like Triumph's Speed Triple 1050, have strong torquey grunt low-down and in the midrange as well as strong peak power.

So it was no surprise when the firm released a triple for the middleweight class in 2006. Fewer cylinders mean less theoretical peak power for a given capacity, so Triumph planned a larger than 600cc (36.6cu in) capacity. World and British supersport racing rules allow 750cc (46cu in) twins to compete with 600cc (36.6cu in) fours, so Triumph split the difference, and went for a 675cc (41cu in) triple.

The Daytona 675 triple was first shown at the 2005 Paris show, and it was the star attraction. Every part of

Triumph 675 Daytona Triple	
Top speed:	265km/h (165mph)
Engine type:	675cc (41cu in), l/c inline-triple, 12-valve DOHC
Maximum power:	123bhp (90kW)@12,500rpm
Frame type:	aluminium twin spar
Tyre sizes:	front 120/70 17, rear 180/55 17
Final drive:	chain
Gearbox:	six-speed
Weight:	165kg (364lb)

the 675 was new, from the compact, powerful three-cylinder, 12-valve, DOHC engine, to the cast-aluminum frame and swingarm, underseat exhaust system and sleek bodywork. The performance statistics on paper were as impressive as its gorgeous styling – a dry mass of 165kg (364lb), and claimed peak power of 123bhp (90kW) was right on par with even the very best of the Japanese opposition.

It wasn't until the bike's riding launch at Malaysia's Sepang F1 circuit that the press could test those claims. Happily, the world's press agreed with Triumph. Both the fast, challenging track and Malaysia's country roads allowed the little 675 to shine, and its strong power, sharp handling and soulful styling immediately impressed. That impression continued through into 2006's various 600cc (36.6cu in) group tests, and many publications rated the 675 Daytona ahead of the competition.

The 675 was so good because it had more than just pure performance, although those claims made in Paris weren't just PR spin: the bike really was that powerful and light. The engine was a beautifully complete package, giving massive pulses of torque in the lower rev ranges, while also making strong peak power, spinning up to 13,000rpm and beyond. The fuel injection was flawless, with smooth, indefatigable power delivered all through the rev range, and the 675 made an enthralling, soulful sound.

The chassis designers had much input from motorcycle racers, and their ideas led to a small, neat, taut-feeling bike, with amazing control, stability and handling. All the chassis componentry was the highest

Elegant frame and subframe castings look rather delicate, but are designed to be immensely stiff without adding weight. The gearchange connecting rod passes directly through the frame.

specification available, from Kayaba suspension to Nissin brakes and Pirelli SuperCorsa Pro tires, and it showed in the final riding experience.

But if the 675 had only been a good paper performer, it wouldn't have been half the bike it was. Much of its attraction is down to its gorgeous design. It has sleek,

Triumph used a sophisticated casting process to manufacture the 675's gorgeous aluminum swinging arm. The triangulated bracing adds stiffness without extra mass, improving handling.

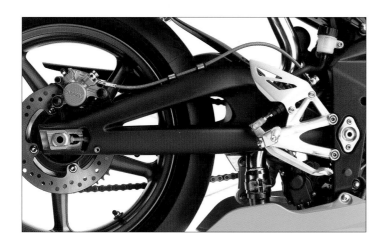

Neat, catseye headlights are mounted below the large single ram air -intake that feeds cool, high pressure air through the steering head to the engine airbox.

curvaceous bodywork, a classy finish and an elegant, sophisticated overall feel. And like the classic motorcycling designs of history: the Ducati 916, Harley-Davidson's V-Rod, Yamaha's V-Max, the 675 Daytona instantly became a stylish, almost cult machine. It even achieved minor racing success in its first year – UK-based Australian racer Paul Young raced the 675 in the British Supersport championship in 2006. Despite limited sponsorship, and a tiny privateer team backup, Young regularly finished mid-pack, finishing just behind many factory-backed teams on well financed Japanese machinery. Young was also a freelance development rider for Triumph, so he had actually helped develop the 675 Triple as a prototype.

The 675 did suffer slightly from its focus. It is so compact and small, that comfort is minimal on long rides. Larger riders will find it hard to tuck in behind the tiny race cockpit, and the high, narrow seat is a chore on rides much longer than a couple of hours.

Yamaha FZ6 (+Fazer 600)

The second-generation FZ6 Fazer boasts a specification close to many sportsbikes. It has a cast-aluminium frame, a fuel-injected engine derived from the R6 supersports bike and sharp, modern styling.

Although the R6-based engine on the FZ6 was much more modern than on the older Thundercat-powered bike, it had a revvier power delivery. Some riders preferred the torquier output of the older engine.

The aluminium frame is cast in two parts, which are bolted together at the steering head and swingarm pivot plates, giving a light, stiff chassis. The swingarm is a simple extruded aluminium design, with a linkless monoshock arrangement.

Yamaha offered an optional ABS-equipped version of the Fazer from 2005.

One area where the 2004 FZ6 impressed less than its predecessor was its brakes. The newer bike's twin-piston sliding calipers gave good performance, but lacked the class of the older bike's four-piston equipment.

The naked FZ6 had a much more modern specification than the elderly Fazer it replaced. This included an ultra-modern LCD combined tachometer/speedo unit.

Although Suzuki's Bandit 600 is normally credited with beginning the 'naked 600' class, Yamaha did have a small head start. Its Diversion 600 of 1992, although a much weaker performer than the Bandit, was practical, cheap and stylish. But when Suzuki released the Bandit, the Diversion was suddenly a long way back, its dated engine and soft chassis found wanting.

Yamaha took a couple of years to hit back. However, when its new middleweight arrived, it hit back with a vengeance. The Fazer 600 first appeared in 1997 and, as many predictable press headlines roared, it 'stunned' the opposition.

The Fazer's main trick was to select its components carefully. So although it was a budget machine, its engine and brakes were both taken from Yamaha's main 600cc (37cu in) supersport competitor, the Thundercat. The engine in particular was a masterstroke, with slight internal changes and smaller carburettors reducing peak power to around 95bhp (71kW), but giving tractable, accessible power everywhere. The brakes, too, gave excellent performance, and their four-piston monobloc design was miles ahead of the class.

These two star-performing components stood out on the Fazer, although the rest of the bike was perfectly competent. A steel-tube cradle frame, while nothing radical, did all that was asked of it, as did the slightly soft suspension. The tires were narrower than usual, but used a sound sport-touring compound that gave fine grip and mileage. And Yamaha also fitted a half-fairing as standard, making the Fazer a real distance contender from the very start. Despite its questionable styling, the small nosecone was a boon for longer trips, and a real advantage over naked competition, such as the Honda Hornet.

Yamaha priced the Fazer sensibly too, putting it in the UK market just below the flashier, but less well equipped, Hornet, and even below the Bandit (Suzuki soon dropped its price though). This combination of value, performance and practicality shot the Fazer to the top of the class, where it stayed for several years.

It wasn't perfect though. That ugly fairing did not win it any awards for styling, and the headlight was terrible at night. The build quality left something to be desired in places, for example, the exhausts suffered badly from rust. But over the next four years, Yamaha gradually updated the Fazer with stainless exhausts, a sleeker fairing borrowed from the Fazer 1000 and little refinements such as a clock, fuel gauge, larger 22l (6gal) tank and classier tank badges. This final 'mark one' Fazer was an excellent all-rounder, with satisfying performance and quiet, assured practicality.

But, for 2004, Yamaha had a new Fazer in the wings, partly forced on it by emissions regulations. The Thundercat engine didn't comply with tightening rules on pollution, so had to be replaced with a new unit, based on the supersport R6 engine. At the same time, Yamaha engineered an all-new bike, with an aluminium frame, fuel injection, new bodywork and an optional naked version. The new bike was renamed the FZ6 (naked) or FZ6 Fazer (faired), and it looked to be a step forward. The new chassis made for a slightly

Yamaha FZ6 (+Fazer 600)

Top speed:	230km/h (145mph)
Engine type:	600cc (37cu in), l/c inline-four, 16-valve DOHC
Maximum power:	98bhp (73kW)@12,000rpm
Frame type:	aluminium twin spar
Tyre sizes:	front 120/70 17, rear 180/55 17
Final drive:	chain
Gearbox:	six-speed
Weight:	180kg (397lb)

A four-into two exhaust system helped reduce noise and emissions, thanks to catalysts inside the silencers. A crossover pipe near the cylinder head improved midrange on the R6-based engine.

lighter machine, and the R6-derived engine was more powerful, lighter and more advanced. The option of a naked version made sense for fans of stylish city machines, and the new fairing was much sleeker.

Sadly, some of the magic that made the old bike such a winner had gone. The new engine was revvier than the old one, and needed more revs and more effort to make decent progress. The fuel injection was occasionally uncertain in its delivery, and the overall powerplant was less user friendly. The chassis was better, the new frame adding some sparkle to the steering, and ground clearance had improved. But the new brakes were a less expensive, two-piston sliding caliper design, and they lacked the style or performance of the old Thundercat calipers.

The naked FZ6 makes a good city bike, where its light handling and comfortable riding position work well.

Yamaha R6 (+Thundercat)

Yamaha was among the first to use large cast-aluminium frame components. These are cast using a controlled fill-vacuum process, reducing imperfections and increasing the strength of the machine.

Separate high- and low-speed compression-damper adjusters front and rear put the R6 at the top of its class for suspension performance.

The sharp 'winglets' on the fairing sidepanels improve the R6's aerodynamic performance, helping air flow around the bike. The central ram-air intake feeds right through the aluminium frame into the engine's airbox.

The most controversial part of the 2006 R6 was its tachometer. It had a red line marked at 17,500rpm, but tests showed the engine was only revving to around 16,200rpm before the rev limiter cut in. Yamaha altered the display for 2007.

Yamaha borrowed technology from its MotoGP programme for the R6's fuel injection system. Its 'fly-by-wire' throttle control is similar to the system used on Valentino Rossi's M1 MotoGP racebike.

Although it had always taken a strong corporate interest in the supersport 600 class, Yamaha hadn't always been top of the pile. Its first modern 600, the 1989 FZR600, did well in competition, although it was harsh and unfriendly on the road. Its replacements (the FZR600R in 1994, and then the YZF600 Thundercat in 1996), were much better machines on road and track. But the competition from other Japanese firms was intense, and the Thundercat was less useful than the CBR600, and less powerful than the Kawasaki ZX-6R. Suzuki's GSX-R600 was the one to beat on track, and so Yamaha had a stiff challenge on its hands.

The first clue to what was coming appeared in 1997, with the Yamaha YZF-R1. This revolutionary machine turned the litre-class market upside-down with its light weight, big power and small-bike handling. It seemed unlikely that a 600cc (37cu in) version

The 2006 R6 was really at its best on the racetrack, where its high-revving engine, super-sharp steering response and firm suspension gave the best results.

wouldn't be forthcoming, and in 1998, the YZF-R6 was unveiled at the Munich trade show. Styled like its 1000cc (61cu in) sister, the R6 was a massive step forward from the somewhat flabby Thundercat styling. Twin headlights framed a radical ram-air engine intake

Yamaha R6 (+Thundercat)

Top speed:	265km/h (165mph)
Engine type:	599cc (36.5cu in), l/c inline-four, 16-valve DOHC
Maximum power:	133bhp (99kW) @14,500rpm
Frame type:	aluminium twin spar
Tyre sizes:	front 120/70 17, rear 180/55 17
Final drive:	chain
Gearbox:	six-speed
Weight:	161kg (355lb)

The R6 had separate high-and low-speed adjusters, to fine-tune the bike's response to bumps and weight transfer forces. This level of adjustment was formerly only available on pure race bikes.

in the nosecone, fully adjustable suspension included 43mm (17in) conventional front forks and a rear monoshock unit, the frame was stiff, light aluminium, and the brakes were the same excellent Sumitomo units used on the R1. It looked incredible next to the competition, and while its performance wasn't as far ahead as the R1, it still shot Yamaha into the lead in this vital class.

Updates to the R6 appeared every couple of years, gradually increasing power, reducing mass and improving equipment levels and usability. The first major update was for 2003, when the bike got a 90% new engine, with 'suction piston' fuel injection. This used a CV-carburetor type vacuum-controlled air valve to match intake gas flow to the engine's requirements. 2003 also saw a new cast frame and swingarm, and new bodywork.

Another minor update for 2005 kept the R6 in contention – new upside-down forks and radial mount calipers being the most important changes. But the R6 had been losing its pre-eminence for a while.

Yamaha also fitted separate high-and low-speed damping adjusters to the rear monoshock, making for an almost-bewildering array of possible settings.

Kawasaki's 636cc (39cu in) ZX-6R had more power, Honda's CBR600RR had racing glory and strong handling, while Suzuki's GSX-R600 was a stunning package on road and track.

So for 2006, Yamaha pulled no punches. It released details of the 2006 R6 in late 2005, and the new bike appeared to be a real step forward. Laden with technology, and swathed in MotoGP styling, the R6 made some incredible claims for power and mass. The new engine was capable of revving to an incredible 17,000rpm on the large central tachometer, and with ram-air effects at high speed, Yamaha claimed 130bhp (97kW) from the 599cc (36.5cu in) motor. The fuel injection used a unique 'fly-by-wire' computerized set-up, dubbed YCC-T (Yamaha Chip Controlled Throttle). On this system, the fuel injection computer analyzes the input from the throttle twist grip, and converts them into the appropriate throttle valve openings in the fuel-injection bodies.

The engine also has titanium valves to allow high-rpm operation, and an underslung exhaust silencer with an EXUP butterfly valve inside to optimize fuel flow, plus a catalyst to cut pollution. The transmission has a slipper-type clutch, which improves stability during gear downchanges on track.

Yamaha's chassis engineers worked hard on the new R6 too. Both the rear shock and forks have separate high-and low-speed compression damping adjustment for optimum track set-up. A new cast-aluminium frame, braced swingarm and radical, aerodynamic bodywork were all new too, and the bike weighed in at a super-light 161kg (355lb).

Yamaha's technology worked amazingly, especially on track, where the stable chassis gives superb control. But the engine is revvy, and it's a less relaxing bike to ride than Triumph's 675, or Honda's CBR600RR.

Italian Exotica:
Italian superbikes

Like their four-wheeled cousins, Italian superbikes have long been associated with extreme performance, exotic design and gorgeous styling. But, again like Italian supercars, that was often matched with outrageous price tags, highly-strung road manners and occasional unreliability.

However, once firms like Ducati had shaken off the appalling unreliability and poor build quality that dogged them through the 1980s and into the 1990s, they started to make a real impact on sales of Japanese machines. Perhaps the archetypal modern Italian superbike is Ducati's 916. Launched in 1993, it took an unsuspecting motorcycling public by storm: no-one had seen anything as jaw-droppingly beautiful before, especially not in production form.

And when that bike turned out to perform every bit as well as it looked, it set parameters for Italian exotica that would turn out to be extremely hard to beat. Over the following decade, the 916 was uprated with bigger, more powerful engines and better chassis components, culminating in the externally-similar 998R of 2001, before Ducati replaced its iconic model with the 999.

The recipe for a modern Italian superbike was laid out by Ducati. It generally meant a big-bore engine – usually a V-twin – housed in a narrow, stiff chassis, and fitted with very high-quality suspension and brake components. Track performance is a big priority, so wide, sticky race-spec tyres are fitted, and a full race fairing is essential. It was this route that Aprilia followed with its RSV Mille, although the RSV had a much more Japanese feel to its design. The resurgent MV Agusta firm went for an inline-four engine for its F4 superbike, but the chassis and design feel was entirely in keeping with the Italian superbike feel. Benelli's Tornado split the difference with a three-cylinder engine, but its Brembo brakes, trellis frame and drop-dead styling were all as Italian as pasta and strong coffee.

However, the truly exotic Italian machinery came from the sidelines. The tiny firm of Bimota has made some of motorcycling's most audacious designs, with varying success over the years. Its Japanese-powered sportsbikes were the epitome of Italian exotica, and at their best they handled, looked and sounded better than anything else. Sadly, they also tended to be the most expensive and least reliable, although the firm has improved matters greatly over the years.

Despite its dubious styling, Ducati's 999 was the archetypal Italian superbike. Powered by a punchy, high-output V-twin engine, and with a track-developed chassis and handling package, it performed admirably in superbike racing, at world and national level.

Aprilia RSV Mille

Aprilia enjoyed some WSB success with the RSV. Australian Troy Corser rode the bike in 2000 and 2001, finishing third and fourth respectively.

Starting in 2004, the RSV used a large single ram-air intake between its dual headlights. This fed cool, dense air through the frame's headstock to the large airbox.

Early versions of the RSV had one large exhaust silencer mounted on the right. Aprilia later moved to a two-into-two exhaust system, with one smaller oval silencer on each side.

The RSV has a very high chassis specification. Öhlins suspension is fully adjustable, Brembo radial-mount brakes are very powerful, and a fabricated aluminium frame and swingarm are stiff and light.

Large V-twin engines can lock up the rear wheel under race deceleration, but Aprilia fitted a 'slipper' clutch to prevent this. When the throttle is closed, a pneumatic system reduces clutch pressure, allowing it to slip slightly, preventing wheel-lock.

For most of the 1990s, Ducati had a free run at the superbike market in Italy. The Bologna-based firm had developed its V-twin desmo sportsbike range into the 916, and if you wanted a large non-Japanese sportsbike, you were very much limited to Ducati.

But other manufacturers had their eye on this market, Noale-based Aprilia in particular. Its expected superbike was the worst-kept secret in motorcycling, and despite several false starts, it was finally unveiled in 1998. It was typically Italian in some ways – its V-twin engine, the rather quirky bodywork – but also rather Japanese. Its aluminium twin-spar frame, complex digital dashboard and practical design marked it out as something rather different.

Aprilia had taken its time over the RSV Mille, as the bike was called. And that longer development period immediately paid off, as the press discovered a bike that was stronger and faster than the competition. The Aprilia's V-twin engine, developed with help from UK engineering consultants Cosworth, had a narrower 60° angle, which made it more compact than the Ducati's 90° layout. A compact, neat cylinder head used twin spark plugs, and had a very efficient combustion chamber. It used dry-sump lubrication, the fuel injection gave good carburation, and the transmission was smooth and glitch-free.

Large capacity V-twins can be difficult to silence, and most designers use dual silencer cans. Aprilia's initial design used an enormous single can, but this was later changed to a two-into-two design.

Aprilia made sure the new bike had a chassis to match its strong, 128bhp (94kW) motor. The more compact engine meant a shorter wheelbase, which adds agility, and the high-quality, fully adjustable suspension front and rear pleased track fans. Brembo four-piston front-brake calipers were as good as, or

Aprilia RSV Mille

Top speed:	261km/h (175mph)
Engine type:	998cc (61cu in), l/c 60° V-twin, eight-valve DOHC
Maximum power:	143bhp (105kW)@10,000rpm
Frame type:	aluminium twin spar
Tyre sizes:	front 120/70 17, rear 190/50 17
Final drive:	chain
Gearbox:	six-speed
Weight:	189kg (416lb)

better than anything else on the market, and lightweight wheels wore wide, sticky rubber, with a choice of a 180- or 190-section rear tyre, the narrower tire giving faster steering, the wider tyre more grip.

The RSV had very distinctive, 'love-it or hate-it' styling – the front fairing housed an unusual triple headlight unit, and Aprilia fitted a large single silencer instead of two smaller ones.

The RSV was a strong seller for Aprilia, and the following year, the firm released two variants, though only one was realistically available to buyers. That bike, the RSV Mille 'R' was an upgraded version that came with higher-quality Ohlins suspension, lighter forged Oz wheels, and an extra £1000 ($1650) on the pricetag over the base model.

The other version, the RSV Mille SP was an entirely different bike, made to homologate the firm's world superbike contender. The SP had a different engine with a much wider bore and shorter stroke, it made 145bhp (107kW), and was supplied with a race exhaust and EPROM chip ready to fit and go racing. Limited to 150 bikes, the RSV Mille SP cost almost £23,000 in the UK ($38,000).

The first RSV was so good Aprilia didn't feel the need to seriously update it for five years. But for 2004,
it revealed the RSV 'R' and the RSV Factory, two new versions. Confusingly, the 'R' was now the basic bike, with the Factory being the luxury version, with radial brakes, and Ohlins-supplied suspension and steering damper. The 2004 range also enjoyed various updates to engine, chassis and bodywork. The new engine, though still a 60° V-twin, was heavily overhauled, with new single-plug cylinder heads, magnesium engine covers, new fuel injection system and many other changes. Power went up to 139bhp (102kW), while dry weight stayed the same at 189kg (417lb). The bodywork was sleeker, while the huge single silencer was replaced by two smaller cans.

The 2004 update kept the RSV on top of the more pricey Ducati 999, but Aprilia kept on revising the bike. The year 2005 saw the radial-mount brake calipers from the Factory version also appearing on the base 'R' bike, and 2006 saw another upgrade of the basic bike, which now also featured the Ohlins front forks. Both bikes also received detail engine changes that added even more power.

The engine's 60° V-twin layout was chosen for its compact nature, but it's still a tight fit in the aluminium frame. Various ancillaries can be seen, including the ignition coils, radiator and cooling system.

Benelli Tornado 1130

The Tornado's angular bodywork has a radical look, and gives good aerodynamic performance. The same angular shapes are echoed in the footpegs, instruments and even the switchblade-type ignition key.

Benelli entered the Tornado in the World Superbike championship in 2001 and 2002. Veteran racer Peter Goddard rode the bike, which was more a development project than a serious race contender.

Italian firm Morini Franco Motori produces the Tornado engine for Benelli. It's the same firm that makes the Moto Morini Corsaro1200 engine.

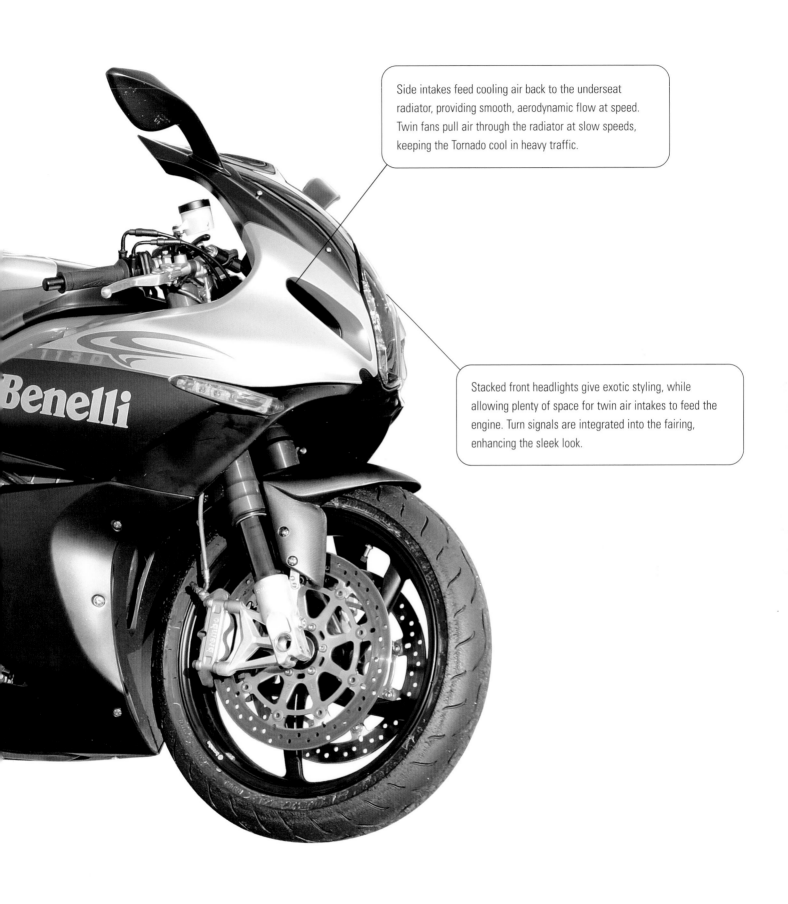

Side intakes feed cooling air back to the underseat radiator, providing smooth, aerodynamic flow at speed. Twin fans pull air through the radiator at slow speeds, keeping the Tornado cool in heavy traffic.

Stacked front headlights give exotic styling, while allowing plenty of space for twin air intakes to feed the engine. Turn signals are integrated into the fairing, enhancing the sleek look.

Like many motorcycle firms, the Benelli company was started in the early part of the twentieth century by a family of enthusiasts. With its origins dating back to 1911, the Pesaro-based company enjoyed varied success over the years. High points included the production of two six-cylinder superbikes in the 1970s; the Benelli Sei 750 and 900. But by the 1980s, the firm was deep in the mire that was enveloping most of the European motorcycle industry. Japanese manufacturers were building better-handling, faster, more reliable machines, and firms like Benelli didn't have the resources to invest in the new machinery required to compete.

It wasn't until 1995 that a firmer future appeared for Benelli. Italian industrial magnate Andrea Merloni invested heavily in the firm, and it announced plans to produce a new range of superbikes.

It took several years before the results of the firm's revival appeared, but most observers felt the wait worthwhile. Unveiled in 2001, the Benelli Tornado Novecento (900) LE was a truly groundbreaking design. Penned by British designer Adrian Morton, it

As you'd expect on such an exotic machine, the cockpit has a dashing, sophisticated layout. The adjustable steering damper is transversely mounted for easy access on the move.

Benelli Tornado 1130

Top speed:	281km/h (175mph)
Engine type:	1130cc (69cu in), l/c inline-triple, 12-valve DOHC
Maximum power:	161bhp (118kW) @10,500rpm
Frame type:	bonded-steel tube/cast-aluminum plate
Tyre sizes:	front 120/70 17, rear 190/50 17
Final drive:	chain
Gearbox:	six-speed
Weight:	198kg (436lb)

had angular, ultra-modern bodywork, clothing a chassis and engine package that was as innovative as it was attractive to look at.

The engine was a three-cylinder 900cc (55cu in), chosen for its eligibility for world superbike (WSB) racing, with high-performance features: fuel injection, 12 valves, DOHC, water cooled, and a balancer shaft to cut vibration. The transmission used a racing dry clutch, and the gearbox was a cassette-type unit, designed for easy ratio changes.

The engine produced a healthy 141bhp (104kW), but its most radical feature was its cooling system. This used a water radiator located under the rider's seat, with an ingenious ducting system that drew cooling air from the front of the bike back through the radiator and out the back of the seat unit. Twin cooling fans at the back of the bike formed an audacious styling point, as well as enhancing aerodynamics. Having the radiator in this position allowed a slimmer front profile, with a more efficient use of cooling airflow than simply placing the radiator flat against the wind.

The Tornado's frame was novel too. It used a combination of steel tubes and aluminium plates, with an aerospace-industry bonding technique joining the parts together. Bolts and high-tech glues attached the steel side rails to aluminum swingarm plates, while a more conventional aluminum swingarm used a combination of cast, forged and extruded parts, welded together.

This first Tornado was a very special, limited edition version, so it used Ohlins suspension, Marchesini wheels, Brembo race brakes and carbon-fiber bodywork. It was intended purely as a homologation machine, to allow Benelli to compete in WSB.

For 2003, Benelli released a less expensive version, with chassis components that were less opulent.

Wheels, suspension, brakes and bodywork were more basic, though still offering excellent performance. This version was slightly heavier, but retained the design impact and engine performance of the LE, and made an interesting choice for riders looking for something somewhat different from the superbike norm.

Riding the Tornado was the usual complex mix of wondrous pleasure and practical nit-picking common to many exotic motorcycles. The steering and handling

Despite its rather high mass, the Benelli's high-spec suspension and brake systems and stiff frame mean it handles beautifully on track.

offered by the high-specification chassis combined stability and dynamism, and worked well on a track. But the riding position was too extreme for many road riders. And though the engine provided strong peak power, the fuel injection was somewhat harsh and unrefined. The underseat radiator certainly looked incredible, but didn't help rider comfort in hot weather, and little things like the poor mirrors were wearing on a day-to-day basis.

Benelli hit further financial problems in 2005, before investment from a Chinese firm, Quianjiang group, got the firm back on track. The 1130cc (69cu in) engine developed for the TNT naked bike (see page 146) was installed in the Tornado chassis for 2006, giving a much-needed 20bhp (15kW) boost, and allowing the Tornado to compete with four-cylinder competitors.

The most striking aspect of the Tornado's design – twin electric fans suck air through the underseat radiator, to keep the engine cool at low road speeds.

Bimota DB5

Chassis components are of the highest standard – Ohlins track suspension front and rear, Brembo race brakes and lightweight OZ wheels, with Dunlop race tyres.

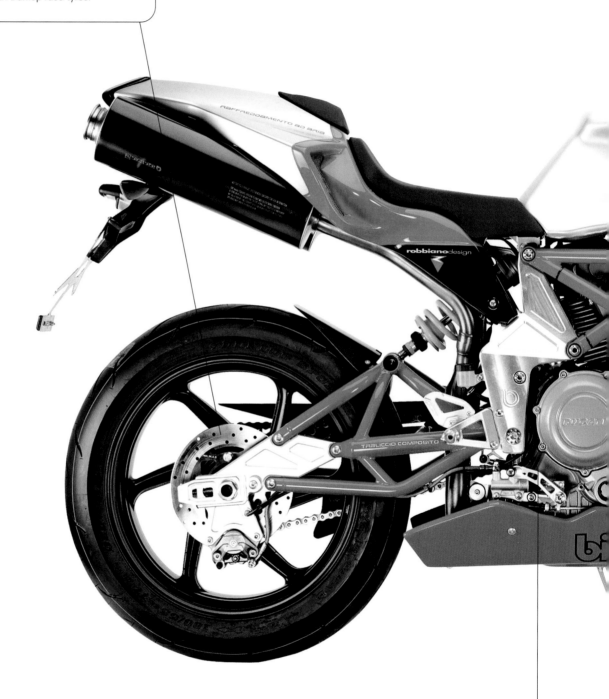

Ducati's 1000DS (Dual Spark) engine is used, with Bimota's own fuel injection and exhaust system. The 92bhp air-cooled 90° V-twin has two valves and two spark plugs per cylinder, and belt-driven desmodromic cams positively close, as well as open, the valves.

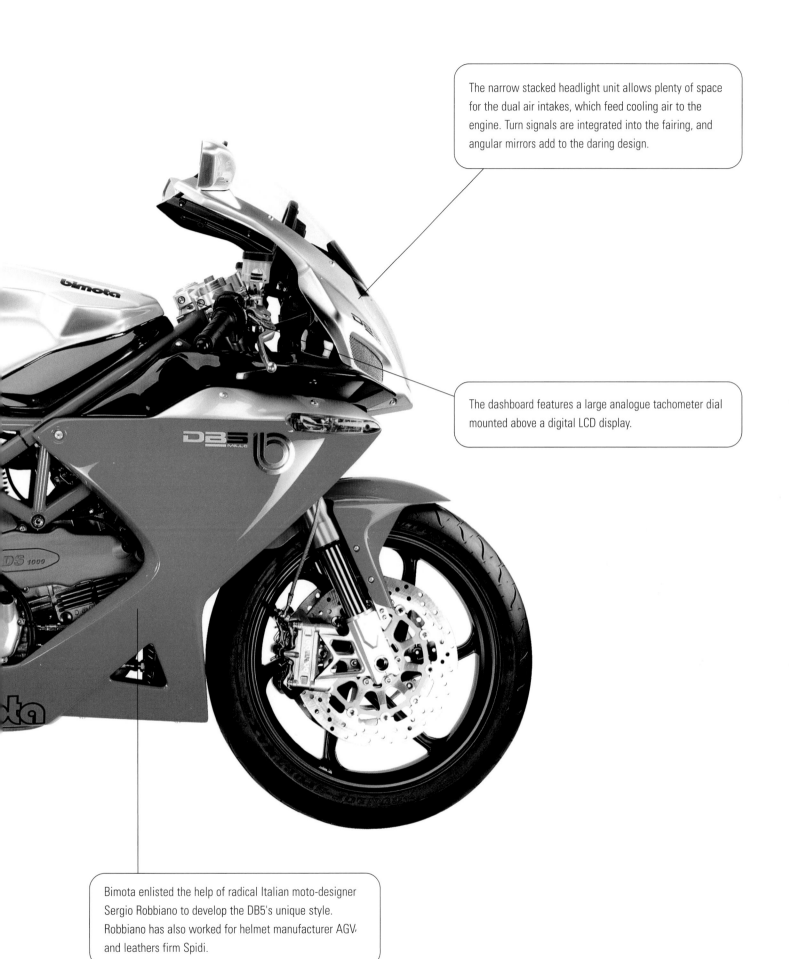

The narrow stacked headlight unit allows plenty of space for the dual air intakes, which feed cooling air to the engine. Turn signals are integrated into the fairing, and angular mirrors add to the daring design.

The dashboard features a large analogue tachometer dial mounted above a digital LCD display.

Bimota enlisted the help of radical Italian moto-designer Sergio Robbiano to develop the DB5's unique style. Robbiano has also worked for helmet manufacturer AGV, and leathers firm Spidi.

As well as its more famous Japanese-engined bikes, Bimota has also used Ducati engines in its machines. The first Ducati-powered Bimota was the DB1 of 1985, a futuristically styled fully faired machine with a 750cc (46cu in) V-twin Ducati motor. The 1993 DB2 used a 900cc (55cu in) V-twin, with an SR version in 1994 using fuel injection. The firm's exotic Tesi hub-center steered design used Ducati's water-cooled four-valve 851 engine and variants, while the DB3 and DB4 used the 900SS engine. All these designs followed the trademark Bimota route of fitting the

This shot clearly shows the combined steel trellis and aluminium swingarm pivot plates used by Bimota on the DB5. The elderly-looking air-cooled Ducati engine is rather underpowered.

Bimota DB5

Top speed:	224km/h (140mph)
Engine type:	992cc (60.5cu in), a/c 90° V-twin, four-valve, SOHC desmodromic
Maximum power:	92bhp (68kW) @8500rpm
Frame type:	steel trellis/aluminium plates
Tyre sizes:	front 120/70 17, rear 180/55 17
Final drive:	chain
Gearbox:	six-speed
Weight:	156kg (343lb)

It's in parts like this steering stem and yokes that Bimota's excellence lies. Machined from solid alloys, these parts add a sophistication and elegance unattainable by standard mass-produced methods.

weight characteristics, as well as showing off the handsome air-cooled engine. The swingarm echoes this design too, with another smaller steel trellis and aluminium-plate construction. This operates a high-quality, fully adjustable Ohlins monoshock unit via a direct cantilever linkage, which is lighter than a conventional rising rate linkage. The front suspension uses a superbike-standard Ohlins upside-down fork, with 43mm (1.7in) inner stanchions and full adjustability. Wheels are lightweight aluminium, and radial-mounted Brembo brake calipers give the light DB5 intense stopping power.

The engine is not what most would call intense, however. It's Ducati's classic air-cooled desmodromic 992cc (60.5cu in) V-twin from the 1000SS, and it has a classy, soulful power delivery, with strong low-down torque and precise fuelling. Bimota fitted larger 48mm (2in) throttle bodies and its own fuel injection system, but the engine still only puts out 92bhp (68kW), putting the DB5 at a serious horsepower disadvantage against even 600cc (37cu in) sportsbikes.

Fortunately, the extremely light chassis means the engine feels livelier than you'd expect. This low weight also helps the DB5's handling, making it incredibly nimble and precise, while remaining stable in bends. The adjustability and high quality of the chassis components makes getting the perfect set-up an easily realized goal. Top speed is high for the power, thanks to the small frontal area, but the DB5 is certainly not a machine for fans of extreme horsepower.

The simple engine design has a few other advantages. The lack of a water-cooling radiator allowed Robbiano to craft an incredible small, aerodynamic machine. A pair of air ducts in the angular fairing direct cooling air onto the engine, and the small windshield and sharply styled mirrors add to the aggressive look of the front end. The headlight has a stacked layout, and the single-seat unit curves over a pair of anodized aluminium silencers.

For 2006, Bimota announced an even higher-specification version of the DB5. The DB5R turned up the chassis specification another notch, with lighter OZ wheels and some carbon-fibre bodywork. The exhaust was made from titanium.

Performance was increased, but so was price. Even the base DB5R was extremely costly for its level of performance, and the 'R' version even more so. Both are exotic specials, but could only appeal to a small coterie of wealthy Bimota enthusiasts and ultimate-handling obsessives. Everyone else will spend less than half as much money to buy a mass-market Japanese machine with twice as much performance.

engine into a stiff, highly appointed chassis package, covered in gorgeous (and occasionally somewhat avant garde) bodywork.

Bimota's 2003 recovery under the guidance of Italian entrepreneur Roberto Comini led to the development of the DB5, launched in 2005. Designed by one of Italy's most exciting bike designers, Sergio Robbiano, the DB5 uses Ducati's 1000SS air-cooled V-twin engine in a radically small and light package, with a host of novel design touches.

The most striking part of the DB5 design is the frame. It uses a network of steel tubes, welded into a stiff trellis, and then bolted to a pair of machined aerospace-aluminium swingarm plates. This composite arrangement gives excellent stiffness and

Bimota Tesi

The 2D Tesi used pneumatic air shock suspension units, which used air pressure, instead of springs to control wheel movement.

The 2D Tesi produced by the revived Bimota firm in 2003 used the Ducati 1000DS aircooled engine rather than the then-defunct 851 superbike engine previously used.

Bimota originally used the Ducati V-twin superbike engine from the 851. The eight-valve, desmo design was chosen partly because its crankcases were designed to mount the rear swingarm, simplifying construction of the Tesi's unusual chassis.

Red control rods are used to transmit steering inputs from the handlebars to the hub-center steering system. The steering head is mounted on a subframe located above the front cylinder. The rods have threaded adjuster sections, which can adjust the steering geometry of the bike.

Braking, drive and suspension forces are transmitted through the front and rear swingarms into the two horseshoe-shaped aluminium plates that make up the Tesi's frame.

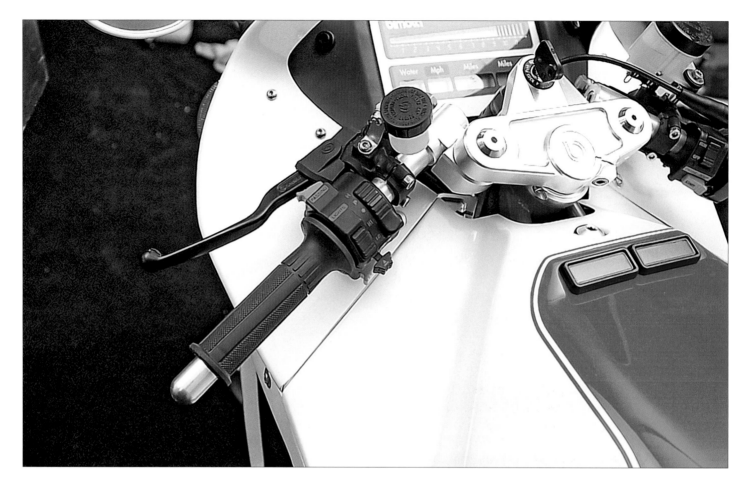

Even for a firm as addicted to unconventional, esoteric engineering solutions as Bimota, the Tesi is a weird bike. The name – 'tesi' (Italian for 'thesis') – indicates the sort of envelope-pushing engineering theories its designer wanted to test. That designer was Pierluigi Marconi, and the bike is named after his university thesis on a hub-centre steered motorcycle.

The Tesi appeared in 1990, though Marconi had worked on several prototypes, including a Honda VF400 powered version with hydraulically operated steering. The first production bike used a Ducati 851 superbike engine, but this was the least interesting part of the bike. Instead it was the Tesi's unique chassis that garnered so much attention.

The main difference is the front suspension. Normal bikes use a pair of telescopic forks, with internal springs and dampers, to hold the front wheel. This whole assembly pivots around the steering head, allowing the bike to be steered, and the forks support the front part of the bike's weight through the springs. However, all the front braking forces are also transferred through these springs, which means they have to cope with much larger forces than caused simply by bumps in the road.

The Tesi uses a different system. The front wheel is mounted on a swinging arm, like a conventional rear wheel. This separates the braking forces from the suspension system: when brakes are applied, the force is transferred directly along the arm into the chassis. The suspension unit mounted on the arm simply has to deal with the forces generated by bumps, and a small amount of weight transfer under braking.

Bimota Tesi

Top speed:	249km/h (155mph)
Engine type:	904cc (55cu in), l/c 90° V-twin, eight-valve, DOHC desmodromic
Maximum power:	113bhp (83kW)@8500rpm
Frame type:	double aluminium plates
Tyre sizes:	front 120/70 17, rear 180/55 17
Final drive:	chain
Gearbox:	six-speed
Weight:	188kg (414lb)

The obvious problem is how to turn the front wheel while it is mounted solidly in a swinging arm. Bimota solved this by using a 'hub-centre' steering system. Inside the front hub is a mechanism that allows the wheel to pivot, operated by pushrods either side, connected to the handlebars. Steering lock is limited by the width of the arm, but there is sufficient movement for reasonable mobility.

This novel front suspension is mounted on a frame consisting solely of two omega-shaped aluminium plates either side of the engine. The rear swinging arm pivots on the plates and the back of the engine, as on the Ducati donor bike, and the two aluminium side plates also support the suspension units, steering gear and other ancillaries.

Despite its extraordinary layout, initial press reports about the Tesi's performance were very positive. On track, the front suspension system worked well, the reduced springing allowed by the separated braking

forces giving excellent wheel control, while allowing very hard braking. There were some worries about the front swingarm perhaps grounding out during hard cornering, but the design seemed to provide sufficient ground clearance.

On the road, the Tesi design had a few weak areas. The poor steering lock irritated, but, more crucially, the steering linkages were subject to wear and slop. The system used a series of spherical rose-joints as well as various bearing surfaces, and the slightest wear or slack affected the steering. The Tesi was also expensive, which confines it to a tiny niche market of wealthy enthusiasts.

Bimota updated the Tesi over the next few years, with a long-stroke 904cc (55cu in) version of the 851 engine, different wheels and a machined front swingarm. But the Tesi never achieved any sort of sales success, and was unable to help the firm when it sank into financial trouble in the late 1990s.

In 2003, the firm bounced back with new investors and a range of new bikes, including a new Tesi. The new Tesi 2D was launched in 2005, with an air-cooled Ducati 1000SS engine, and even more esoteric styling.

This closeup detail of the front suspension shows the fabricated swingarm, steering control arms, brake caliper mount and the kingpin mounted inside the front wheel's hub.

Bimota SB8R

The original SB8R of 1999 had a pair of ram-air intakes that swept back from the windshield over the fuel tank and into a large carbon airbox.

Enormously thick 46mm (1.8in) upside-down forks are by Italian firm Paioli. Rear suspension unit is a racing Ohlins part. Wheels are by Antera, and brakes are Brembo.

Suzuki intended its TL1000R engine to be a serious contender in Superbike competition. But it was Bimota that took the advanced eight-valve 90° V-twin to racing success.

Bimota used a novel carbon/aluminium composite design for the SB8's frame. Carbon fibre was also used in the self-supporting seat unit, and the front fairing bodywork.

The Italian firm fitted its own high-performance fuel injection system and underseat exhaust system to the Suzuki engine. On the 2004 bike, the throttle bodies measure 55mm (2.1in) in diameter, and the injectors are moved by a linkage to different positions. This helps give optimum fuelling.

By the mid-1990s, Japanese chassis technology had advanced sufficiently to render Bimota's original raison d'etre almost null. Bikes like the Honda FireBlade proved that the engineers of mass-market bikes could now match their undoubted engine design prowess with chassis performance to match. So the notion that Bimota could take an excellent engine from Japan, and fit it into a rolling chassis to take the handling to a new level was becoming less true.

But no one's perfect. And when Suzuki released its TL1000S superbike in 1997, it showed that Japan could still get things wrong. The radical nature of the TL's chassis design wasn't a total success, and the somewhat wayward handling it gave didn't live up to the promise of its powerful, character-laden engine.

Enter Bimota. The Rimini firm had an illustrious canon of Suzuki-powered superbikes, from the original racing SB1 with its T500 two-stroke engine, through to the GSX-R1100-powered SB6, its most successful model ever. So it was only natural that it should build a fitting home for the TL1000 engine – the SB8R.

Here, the SB8's centralized mass is seen clearly, as is the virtually straight line between the swingarm and the steering head. Note massive radiator, and super-deep four-bolt lower fork clamps.

Bimota SB8R

Top speed:	265km/h (170mph)
Engine type:	996cc (61cu in), l/c 90° V-twin, eight-valve, DOHC
Maximum power:	143bhp (105kW)@9750rpm
Frame type:	aluminium twin-spar/carbon-fiber plates
Tyre sizes:	front 120/70 17, rear 180/55 17
Final drive:	chain
Gearbox:	six-speed
Weight:	175kg (385lb)

When the bike was first revealed in 1998, it certainly ticked all the exotic boxes that a Bimota should. Swathed in carbon-fibre bodywork, it had an elegant brutality, from the gargantuan ram-air intake ducts arching up from the headlights and back into the fuel tank, to the underseat exhausts and luxury chassis componentry. But it wasn't just a pretty, parts-list exercise. Bimota made its reputation with innovative frame technology, and the SB8R had an entirely new

The best place for most Bimotas. Their highly-strung, exotic nature makes them a poor choice for high-mileage road riding. Conversely, they can be a dream to ride on track.

frame design. At first, it looks like any other aluminium beam-frame, but a closer inspection reveals its unique feature: Bimota replaced the usual welded-on cast-aluminium swingarm plates with two fabricated carbon-fibre parts. These carefully engineered structural plates are bolted onto the aluminium beams that reach back from the steering head. Bimota claimed that they offered a lighter, stiffer solution than the normal welded cast plates used by other manufacturers. The front forks were massive 46mm (1.8in) upside-down Paioli parts, which, like the rear Ohlins monoshock were fully adjustable. Brakes were Brembo racing calipers and 320mm (12.5in) floating disks, fitted to extra-light forged aluminum wheels by Antera.

Not content with building a custom-made, novel rolling chassis, Bimota had also paid close attention to the TL1000 engines arriving from Japan. These were TL1000R engines, the more sporting version of the TL that had been launched in 1998, and had a torquier power delivery than the original TL1000S. The SB8R was fitted with an all-new exhaust and intake system,

crafted to fit the underseat silencers and outrageous front ram-air intakes. Bimota also junked the (perfectly serviceable) Suzuki fuel injection system, and replaced its 52mm (2in) throttle bodies with gaping 59mm (2.3in) alternatives by Magneti Marelli. The resulting power map was not only 8bhp (6kW) stronger than the Suzuki at peak, but had more midrange grunt too.

Bimota launched the SB8R at its local track, Misano. This fast circuit allowed the bike to show its excellent high-speed performance, while testing the brakes and handling to the limit. The SB8R was a stable bike, with much of its weight over the front, which gives good track handling. The high-quality running gear made it very dynamic and quick to change direction.

The strength of the SB8R's design was underlined spectacularly when it won a world superbike race in 2000 at Philip Island, in Australia. Rider Anthony Gobert, at his home circuit, won in dreadful wet conditions, earning the SB8R a well deserved note in motorcycle racing history.

Bimota suffered from the Italian 'disease' of financial difficulties, briefly going out of business before reopening in 2005. The new owners resurrected the SB8R, producing a special 'Gobert' version in honor of its WSB winner.

Ducati 748

The riding position of the 748 is extremely uncompromising. The bars are low, pegs are high and the seat is small and thinly-padded. Outside a racetrack, it's a chore to ride far. Pillion accommodation is especially poor.

Most 748s were painted yellow, distinguishing them from the 916 range, which was normally red. However, both models appeared in both shades, so it's not a foolproof distinction. Apart from the decals, it's incredibly difficult to tell a 916 from a 748.

Early 748s suffered from poor reliability. Electrical parts often failed, and the engine needed fastidious, regular maintenance to avoid problems.

The 748 used a dry clutch, a high-performance racing design, but one that can fail under extended use or abuse. The transmission used a conventional six-speed sequential gearbox.

The 748 uses Ducati's legendary Desmoquattro engine design in its smaller version. The eight-valve, water-cooled 90° V-twin used fuel injection and desmodromic valve actuation.

On the face of it, Ducati's middleweight superbike had a rather curious moniker. The 748 referred to the bike's capacity of course, but it also had historical significance for Massimo Bordi, the chief engineer of Ducati's late 1980s four-valve superbike range. The very first testbed engine Bordi used to try out his design was of 748cc (46cu in) capacity, and this primitive test motor proved the desmodromic four-valve principle that was to be so successful for Ducati.

But when the 748 first appeared to the world in November 1994, it was simply as the smaller sibling to the year-old 916. That bike had appeared the season before, so the classically beautiful lines of the range were already part of motorcycling's collective psyche. And it would be easy to think that a slower, less-powerful version of the 916 would be less exciting.

Far from it: the riding launch of the basic 748 showed that the minor changes – a narrower rear tyre and a slightly revvier engine – had made the machine every bit as exciting. The virtually identical chassis had all the stability, poise and class of the bigger bike, and although the smaller engine was almost 10bhp (7kW) down on power, it could be hustled around a twisty track at a similar pace. The frame was the same steel-tube trellis design, and the trademark single-sided cast swingarm held the thinner rear wheel. Suspension was Showa, with a 43mm (1.7in) upside-down front fork and fully adjustable monoshock.

The first 748 to appear was actually a special SP 'Sports Production' version. This bike was released

The frame is made of welded short steel tubes, and the V-twin engine is neatly mounted as part of the chassis – the single-sided swingarm pivots on the rear of the crankcases.

early to ensure Ducati could enter it in the Supersports racing the following year. This class is limited to 600cc (36.6cu in) four-cylinder machines, or 750cc (46cu in) twin-cylinder bikes, and Ducati's 748SP had the Ohlins suspension, carbon-fiber bodywork, cast-iron disks and a single race seat typical of such a homologation machine. It was also painted bright yellow for the next few years.

The following eight years saw the 748 follow Ducati's typical development cycle. An SPS (Sports

DUCATI 748

Top speed:	254km/h (158mph)
Engine type:	748cc (45.6cu in), l/c 90° V-twin, eight-valve, DOHC desmodromic
Maximum power:	106bhp (78kW)@11,500rpm
Frame type:	steel-tube trellis
Tyre sizes:	front 120/60 17, rear 180/55 17
Final drive:	chain
Gearbox:	six-speed
Weight:	192kg (423lb)

Production Special) version appeared in 1997, taking the SP concept to the next level, with new brakes, a lighter frame borrowed from the 916SPS, and tough titanium conrods allowing the engine to rev higher. The bike achieved some race success too, winning the European Supersport championship in 1995 under Michael Paquay, and the new world championship in 1996 with Fabrizio Pirovano and 97 with Paquay again.

In 1999, Ducati split the 748 range into three models – the E, S and R. The 748E was the base model, with a 92bhp (68kW) motor and a dual seat. The S was the interim model, and it had higher-specification Showa suspension and Marchesini wheels. At the top of the range though, was the 748R. This homologation bike had Ohlins suspension front and rear, with golden-

tinted titanium-nitride coatings on the fork stanchions, a wider frame to accommodate a carbon-fibre airbox, and racing Brembo brakes. An Ohlins steering damper and Marchesini racing wheels rounded off the superlative chassis specification. Inside the motor, the titanium conrods of the SPS were matched to gaping 54mm (2in) throttle bodies, with a new 'shower'-type fuel injector and larger airbox. These changes, together with different camshafts, a high compression ratio and raised rev limit meant the motor pumped out a mighty 106bhp (78kW) at 11,500rpm.

This 748R was the last of the 748 line, and the best. Ducati launched it at the legendary Misano circuit, and its beguiling blend of chassis finesse and engine prowess was a perfect match to the track.

The more efficient, yet ultimately less satisfying 749 was just around the corner, but the 748 was certainly going out on a high.

The Ducati abounded with simple, effective design details, such as the transversely-mounted steering damper and, on more expensive versions, adjustable Ohlins dampers.

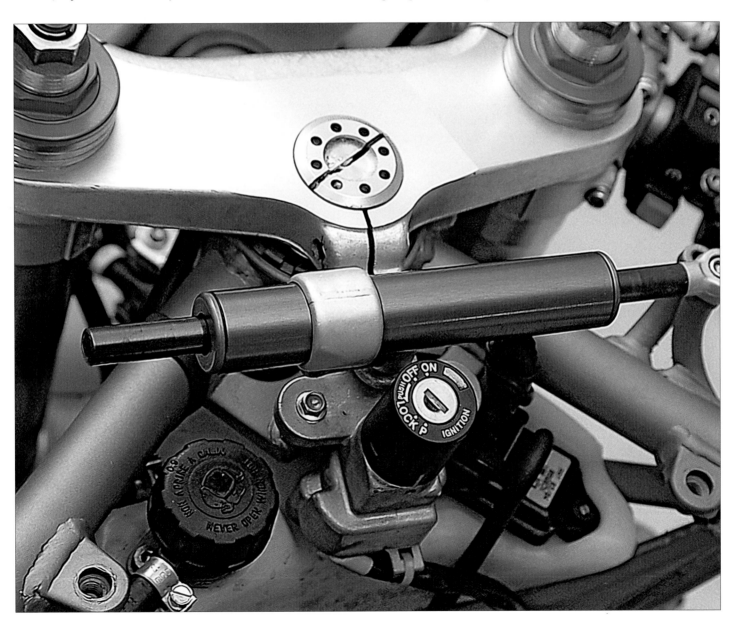

Ducati 749

Despite its '749' nomenclature, the first 749 was actually a 748cc (45.6cu in) design. The later 749R was a 'true' 749cc (46cu in) though, with a wider 94mm (3.7in) bore and shorter 54mm (2.1in) stroke.

The mirrors incorporate the turn signals, and are easily removable for track riding. A new analogue/digital CAN-BUS dashboard displays diagnostic information, as well as a lap timer function, and other useful readouts.

The chassis components on the 749 range use the best of European and Japanese design: Showa, Ohlins and Boge suspension units, Marchesini wheels and Brembo brakes.

Ducati has made the steel-tube trellis frame its trademark, and the 749 is no exception, using the familiar welded chrome-moly steel layout. The rear swingarm is a double-sided fabricated aluminium design.

The exhaust system uses clever 'asymmetric' design to match gas flow from the unequal header pipes. A catalyst in the silencer also reduces harmful emissions.

It's a touch ironic that Ducati, one of the most passionate and emotional of all the motorcycle manufacturers, often behaves in the most logical, predictable way. So when the firm replaced its full-bore 916-series superbike with the 999 range, everyone knew something similar would happen to the smaller 748 models too. Massimo Tamburini's timeless, evocative design had been extended over both ranges for nearly a decade, with incredible success in racing and showroom sales, and Pierre Terblanche, Ducati's design chief, had a Herculean task to match it.

The base model 749 Biposto appeared in the news pages shortly after the 999, so its overall shape was by now reasonably familiar. The vertically stacked headlights with the fairing slats and winglets, underseat silencer and double-sided swingarm all echoed the 999.

Underneath the bodywork, there were few changes from the bigger bike – in much the same way as the 748 was just a small-capacity 916. The frame remained the same welded steel-tube trellis type that Ducati uses for everything from its least powerful Monster 600 to its Desmosedici MotoGP bike. That frame mounted

The 749 in its natural habitat: riding hard around a GP circuit in Italy. Perhaps as close to motorcycling perfection as it's possible to get.

Ducati 749

Top speed:	265km/h (165mph)
Engine type:	749cc (46cu in), l/c 90° V-twin, eight-valve, DOHC desmodromic
Maximum power:	121bhp (89kW)@10,500rpm
Frame type:	steel tube trellis
Tyre sizes:	front 120/70 17, rear 180/55 17
Final drive:	chain
Gearbox:	six-speed
Weight:	183.5kg (405lb)

upside-down front forks by Showa, which featured fully adjustable spring preload and damping, and the rear monoshock was a fully adjustable Boge part. Brakes were the same Brembo four-piston front calipers with 320mm (12.6in) discs and a 240mm (9.5in) rear disc with dual-piston caliper.

What was different, both from the 999 and the previous 748, was the engine. On the base 999, Ducati used the 998cc (61cu in) 'Testastretta' ('narrow head') engine it had already developed for

The tiresome statutory requirements for registration plate, turn signals and tail light produce a rather inelegant rear end. The beautiful exhaust unit saves matters though.

the 996R, 998 and 998S models, with a 100x63.5mm (3.9x2.5in) bore and stroke. But the last 748R didn't have this next-generation Testastretta layout, so the 749 launched with an all-new engine. The smaller Testastretta motor had a 90x58.8mm (3.5x2.3in) architecture, giving a higher rev ceiling than the longer-stroke 748 engine, as well as a new, more efficient cylinder-head design, which retained the desmodromic four-valve layout.

Ducati's predictable modelling system applied to the 749 too. The base bike was joined by an upgraded 'S' version, then a full-blown 'R' race homologation model the following year. The 749S had the same basic package as the base bike, but with higher-specification suspension. The front Showa forks received a special titanium nitride coating, which reduced static friction (stiction) and gave a slightly smoother ride (as well as stylish gold finish). The rear shock was also upgraded to a better Showa part from the budget Boge unit.

The 749R was a much-modified version, with all the usual 'R' type refinements, aimed at making the bike

go quicker around a racetrack. Homologation rules are very strict for the supersport class this bike was aimed at: race teams are restricted in parts they can change from the standard bike. So the better Ducati made the showroom bike, the more chance its raceteams had of success. The 749R featured carbon-fibre bodywork to save weight, fully adjustable Ohlins suspension, forged-aluminium Marchesini wheels and radial Brembo brakes. The swingarm was borrowed directly from the 999F factory racebike of 2003 that had dominated world superbike racing that year.

The engine was also radically different, with a wider 94mm (3.7in) bore and shorter 54mm (2.1in) stroke, higher compression ratio, and a slipper clutch. Titanium con rods and valves (a Ducati first) were lighter and tougher, and allowed a higher rev ceiling. This all resulted in a mighty power output of 118bhp (87kW) at 10,250rpm.

Like its bigger sister, the 749 range was a much better bike than the 748 it replaced. The engine offered a big leap forward in power and refinement, while the chassis was easier to get along with, and ultimately more effective. The styling, however, again drew some criticism, and the 749 was unquestionably less of a design icon than the 748.

Ducati 916

The last of the 916 series, the 998, was produced in several versions, including an FE 'Final Edition'. This was sold in 2004, and was limited to 300 units. The FE had an upgraded Ohlins suspension and a numbered plaque on the top fork yoke.

Like the rest of the bike, the 916 dashboard was an exercise in classic simplicity, with analogue speedometer and tachometer dials and a temp gauge.

The transmission used a six-speed gearbox, chain final drive and a race-style dry clutch, which gave a distinctive 'jangling' sound when it was disengaged.

The 916 range was available in 'Biposto' dual-seat and 'Monoposto' single seat versions. The pillion accommodation was vestigial at best, underlining the focussed nature of the Ducati superbike.

The 916 became a byword for stable, yet seductive handling. This was helped by its stiff trellis frame, Showa suspension (Ohlins on more exotic versions), Brembo brakes and grippy race tires.

The first 916 engine was a development of Ducati's 888 Superbike racer. It shared that bike's 90° V-twin water-cooled layout, with fuel injection, four valves per cylinder and desmodromic camshafts.

In the same way as the Porsche 911 defines the German supercar, Ducati's 916 defines the Italian superbike. From the very first glimpse of the red V-twin in 1993, right through to its eventual discontinuation and replacement by the 999 in 2004, the 916 achieved legendary status in motorcycling.

That first model was officially released at the Milan show in 1993, and it was like nothing seen before in a production model. In theory, it was merely an update of the successful 888 desmoquattro superbike, but in practice, it was the beginning of a new era for Ducati. The firm had taken that base 851 chassis and engine, and overhauled it with an all-new design by Massimo Tamburini. The desmodromic, eight-valve, water-cooled engine pioneered by Massimo Bordi went up in capacity to 916cc (56cu in), thanks to a fractionally longer stroke (94x66mm vs 94x64mm/3.7x2.5in vs 3.7x2.6in). New Weber Marelli fuel injection had 50mm (2in) throttle bodies, and the engine pumped out a very healthy 114bhp (85kW). Ducati had long used desmodromic operation, a system that uses a complex camshaft set-up to physically close the engine valves rather than using springs. This theoretically gives better control over the valves, allowing more radical valve lift and timing.

The chassis was upgraded too, with thicker frame tubes, an adjustable steering head angle, Showa suspension and that audacious single-sided swingarm.

But it was the styling that really wowed the motorcycling world. Beginning at the front with a pair of slit headlights curving back to a small racing windshield, and down to a pair of gorgeous red flanks, the fairing was both beautiful and aerodynamic. A flat-topped, broad fuel tank flared out, then in, before the seat unit took up the curves, ending in a pair of neat tail lights. Twin silencers

Stiff, adjustable upside-down forks and dual Brembo brake calipers made for a communicative, stable front end. Top-spec 'R' and SPS versions had Ohlins forks, base bikes had Showa.

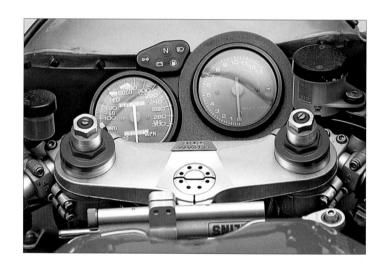

Even the steering damper mount was new and innovative. Located transversely behind the top yoke, it's easily reached to adjust while on the move. Ohlins dampers were fitted to higher-spec models.

were tucked underneath the seat, and that single-sided swingarm allowed the three-spoked rear wheel to be shown off to great effect.

The 916's styling was hailed as a masterpiece by both the critics and the biking press. Strong performance was assumed, but just how much better this bike was didn't immediately become clear. Press reports from the first riding launch echoed the flattering opinions of the styling, but its performance was confirmed when Carl Fogarty rode it to the first of his four, and Ducati's six, WSB championship wins with the 916 series.

Fogarty's bike was based on the homologation version of the 916, the SP. It had Ohlins suspension and carbon bodywork. On the racebike, the heavily

Ducati 916

Top speed:	261km/h (175mph)
Engine type:	999cc (61cu in), l/c 90° V-twin, eight-valve, DOHC desmodromic
Maximum power:	139bhp (103.5kW)@10,000rpm
Frame type:	steel tube trellis
Tyre sizes:	front 120/70 17, rear 190/50 17
Final drive:	chain
Gearbox:	six-speed
Weight:	198kg (436lb)

modified engine's capacity was raised to 955cc (58cu in), producing an incredibly strong 150bhp (112kW).

There were some murmurings over the 916's success. As evidence of mild plagiarism on Ducati's part, critics pointed to the Honda NR750 of 1992, which had a single-sided swingarm, underseat exhausts, twin slit headlights and curvaceous, blood-red bodywork. And there was continual carping from WSB contenders about the rules that allowed twin-cylinder engines to run to 1000cc (61cu in) while keeping four-cylinder bikes under 750cc (46cu in).

The next few years saw several minor chassis and engine changes, before a higher-spec SPS version, with titanium conrods and a 996cc (61cu in) capacity engine appeared in 1996. Ducati replaced the basic

916 with the 996 Biposto for 1999, and built a 996SPS version with Ohlins suspension. For 2000, the 996 range comprised a base Biposto, a 996S and a 996R. The S was based on the Biposto, with some SPS engine parts. The R, however, had an all-new 998cc (61cu in) 'Testastretta' engine, together with the obligatory Ohlins race suspension, Brembo race brakes and carbon bodywork.

The final update for the 916 series was the 998 range built from 2001 to 2003, topped by the 998R. This bike had the next-generation 999cc (61cu in) engine, which would also power the 999R that replaced it.

A sunny day, a twisty back road, a committed rider, and a 916. Summer biking doesn't get much more satisfying than this.

Ducati 999

One major change from the 916 series was the use of modern CANBUS electronics. This system has 'smart' components, reducing wiring and improving reliability and functionality.

The 999's stacked dual headlight makes space for air intakes in the front fairing, but the final look was criticized by many Ducati fans. Mirrors have integrated turn signals, and are easily removed for track riding.

The most powerful 999, the 'R' produces an incredible 150bhp (110kW), thanks to its short-stroke layout, 54mm (2in) fuel-injection bodies, titanium valves and conrods, and light magnesium covers.

Unusually for a superbike, Ducati made the 999's seat and tank unit adjustable over three positions. The footpegs have five possible positions, and the brake and clutch levers are also adjustable, allowing owners to tailor the fit exactly.

The 999's fabricated dual-sided swingarm is lighter than the 916's single-sided part, and is developed from the 999F factory racebike.

The most famous problem facing a rock band, apparently, is following up its greatest album. When you've made the best piece of work you could, what do you do next?

Ducati faced this problem with the 916. The firm's legendary superbike was such an incredible success, in terms of sales, race wins and critical acclaim. So when its inevitable replacement became due, it was sure to be a tense time for the firm.

The 916 was designed by Massimo Tamburini, perhaps Italy's finest motorcycle designer. Tamburini no longer worked for Ducati, so the task of developing a new bike fell to Pierre Terblanche, Ducati's chief designer. Terblanche, a South African, had designed the SS range update of 1998, as well as the radical MH900 modern-retro Mike Hailwood 'replica'.

Terblanche's machine, the 999, was replacing a bike at its peak. The final edition of the 916, the 998, had reached the end of its development, and was an incredible machine. So it was perhaps inevitable that

Hidden by the steel tube frame trellis, and swathed in hoses, wires and cables, the 999 motor isn't particularly pretty. But it is an amazing performer, both on the road and on the racetrack.

Ducati 999	
Top speed:	281km/h (175mph)
Engine type:	999cc (61cu in), l/c 90° V-twin, eight-valve, DOHC desmodromic
Maximum power:	150bhp (110kW)@9750rpm
Frame type:	steel-tube trellis
Tyre sizes:	front 120/70 17, rear 190/50 17
Final drive:	chain
Gearbox:	six-speed
Weight:	181kg (398lb)

the 999 would be a little bit of an anticlimax when it appeared in 2002. Rather than the seductively beautiful, sleek lines everyone had been used to with the 916, Ducati showed a somewhat curiously styled machine. A pair of vertically stacked headlights with slats either side dominated the 999's front end, and the 916's trademark single-sided swingarm was replaced by a conventional double-sided arm. The race fairing

was somewhat slab-sided, and a pair of small winglets down each sidepanel added to the modern style.

While the styling may have been a little disappointing, the 999's new technology certainly impressed. The engine was the latest-generation 'testastretta' motor that had been used on the 998. 'Testastretta' means 'narrow head', and describes the motor's clever cylinder-head layout, which used smart design to reduce the angle between the inlet and exhaust valves, allowing a more compact combustion chamber and more efficient power production.

The chassis was heavily updated too. The change from a single-sided swingarm may have reduced styling impact, but a twin-sided arm is much lighter, as well as less expensive and easier to make. The frame was still made from welded-steel tubes in a trellis layout, but the 999 had a slightly longer wheelbase, a change adding stability at the cost of some steering agility. Suspension components were of a similar high quality to the 998, with Showa forks and rear shock on the first base model 999 Biposto (dual seat). Brembo brakes, grippy sports tyres and light aluminum wheels rounded off the typically Italian chassis specification list.

Reaction to the 999 was dominated by its styling, with debate raging in magazine letters pages and internet forums. The balance of opinion seemed to be

The upper pair of air ducts on the 999 were removed on later models. 2005-on bikes had only the lower pair, reportedly to improve stability on the firm's WSB machines.

that, while the 999 was an amazing looking machine, some of the magic that made the 916 such an icon had unquestionably been lost.

It wasn't until the riding launch of the new bike that the world discovered that, styling aside, the 999 really was a much better bike. It was easier to ride, more comfortable and forgiving, as well as faster and better handling. The chassis in particular was much praised for its solid stability, while remaining commendably nimble. Aerodynamics were vastly improved, while little things like the CAN dashboard and controls all made life easier than before.

In typical Ducati style, the firm released several versions of the 999 over the next year or so. The 999S had better Ohlins suspension front and rear, while the full-bore 999R race replica was a different machine in several important areas. The R used a new big-bore version of the Testastretta engine, with a 104x58.8mm (4x2.3in) bore and stroke versus the 100x63.5mm (3.9x2.5in) layout of the base models. It revved higher and harder and had titanium internal parts, carbon-fibre bodywork, forged Marchesini wheels, and radial-mount Brembo brakes.

MV Agusta F4 1000

The F4 uses a combined steel-tube/cast-aluminium frame. On the more exotic Oro version, lightweight magnesium replaced the aluminium. The rear swingarm is also cast aluminium or magnesium, depending on the model, and has a gorgeous single-sided trellis form.

A beautiful four-into-four stainless exhaust system ends in a set of underseat silencers, which emit a unique, hard-edged sound.

Agusta's inline-four cylinder engine is compact and powerful. The 998cc (61kW), 16-valve, water-cooled design makes 166bhp (122kW) in its base form. Special tuned versions make even more. Its valves are arranged in a radial layout to improve combustion chamber design.

The limited edition 'Tamburini' version of the F4 had a variable-inlet tract system, which moves the inlet trumpets to different positions, giving optimum power production at all revs.

Early F4s used six-piston Nissin brake calipers and 320mm (12.6in) disks, although later models were fitted with radial-mount Brembo four-piston calipers.

Of all the classic names in Italian motorcycling that disappeared in the late twentieth century, MV Agusta was perhaps the most evocative. The firm, set up to build airplanes in 1907 by a Sicilian Count, no less, had an incredible run of 270 Grand Prix race wins and 75 championships (38 rider's, 37 manufacturer's) between 1952 and 1976. It also built high-performance roadbikes, but like many European firms, it was swept aside in racing and roadbikes by the Japanese, and ceased selling bikes in 1980.

Fast-forward 12 years, and the charismatic boss of Cagiva, Claudio Castiglioni, announced that his firm had bought the MV Agusta name. And the firm's plans for a new 750cc (46cu in) four-cylinder superbike were soon widely known. Cagiva had legendary designer

MV Agusta F4 1000

Top speed:	300km/h (187mph)
Engine type:	998cc (61cu in), l/c inline-four, 16-valve, DOHC radial valves
Maximum power:	166bhp (122kW)@11,750rpm
Frame type:	steel-tube trellis
Tyre sizes:	front 120/70 17, rear 190/50 17
Final drive:	chain
Gearbox:	six-speed
Weight:	192kg (423lb)

The beautiful, sinuous shape of the F4's bodywork was penned by the master designer, Massimo Tamburini, the man who was also responsible for that other piece of motorcycle art, the Ducati 916.

Clever design touches abound – the indicators are integrated into the mirrors. In common with many beautiful bikes though, those small mirrors aren't very effective at actually showing what's behind you...

Massimo Tamburini working for it, and had secured the rights to a new four-cylinder engine, initially developed by Ferrari. Castiglioni chose to develop this engine as his own, rather than buy in an engine from a Japanese manufacturer. The F4 motor had some novel features, including a radial valve layout, which splayed out the ends of the four engine valves in each cylinder, rather than mounting them in two parallel pairs. This allowed a more compact combustion chamber, improving power and efficiency, but proved difficult to manufacture. The engine also had a cassette-style removable gearbox, fuel injection and a radical four-into-four underseat exhaust system.

This unique engine was fitted to an equally special chassis. The frame used steel-tube trellis sections, and cast side plates, as well as a trellis-style cast rear swingarm. On the initial 'Oro' (gold) series bikes, these cast parts were in expensive, lightweight magnesium, as were the wheels. Tamburini had penned another gorgeous set of exotically curved bodywork, finished in traditional red and silver paint, and on the F4 Oro, this bodywork was carbon fibre.

The bike caused a massive stir at the 1997 Milan show, but it was to be nearly two years before it

Among the best motorcycle brakes available: Brembo radial-mounted calipers and 320mm (12.5in) floating discs. Note silver-coloured fork damping adjuster screw, and carbon-fibre front fender.

became available. Initial press tests in 1999 praised the design and handling of the bike. The basic production model appeared soon after, with aluminium replacing the magnesium parts, and plastic, instead of carbon, bodywork.

MV continued to develop the F4 over the next few years, but the firm needed to build a larger-capacity engine. The 750cc (46kW) market was fading, and the Japanese were building 1000cc (61cu in) bikes like the R1 and GSX-R1000, which had handling equal to any 750, and with massively increased power and torque. The F4's 126bhp was uprated to 140bhp (103kW) by the SPR version of 2000, and this was very good power for a 750. But its somewhat revvy delivery was a slight disappointment to fans of the bike's superlative handling, design and equipment. That handling was dominated by a stable front end, and communicative suspension set-up. On track, the F4 shone. Its lack of comfort made it to be a poor distance tool, but twisty backroad rides on it were very special.

Problems with sizing up the radial valve layout reputedly held up production of a 1000cc (61cu in) F4, but the full bore F4 finally appeared for 2004. Power was up to a claimed 166bhp (122kW), with a corresponding increase in torque. The result was an intoxicating blend of style, handling and power. But it wasn't for all riders: the uncompromising motor and chassis package was at its best on a track, and its hard edges made it a difficult bike to ride hard. Novice riders would get along much more easily with a more conventional Japanese model, but the advanced loved the handling, brutal power and class of the big F4.

Musclebikes: large-capacity naked roadsters

The term 'naked', when referring to motorcycles, generally means a bike with little or no fairing or bodywork. This covers a wide range of machines, from basic, budget bikes built to a price, through 'retro'-styled musclebikes that harked back to the original superbikes, to top-end streetfighters, 'super-naked' machines, based on cutting edge sportsbikes, with minimalist fairings and loads of attitude.

Of course, the original superbikes of the 1970s and 1980s were all naked. Honda's CB750 and Kawasaki's Z1 had nothing more than a large headlight for the rider to duck behind, and had an upright riding position to suit. From the mid-80s onwards, all serious sportsbikes had plastic fairings, but in the late 1990s, some riders began to rebel against them. The desire for a 'proper' motorcycle, with classic retro styling, lots of chrome plating and no plastic on show began in Japan, and spread quickly. Lavishly-engineered machines like Honda's CB1000 appeared, with modern chassis and engines, designed to look like bikes from ten years previously. Alongside the base-model naked bikes of the time – Suzuki's Bandit 1200 or BMW's R1100R – these formed a wide range of shiny, neck-stretching machines. The strong shoulder muscles these bikes developed in their riders, as well as the high power output of their engines, led to the 'musclebike' name.

Up she comes! Triumph's Speed Triple is one of the most exciting big-bore naked bikes available. The British bike's strong engine and compact chassis makes it an excellent choice for stunt fans as well as more sensible riders.

A slightly different type of naked bike sprang up in Italy. Ducati's Monster had become a firm favourite there since its launch in 1993, and it was joined by designer naked bikes like Triumph's Speed Triple. And as the Monster developed, it borrowed more technology from Ducati's sportsbike division, until it resembled nothing so much as a full-on superbike with no fairing and wide handlebars.

The 'streetfighter' class emerged, fittingly, from the streets. Many riders, having crashed their faired sportsbikes, couldn't afford to replace the bodywork. Making the bike roadworthy, minus its bodywork, resulted in a purposeful-looking machine ideal for city streets. Manufacturers latched onto these designs, producing factory streetfighters like the Aprilia Tuono and BMW K1200R.

Several factors led to increased popularity for naked bikes in the 21st century. Many riders were older, and the more relaxed, upright riding position of a naked musclebike is kinder to elderly joints. And stricter speeding law enforcement meant riders were less inclined to choose machines with increasingly-irrelevant 290km/h (180mph) top speeds.

Aprilia Tuono

The Tuono's small nosecone houses a four-bulb light cluster, and also incorporates a ram-air intake that feeds cool, dense air through the frame headstock directly to the airbox.

Aprilia's V60 Magnesium engine has a 60° V-twin layout, with four valves per cylinder, water cooling and a pneumatically operated back-torque limiting clutch.

The fuel injection system is by Siemens, and uses 57mm (2.25in) throttle bodies, with a single injector per cylinder. There's a catalyst in the exhaust to reduce emissions, and the two-into-one-into-two system is fabricated from stainless steel.

The frame and swingarm are the same as on the RSV – fabricated from cast- and extruded-aluminium components. The swingarm is curved to improve ground clearance, and both items together weigh less than 15kg (33lb).

Aprilia also offered a special racing version of the Tuono, called the Tuono Factory. This had an even more powerful engine, producing 139bhp (103.5kW), and full Ohlins suspension all around.

Italy has always been very fond of naked bikes. The country's motorcycling culture, good weather and innate sense of style all contribute to a love of the various unfaired roadsters, from basic machines like the Suzuki Bandit and Honda Hornet, right up to the highest-performing superbike-powered 'streetfighters', such as Ducati's Monster S4Rs and Triumph's Speed Triple. These top-performing machines have grown into a class of their own, dubbed the 'hyper-nakeds', and have even spawned national racing classes.

It's not just the Italians who love naked bikes. The European market for such machines expanded greatly through the 1990s, so for a small manufacturer like Aprilia, the chance to develop into this market was an important one.

It was the success of the firm's RSV superbike platform that allowed it to do so. It had spent such a long time developing the RSV that it turned out to be extremely reliable and an excellent performer, and was suited to use in various other guises. Ironically, Aprilia chose the easiest imaginable route to develop its hyper-naked roadster. It simply took the RSV Mille superbike, removed its race bodywork, then added some wide handlebars and a small nosecone. The

Aprilia Tuono

Top speed:	256km/h (160mph)
Engine type:	998cc (61cu in), l/c 60° V-twin, eight-valve, DOHC
Maximum power:	133bhp (99kW)@9500rpm
Frame type:	aluminium twin spar
Tyre sizes:	front 120/70 17, rear 190/50 17
Final drive:	chain
Gearbox:	six-speed
Weight:	185kg (407lb)

aluminium frame, gull-arm swingarm, fuel-injected V-twin engine and track-ready suspension all stayed virtually the same.

The result, dubbed the Tuono (Italian for 'thunder') 1000 Fighter, appeared in 2002, and amazed the market with its wild performance, no-compromise specification and spikey styling. The altered riding position, with a more upright stance from the

Although the dashboard looks like a rather minimalist installation, it's a complex, advanced system, with comprehensive rider information, diagnostic checks and lap timer functions.

Combining the RSV sportsbike chassis with a more upright riding position makes the Tuono a fantastically dynamic cornering machine. Many riders replaced the stock Dunlop tyres for even more grip.

handlebars, and gearing modifications, changed the balance of the bike, putting the weight bias further back, and allowing the bike to wheelie more easily. In fact, together with the hard-hitting performance of the RSV's 60°V-twin engine, this more dynamic layout was rated as really not suitable for novice riders.

Aprilia endorsed this view, saying the Tuono was a pure performance machine, developed not by sales research or marketing analysis, but for passionate, uncompromised performance. A year later, it then went one step further, and released a Racing version of the Tuono, based around the RSV Mille 'R'. This version was even more extreme, and had Ohlins suspension front and rear, lighter wheels, and an engine with 18bhp (14kW) more than the base bike, up to 130bhp (97kW). It also came with a set of race exhausts and a different fuel-injection chip to match the engine-management settings to the pipes. Press reports were slightly stunned – here was a bike with such extreme performance, it was actually difficult for even skilled test riders to handle.

For 2006, Aprilia applied the latest updates from the RSV superbike range to the Tuono. So it released a new base-model Tuono, the Tuono R, with the revised engine and chassis components from the 2005 RSV R. That meant an updated engine, with new cams, heads, conrods and lightweight magnesium covers, as well as a new fuel injection system with 57mm (2.25in) throttle bodies. The chassis was updated with new Brembo radial-mount brake calipers, revised frame and swingarm, and new fully adjustable suspension (Showa forks and a Sachs monoshock). The result was a slightly more friendly machine, with a smoother, more progressive power delivery. Peak power was now up to 133bhp (99kW) though, helped by the bike's ram-air intake system, which was integrated into the nosecone.

Aprilia completed the family revisions to the Tuono by releasing a Factory version in late 2006. Again, this followed the pattern of the RSV Factory version, and had carbon bodywork, Ohlins suspension front and rear, forged aluminium OZ wheels and a more powerful engine. Changes to the exhaust valves and altered cylinder heads gave an extra 6bhp (5kW) over the base Tuono R, and fuelling differences from the RSV Factory improved low-down power.

Benelli TNT

The TNT's frame is similar to the Tornado, with a composite steel tube trellis section bolted and bonded to aluminium sideplates. But the swingarm is an all-new steel tube design, with eccentric chain adjusters.

The TNT was also available in several special editions with higher specification chassis components, and different styling.

Early TNT models suffered from starting problems, because the battery and starter motor system from the Tornado 900 engine hadn't been upgraded to suit the longer stroke TNT 1130 engine.

The TNT featured a unique 'power' button on the dashboard. The button switched between two fuelling maps – one full-power setup for track riding or dry weather use, and another softer map, which gave less peak power and better fuel economy. This was more suited to damp conditions or city commuting.

Rather than use the underseat cooling radiator from the Tornado superbike, Benelli fitted a pair of smaller side-mount radiators to the TNT.

Benelli had bounced back onto the motorcycle production scene in the early part of the 21st century with its Tornado superbike. That bike's unique design, strong performance and top-spec chassis components were all in its favor, but Benelli knew it had to expand its range to survive. Sales of one expensive, special sportsbike wouldn't be able to support the firm on their own, so it didn't take long for a streetfighter version of the Tornado to appear. Designed by the same British designer as the Tornado, Adrian Morton, the Tornado Naked Tre, or TNT was based on the Tornado, but with several important differences – both visible and hidden.

The visible changes were easy to spot – the Tornado's trademark underseat radiator and cooling fans were gone, replaced by a pair of side-mount radiators. In their place under the seat was a single exhaust silencer. The frame remained a steel tube and aluminium plate design, but the swingarm was now a steel tube trellis type, rather than the aluminium fabrication on the Tornado. And in place of the sleek, sophisticated design of the Tornado was a rather brutish, hooliganistic style, with a multi-beam headlight design that looked rather like the alien from the movie *Predator*. The other big change was the hidden one – Benelli had extended the Tornado's 898cc capacity to a full 1130cc (68 cu in), by lengthening the stroke on the engine by a comparatively large 12.8mm (.5 in). Bore remained the same on both bikes, at 88mm (3.46in).

The result of all these changes was a fairly hard-core naked roadster. It looked like a brute, and the power

Benelli TNT

Top speed:	256km/h (160mph)
Engine type:	1,130cc (68 cu in), l/c inline-triple, 12-valve, DOHC
Maximum power:	135bhp (100kW) @9,250rpm
Frame type:	steel tube/aluminum plates bonded composite
Tire sizes:	front 120/70 17, rear 190/50 17
Final drive:	chain
Gearbox:	six-speed
Weight:	199kg (438lb)

delivery from the large-capacity triple engine came in with a bang. Claimed power of around 135bhp (100kW) and very high levels of torque made for an exciting ride, with loads of grunt to pull the bike out of a tight bend. Stunting fans also found wheelies were a simple matter, either off the clutch or off the throttle.

It wasn't all perfect though. The small size of the Benelli company meant that it didn't have the development resources of a firm like Aprilia or Ducati, far less one of the Japanese companies. This lack of development showed in certain areas of the TNT, such

The Benelli's strong, powerful three-cylinder engine is produced in Bologna, Italy by the Franco Morini company. Note the balancer shaft located in front of the crankshaft.

as the fuel injection. The torquey engine was a great performer at full throttle, but metering smaller amounts of fuel was tricky. And while the chassis had plenty of high-quality components, it felt slightly ungainly, as if the weight was held too high up. There were also reliability niggles, like the 'designed for a 900' battery and charging system being unable to cope with starting the larger-capacity 1130cc (68 cu in) motor.

Benelli hit financial problems in 2005, and development of the TNT faltered. But investment from Chinese firm Qianjiang has got the firm's plans back on track, including development of the TNT's various different versions. Benelli produced three special TNT models – the Café Racer, the Titanium and the Sport. The Sport version had radial-mount Brembo front brake calipers, as well as a unique 'power button'. This switched between two different engine management maps, which gave either full power for track use, or a

A snappy, torquey engine and upright riding position makes the TNT a very exciting ride. Although it lacks the finesse of more established models, it's still a strong performer for sporty riding.

softer setting with less savage power, for wet conditions. The softer setting also gave improved fuel consumption.

The TNT Titanium had the same brakes and mapping button, but added a titanium exhaust, carbon bodywork, forged wheels, dry clutch and a host of other exotic special parts. The Café Racer had the wheels, power button, radial brakes, and different styling over the basic bike.

These new models were joined in 2006 by another variant of the TNT, with a more adventure-sport style. The Benelli TREK used the Tornado's 1130cc (68 cu in) engine and a variant of the frame, with longer-travel suspension and a more practical half-fairing.

BMW K1200R

On this bike, an aluminium twin-spar frame passes over the top of a laid-down cylinder bank. The 16-valve DOHC engine used BMW's latest BMS-K engine management system, and an F1-developed cylinder head.

The K1200R's naked design shows off the bike's high-tech engine and chassis package.

BMW claims the K1200R can reach 100km/h (62mph) in under three seconds. This incredible performance figure is down to the engine's high torque output, as well as the long, heavy chassis, which helps transmit the power to the road.

An asymmetric headlight, with a single-ram air-intake scoop gives the K1200R a distinctive, aggressive frontal aspect. The instrument surround and radiator shroud gives the rider a small element of wind protection.

The extreme laid-down nature of the engine can be seen in this picture. Note the compact cylinder head and the 'stacked' gearbox, with the clutch located above the crankshaft.

BMW's renaissance in the twenty-first century in the high-performance motorcycle stakes had been cemented by the launch of the K1200S, as well as the massive improvements in the R1200 range starting in late 2004. But it wasn't until the firm released details of the K1200R that the extent of the change BMW had undergone became clear to the press and to customers alike. Here was a bike so audacious, so radical and simply so plain crazy, that not even the most demented Japanese engineer would have dared to put the plans forward for approval.

Like some sort of backstreet autobody tuning shop, BMW had simply taken the full-bore, 167bhp (124.5kW) K1200S (a formidable machine in anyone's book), removed the protective sports-touring fairing and offered it for sale. A boss-eyed headlight, with a tiny visor, a pair of clocks and some plastic covers for the radiator was about the limit of the changes. There was no 'retuning' of the 1157cc (71cu in) engine's enormous power, and no changes in gearing or fuelling. The result was the world's most powerful production-naked roadster, and the wildest BMW ever to leave the Munich firm's factory.

The lack of a fairing shows off the K1200R's chassis even better than on the faired S, clearly displaying the 'Duolever' front suspension. This uses a cast-aluminium 'wheel carrier' subframe, which locates the front wheel and brakes, and is mounted to the frame by a pair of wishbones, not unlike a car suspension system. A single monoshock unit mounted in front of the steering column provides springing and damping, and the handlebars mount on a carrier that transmits steering forces to the wheel carrier. This separates the steering and braking forces from the suspension system, allowing more control over steering during braking, as well as improving suspension movement.

The Duolever front suspension is mounted to a massive aluminium frame. The frame uses the engine as an additional bracing member, and the unusual, laid-down design of the motor lets the frame spars pass over the top of the engine, rather than around the sides, making the bike slimmer and more aerodynamic.

BMW K1200R

Top speed:	265km/h (165mph)
Engine type:	1157cc (71cu in), l/c inline-four, 16-valve DOHC
Maximum power:	163bhp (122kW) @10,250rpm
Frame type:	aluminium twin spar
Tyre sizes:	front 120/70 17, rear 180/55 17
Final drive:	shaft
Gearbox:	six-speed
Weight:	211kg (465lb)

While it could never be described as pretty, the K1200R has a certain brutal charm to its design. However, it's the bike's extreme performance which dominates its character.

The frame also locates the rear Paralever suspension system. This uses a single-sided swingarm that incorporates the driveshaft, with a linkage system that works to decouple the rear suspension from the effects of the shaft drive.

The K1200R engine is unchanged from the S, with the same inline-four, DOHC layout, a super-compact cylinder head, rocker-arm valve operation and advanced fuel injection. The lack of the S bike's fairing and full ram air-intake system means the R only has one engine air intake to the side of the headlight, which cuts peak power by 4bhp (3kW). The engine uses high-octane 98RON super-unleaded fuel, but a knock sensor in the engine detects the pre-ignition caused by lower-octane fuel and adjusts the ignition settings to suit.

Riding the R is an exhilarating experience. The big-bore engine has masses of grunt just off idle. As the revs rise towards the red 11,000rpm line, a savage tone barks from the massive single silencer. After a brief episode of harsh vibration as the engine passes peak torque around 8000rpm, the fuelling is almost perfect, with no hiccups or pauses in the 1200's power delivery. Luckily, the chassis copes with the power generated by the engine very well. The quirky front end gives a much more nimble feel than you'd expect from such a big bike, and performance under braking is impressive.

BMW chose to underline the K1200R's sporting potential by organizing a single-marque race series for the bike. The BMW Powercup championship supported the MotoGP world championship (itself sponsored by BMW) and featured top racers from around the world, competing on tuned K1200Rs. The Powercup bikes featured race exhausts, tires and carbonfibre bodywork, and produced 175bhp (130.5kW). The Powercup rounds provided close racing, with the huge BMW roadster lapping almost as fast as more specialized track machines.

Cagiva Raptor 1000

Cagiva also produced a 650cc (40cu in) Raptor and V-Raptor, using the Suzuki SV650 engine. The smaller Raptor made an excellent novice machine. A Raptor 125 was also built, based on the Mito sportsbike.

The Raptor chassis is based around a neat steel-tube trellis frame, with 43mm (1.7in) upside-down front forks, and a Sachs monoshock rear suspension system. Brakes are four-piston Brembo calipers and 298mm (12in) disks while cast-aluminium wheels wear sporting radial tires.

Cagiva used the excellent 90° V-twin engine from the Suzuki TL1000. The eight-valve water-cooled unit was fitted with Cagiva's own fuel injection and two-into-two exhaust system, and produced a healthy 106bhp (78kW).

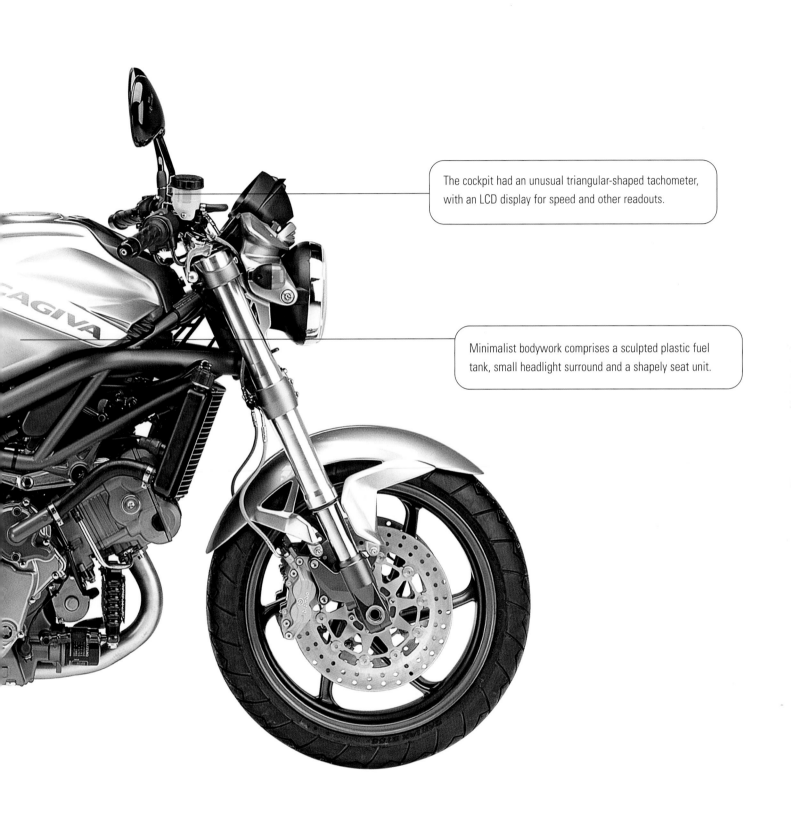

The cockpit had an unusual triangular-shaped tachometer, with an LCD display for speed and other readouts.

Minimalist bodywork comprises a sculpted plastic fuel tank, small headlight surround and a shapely seat unit.

The Italian firm, Cagiva, based near Milan, has a long history of buying in large-capacity engines for its bikes. A close working relationship with Ducati through the 1980s and early 1990s (both firms were owned by Claudio Castiglioni) meant it often used Ducati engines. But in the latter half of the 1990s, it became clear that Cagiva, now split from Ducati, was looking elsewhere for engines.

Japan was Cagiva's supplier; Suzuki in particular. The Hamamatsu firm had a long history of supplying engines to Italian firms – Bimota used its motors in several bikes, and Aprilia used the Suzuki RGV250 engine in its RS250 sportsbike. And with its troubled TL1000 engine in full production, Suzuki had a powerful, compact, modern V-twin engine available. Cagiva was used to V-twin engines (its Elefant and Gran Canyon used the Ducati SS V-twin engine), and although Suzuki's TL range itself was less than a massive success, the engine it used was excellent. A

The V-Raptor was distinguished by its more extreme bodywork, including a pair of struts passing back over the clocks. These struts are purely cosmetic, and don't feed air to the engine or air intakes.

Cagiva Raptor 1000

Top speed:	237km/h (147mph)
Engine type:	996cc (61kW), l/c 90° V-twin, eight-valve, DOHC
Maximum power:	106bhp (78kW)@8500rpm
Frame type:	steel-tube trellis
Tyre sizes:	front 120/70 17, rear 180/55 17
Final drive:	chain
Gearbox:	six-speed
Weight:	192kg (423lb)

modern, water-cooled, fuel-injected eight-valve design of 996cc (61cu in), it wasn't so far off Ducati's own superbike engine, except it was cheaper, more reliable and more powerful.

So Cagiva had its engine. And it also had a designer for a new roadster. Argentinian designer Miguel Angel Galluzzi was the man behind Ducati's hugely

Even the V-Raptor's nosecone didn't provide much protection from the windblast, especially at the high top speeds the Cagiva was capable of.

successful Monster range, and he now worked for Claudio Castiglioni at Cagiva. Galluzzi turned his pen to a new-generation roadster, intended to take on his own creation at Ducati. With a sense of drama familiar to anyone used to Italians, Cagiva called its Monster challenger the Raptor – with all the echoes of birds of prey and small vicious dinosaurs the name carried.

The basic layout of the Raptor was similar to the Monster's typically Italian design: a V-twin engine in a steel-tube frame with upside-down forks, sporty running gear and neat design. But the Cagiva boasted much more performance. The Suzuki-sourced engine was fitted with Cagiva's own fuel injection, inlet and exhaust systems, and the first Raptor 1000 produced a claimed 106bhp (78kW) at the rear wheel – almost 30bhp (22kW) more than the 900 Monster.

That first bike appeared in 2000, and Ducati hit back with the 916-powered 101bhp (74kW) Monster S4. But in the meantime, the Raptor was faster, sportier and much more aggressive than its Bolognan rival. The TL1000 engine had lowered final gearing, which made wheelies almost unavoidable, and both front and rear suspension used high-specification parts, with Brembo brakes and sports tires. This chassis package, attached

to a stiff frame, meant that the Raptor boasted fine handling, and was at its best on backroad bends.

Cagiva also produced a semi-faired version of the Raptor, the V-Raptor. This version had a small, radical nosecone. This offered minimal wind or weather protection, but lots of style. It followed the jagged, triangular styling of the bike, whose footpegs, frame brackets, tank moldings and dash surround all looked more like teeth or claws from a terrible dinosaur than simple moto components.

For Raptor fans with deep pockets, Cagiva offered an even more radical version, the X-Raptor. Swathed in carbon-fibre bodywork, this limited edition version boasted fully adjustable, higher-specification suspension, as well as an adjustable steering damper.

The Raptor had better performance and design than the Monster, but it had problems. Cagiva entered a period of financial troubles in the early part of the 21st century, and while Ducati was able to produce better Monsters, Cagiva lurched from crisis to crisis. There was a brief period of operation with Malaysian car firm Proton in 2004, and then the firm was sold back to an Italian maker. Supplies of the Raptor were uncertain, spares supply was rather haphazard, and build quality and reliability issues dogged the bike.

But for the lucky few who rode the Raptor, its aggression and dynamism made it one of the most exciting naked roadsters ever built.

Ducati Monster S4Rs

Unlike most sportsbike firms, Ducati offers a wide range of performance accessories, including serious engineering enhancements. The most popular upgrades are race exhausts, but there are also slipper clutches, carbon bodywork and titanium engine parts.

The S4-series of Monsters has a special single-sided swingarm design, using aluminium round tubes formed into a trellis. The same arm is also used on the air-cooled S2R range.

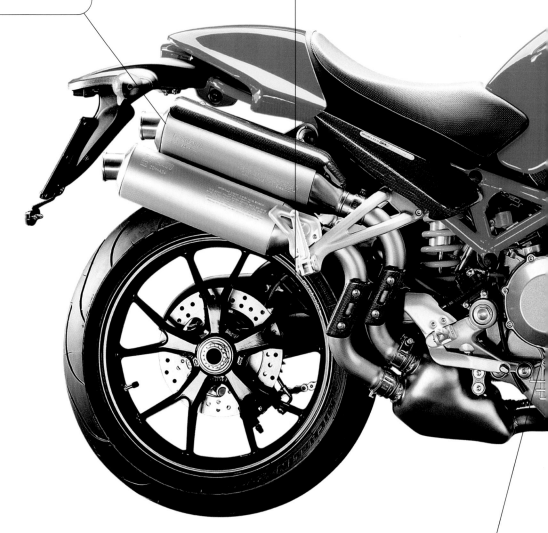

Ducati chose the engine from its 999 superbike for the Monster S4Rs. This 'Testastretta' engine is the 998cc (61cu in) version, with a bore and stroke of 100x63.5mm (4x2.5in). It produces 130bhp (96kW) at 9500rpm.

The neat nosecone is more of a styling device than any sort of aerodynamic aid, but it does deflect some windblast over the rider's shoulders.

The Marchesini aluminium wheels have Y-shaped wheel spokes, which increase stiffness by doubling the number of connecting members from the rim to the hub.

The original Monster was conceived as a city bike. But the bike's development over the years means the latest high-spec model is as good on track as many 'proper' sportsbikes.

The Monster range has generally been accepted as having rescued Ducati in the 1990s and beyond. While the glowing headlines and the World Superbike racing glory went to the 916/996/998/999 superbike range, it was the sheer volume of Monsters churned out by the Bologna firm (more than 130,000 have been built so far) that funded the development of the superbikes.

The first Monster was a 900, launched in 1993, and designed by Argentinean designer Angel Miguel Galluzzi. Galluzzi's design used the firm's air-cooled two-valve 900SS engine in a naked steel-tube trellis frame, borrowed from the 851 Superbike. It was one of motorcycling's instant hits, combining Italian prestige and style, with a useful, practical, fun little roadster.

Even the latest Monsters, with more performance and design than the original bike, are still instantly recognizable as Il Mostro's descendants. This Rs is Ducati's most extreme Monster to date. It's part of a

long line of high-performance Monsters that started with the 916-powered S4 of 2000, and the S4R of 2003.

The S4R not only had a 996cc (61cu in) superbike engine, borrowed straight from the 998 Superbike, it also had a stylish single-sided rear swingarm, using welded round aluminium tubes. Ducati also installed

Ducati Monster S4Rs

Top speed:	250km/h (155mph)
Engine type:	998cc (61cu in), l/c 90° V-twin, eight-valve desmodromic, DOHC
Maximum power:	130bhp (96kW)@9500rpm
Frame type:	steel-tube trellis
Tyre sizes:	front 120/70 17, rear 180/55 17
Final drive:	chain
Gearbox:	six-speed
Weight:	177kg (390lb)

a rogueish set of twin-barrelled silencers to the right-hand side, and painted an audacious wide 'speed stripe' down the nosecone, fuel tank and seat unit. A carbon-fibre front mudguard, cambelt covers, sidepanels and radiator cover rounded off the look of the S4R

For 2006, Ducati finally took the plunge, and fitted the Monster with its most modern engine design, the advanced V-twin powerplant from the 999. This 'Testastretta' motor is the same narrow-headed 998cc (61cu in) engine used in the 999 and 999S sportsbikes, and produces a very healthy 130bhp (96kW), 13bhp (9.5kW) more than the S4R. The exhaust system was modified, with 5mm (.2in) wider diameter 45mm (1.8in) header pipes for peak power, and the engine used Ducati's latest fuel injection system.

This Termignoni race exhaust comes with a competition air filter and a new fuel injection ECU, which will give around an extra 10–15bhp.

Not content with adding a large dose of extra power, Ducati engineers also upgraded the chassis with some of the finest components available. The steel-tube trellis frame was modified around the airbox area, adding 5 percent more stiffness. Both front forks and rear monoshock suspension units are by the Swedish suspension firm Ohlins, and they offer a wider range of adjustment, as well as more sophisticated damping than the Showa units of the S4R. Radial-mounted Brembo front brake calipers are straight from the firm's sportsbike department, and look identical to those

Designed to win world superbike races, the Testastretta engine is an incredibly advanced V-twin. Note how the camshafts are positioned close together to optimize combustion chamber space.

used on the firm's Desmosedici GP6 MotoGP racebike, as are the Marchesini wheels. These are made from lightweight aluminium and finished in an attractive glossy white paint. The single-sided swingarm of the S4R remained, finished in Ducati Racing black as did the twin, high-mount silencers, now with a carbon-fibre heat shield.

The chassis specification sounds more like a race bike than a classy city commuter, and it's capable of much more than just riding to work and back. Get the S4Rs onto a racetrack, and you'll find yourself dicing with full-bore sportsbikes, the strong low-down pull of the 999 engine slingshotting you out of bends, the Brembo brakes letting you wait to the last possible second before braking for a bend. The high-mounted silencers and skinny footpegs mean that there is amazing ground clearance, and the wide, sticky Michelin tires mean you'll run out of skill before they run out of grip.

But a bike as special as the Rs turns even the most mundane trip into a dream ride. The deep-toned rumble from the V-twin engine, and the light steering is as perfect on Chelsea's King's Road in London as on Bologna's Passo della Futa.

The S4Rs wasn't an inexpensive bike to purchase. But considering the extremely high level of chassis components, together with the gorgeous design and strong engine, this top-priced Monster was almost a bargain.

Harley-Davidson V-Rod

The neat aluminum 'fuel tank' is just a cover over the engine's airbox. The real fuel tank is a plastic cell under the seat. The filler cap is accessed by flipping the seat up.

Early V-Rods had a conventional 46cm (18in), 180-section rear tyre. But later models had a super-wide, dragrace-style 240-section Dunlop. The front tyre is a 48cm (19in), 120/70 fitment.

As suited Harley-Davidson's first-ever water-cooled four-stroke roadbike engine, the V-Rod powerplant was dubbed the 'Revolution'. It's a 60° V-twin with eight valves, four camshafts and a 1130cc (69cu in) capacity.

The V-Rod's instrument binnacle has a large central speedometer, with side pods housing a tachometer and fuel gauge. There's also an LCD panel showing time, trips and other information.

Harley-Davidson cleverly disguised the engine cooling radiator between the front frame rails, and covered it with a large shroud. This had ducts to direct cooling air through the radiator efficiently.

racebike design; that bike's engine was increased in capacity and modified for street use. An advanced fuel injection system optimized power and rideability while cutting emissions, and swooping exhaust silencers contained a catalyst to further cut pollution, while producing a pleasing engine note.

It wasn't just the engine that was new though. The V-Rod's frame was formed by a novel 'hydroforming' process, which used high-pressure fluid to shape the sinuous form of its steel tubes. The V-Rod also made extensive use of aluminium to cut weight, although it's still a heavy bike at 270kg (595lb) dry. Running gear was a curious mix of cruiser styling and sportsbike specification. The wheels were a solid aluminium cruiser 'disc' style, yet were fitted with Dunlop D207 sports tyres. And while the front forks were raked out at a most unsportsbike angle of 34°, they had stiff 49mm (2in) stanchions and firm damping. Brakes are often the most dismal part of a cruiser's chassis specification. However, the V-Rod again proved it was no normal cruising bike by having a pair of powerful four-piston brake calipers up front, biting on 292mm (11.5in) discs.

The riding position seemed at odds with the performance of the sporty engine and chassis. The forward-set footrests, low seat and pullback bars put the rider down low and stretched out. And if the rider begins to exploit some of the lean angles allowed by the sports tyres, she'll find her motorcycle boot heels are the first thing to drag on the tarmac, which is rather disconcerting when it first occurs.

But while the V-Rod can make good progress on twisty back roads, it's much more at home cruising on freeways, or, even better, posing on city streets. The drop-dead styling of this unique 'power cruiser' stands out from the run-of-the-mill sportsbikes and standard

The V-Rod's handsome powerplant is based on the firm's VR1000 racebike engine. Chrome-plated covers and finned heads give a classic, stylish appearance.

Despite being one of the world's oldest motorcycle manufacturers (having started making bikes in 1903), Harley has spent most of its time building old-fashioned motorcycles. Deliberately eschewing many of the technologies – such as water-cooled engines and aluminum chassis components – considered essential by most other manufacturers, Harley's machines were built with heritage and history first.

But in 2001, a small revolution took place in Pasadena, California. The firm unveiled the new VRSCA V-Rod, an advanced, powerful cruiser with more technology, performance and design than any previous Harley-Davidson. The heart of the V-Rod is a water-cooled 1130cc (69cu in) 60° V-twin, with four valves and double overhead cams in each cylinder head. The engine's roots are found in Harley's VR1000

Harley-Davidson V-Rod

Top speed:	217km/h (135mph)
Engine type:	1130cc (69cu in), l/c 60° V-twin, eight-valve, DOHC
Maximum power:	115bhp (86kW) @8250rpm
Frame type:	hydroformed steel-tube perimeter
Tyre sizes:	front 120/70 19, rear 180/55 18
Final drive:	belt
Gearbox:	five-speed
Weight:	270kg (595lb)

Long, low and swept back. Harley's V-Rod was a genuine show-stopper when it was revealed to the press in Pasadena, California in June 2001.

cruisers, helped by the satin aluminium bodywork and wheels, chromed engine, concealed radiator and sleek exhaust system.

Harley expanded its V-Rod range over the next few years. 2005 saw the appearance of the Street Rod – a more sporting version of the V-Rod. A 43mm (1.5in) upside-down front fork, Brembo brakes and alloy wheels improved handling from the front end, while an extra eight degrees of lean angle either side, a shorter wheelbase and sharper steering geometry added sportiness. Rear-mounted footpegs replaced the V-Rod's forward controls, giving the rider a more committed riding position. The engine was slightly modified, with an altered exhaust system and different

ignition settings combining to provide an extra 5bhp (4kW) of peak power.

Harley also launched a stylish version finished in black, called the Night Rod in 2005. It had the Street Rod's footrests and exhausts, a 36° steering-head angle and a small headlight visor.

2006 saw another edition of the VRSCX, designed to celebrate the firm's dragracing achievements. Based on the standard V-Rod chassis, this 'X' version had a factory-fit big-bore kit, which increased the piston size to 105mm (4in). That took the capacity to 1250cc (76cu in), with accompanying power and torque improvements. A drag-style wire-spoked front wheel replaced the stock cast-aluminium design.

As Harley-Davidson settles into its second century of motorcycle production, the V-Rod range seems set to continue offering the H-D fans a near-perfect mix of heritage and technology.

Honda CB1300

Honda produced two versions of the CB1300. The original CB1300F appeared in 2003, and was an unfaired big-bore roadster. For 2005, a half-faired CB1300S version appeared with more potential for touring and highway riding.

Honda produced the CB1300 with a very high level of finish: the engine, exhaust and chassis components are all beautifully made and finished.

The CB1300 engine is unique to the bike, and isn't used on any other machine. The inline-four 1284cc (78cu in) 16-valve motor was specially designed to look good on the outside, since it wouldn't be covered with plastic panels.

The steel tube frame looks like the cradle designs used on 1980s superbikes. But modern materials and design meant it was much lighter and stiffer, giving better handling than on the older bikes.

The CB1300S half fairing has useful storage space incorporated, and the headlight was swapped to a classic 1980s rectangular design.

Like Kawasaki and Suzuki, Honda turned to its racing heritage for inspiration in the early 1990s. Retro-styled bikes were fashionable in Japan. So the firm went back to its racing models from the 1980s, and especially the AMA Superbike class, which had spawned such close, exciting racing between such famous names as Freddie Spencer, Eddie Lawson and Wes Cooley.

Kawasaki's 80s-inspired retro racer was the ZRX1200, and Suzuki's was the GSX1400. And Honda's is the CB1300 – though the first version of this bike was a CB1000, launched in 1993. Both the CB1000 and the CB1300 echo the styling of Freddie Spencer's CB900 racebike, which performed so well in the early 1980s.

The 1993 CB1000 was a basic naked roadster, using the firm's CBR1000F sports-touring engine in retuned form. Dubbed 'The Big One', it wasn't a great success, but sold well in some markets. The CBR-derived engine was incredibly smooth and refined, and

It could almost be the 1970s – but Honda's mighty CB1300 is bang up to date. Handsome design and top-quality components make the CB a classic connoisseur's choice.

Honda CB1300

Top speed:	225km/h (140mph)
Engine type:	1284cc (78cu in), l/c inline-four, 16-valve, DOHC
Maximum power:	114bhp (994kW)@7500rpm
Frame type:	steel-tube double cradle
Tyre sizes:	front 120/70 17, rear 180/55 17
Final drive:	chain
Gearbox:	five-speed
Weight:	224kg (493lb)

The beefy rear swingarm is fabricated from aluminium components and operates twin suspension units, one from each side. Note the ABS sensor ring on the inner edge of the brake disc.

produced a reasonable 98bhp (72kW). The chassis was a simple, high-quality design, with steel-tube frame, 43mm (1.7in) forks, piggyback twin-shock rear suspension, and a pair of four-piston front brake calipers with 310mm (12in) disks.

Honda discontinued the CB1000 in 1997. But the desire for fashionable, well designed retro machines remained strong in the market, and machines from Kawasaki, Suzuki and Yamaha were selling well. So Honda decided to build another big bore CB, but this time with an all-new engine and chassis.

That bike – the CB1300 – appeared in 2003, a decade after the first CB1000. It looked very similar to the 1000, and again was designed to pay homage to Spencer's AMA racebike of over two decades previous.

Despite that visual similarity, every part of the CB1300 was new. The engine was specially developed just for this bike, and it incorporated a host of modern engine design and production techniques. Despite its modernity though, it was styled externally to look like the CB1000. The new engine had a compact combustion chamber with a narrow angle between the valves, and the dual camshafts are positioned close together. Honda's PGM-FI fuel injection system was installed, and was carefully tuned to provide the CB1300 with strong low-down grunt and a savage midrange. A four-into-one exhaust system both reinforced the traditional racebike styling, as well as giving good power characteristics.

The engine itself was rubber-mounted to cut high-frequency vibrations, although Honda wanted to retain some vibes to give a raw feel to the bike. Honda also

fitted a five-speed gearbox, the strong torque of the CB1300 motor negating the need for six gears. The chassis was very similar to the CB1000, but all new, and with more modern components.

Honda has very high standards of fit, finish and build quality on all its bikes. But it declared the CB1000 and 1300 to be top-specification bikes, and so they featured even higher standards of finish. All the parts on the bike, from footrests, brackets, handlebars and fasteners to the major components like swingarm and shocks, are incredibly well finished. Brushed aluminum, stainless steel and chrome finishes are deep, lustrous and long lasting.

On the road, the CB1300 performs much better than its statistics would suggest. The peak power figure of 114bhp (85kW) doesn't sound very impressive, especially with the 224kg (494lb) dry mass, but the engine's strong torque figure of 86lbf ft means it has strong, relaxed acceleration.

Honda released a half-faired version of the CB1300 in 2005. The CB1300S weighed 6kg (13lb) more, and its small half fairing not only added an extra touring dimension to the bike, but continued its retro style, with its echoes of Honda race bikes of the early and mid-1980s. Honda took the opportunity to add its latest ABS antilock barking system to the 'S' model too, further enhancing its all-round ability.

The upright cylinders and large polished covers echo Honda's great inline-fours of the past. But small details such as the compact cylinder head and the concealed fuel injection belie its modern design.

Kawasaki Z1000

Radical bodywork includes an angular nosecone, radiator shrouds and a supersports-style seat unit with an LED tail light, borrowed from the firm's Ninja range. The shapely fuel tank holds 18.5l (5gal) of fuel.

The first modern Z1000 had a dynamic four-into-four exhaust system, while the 2007 version switched to outlandish triangular silencers. These echo the four silencers on Kawasaki's 1970's 'Z' superbikes.

The 2007 Z1000 used the same basic engine as on the 2006 bike – a 953cc (58cu in) inline-four, developed from the firm's old ZX-9R sportsbike engine. It featured dual-valve fuel injection and complied with latest European emissions regulations.

The high-specification chassis includes upside-down forks and monoshock rear suspension. The frame is made from welded steel tube. The 2007 model Z1000 also features a dual-mount for piston brakes and petal discs.

Cast-aluminium wheels are fitted with superbike-sized sports tyres – a wide 190/50 17 rear and 120/70 17 front.

It's a common misconception to dismiss the Japanese motorcycle manufacturers as somehow lacking in 'heritage' or character compared with firms like Harley-Davidson, Ducati or Triumph. Each of the big four Japanese companies has a history of passionate commitment to building exciting, powerful motorcycles, competing in racing at all levels, and jealously guarding their own history and heritage, not least Kawasaki.

The motorcycle division of Kawasaki Heavy Industries is a tiny offshoot of an absolutely enormous

The Z1000 used a new engine derived from the ZX-9R motor. Note the two rotary potentiometer sensors on the fuel injection bodies, which tell the ECU how far each throttle valve is open.

Kawasaki Z1000

Top speed:	248km/h (155mph)
Engine type:	953cc (58cu in), l/c inline-four, 16-valve, DOHC
Maximum power:	127bhp (93kW)@10,000rpm
Frame type:	steel-tube diamond type
Tyre sizes:	front 120/70 17, rear 190/50 17
Final drive:	chain
Gearbox:	six-speed
Weight:	198kg (436lb)

heavy-engineering conglomerate that builds commuter railroad systems, ships, airplanes and even space rockets. As such, it's always taken its engineering extremely seriously, and has produced some of the finest motorcycles of the modern era.

'Z' has been Kawasaki's letter. All its four-stroke performance motorcycles have contained that ultimate letter in their designations, and the Z1000 of the 1970s was one of the very first true superbikes. Its air-cooled eight-valve inline-four engine and steel-tube cradle-framed chassis defined a generation of powerful roadbikes that ruled until smaller, liquid-cooled designs appeared in the 1980s.

Twenty years later, and Kawasaki realized what a popular market the naked streetfighter class had become. So it resurrected the Z1000 moniker, and attached it to an all-new motorcycle. The 2003 Z1000 had an inline-four engine, and a steel frame, but everything else was very different from the original. That engine was a 16-valve, fuel-injected, water-cooled design. It was based on the firm's muscle-bound ZX-9R superbike engine, but with a larger 953cc (58cu in) capacity. Keihin dual-valve fuel injection provided immaculate fuelling, and the motor's 127bhp (93kW) was delivered through a six-speed gearbox. This strong, capable powerplant was bolted into a straightforward 'diamond' type steel-tube frame, which used the engine as an additional bracing member. A 41mm (1.6in) upside-down front fork had preload and rebound damping adjustability, as did the rear monoshock, while four-piston front brake calipers operated on dual 300mm (12in) discs. Superbike-sized Bridgestone sports tyres on cast-aluminium wheels completed the comprehensive chassis package.

Styling is very important on a machine like this, and the Z1000 had an unmistakable look. A stylish nosecone fairing mounted the headlights, and a neat LCD dashboard, natty radiator covers, shapely frame covers and a Ninja-styled seat unit all added dynamism. Most striking of all was the four-into-four exhaust system, manufactured in polished stainless steel, and finishing off the rear view with four 'rocket-launcher' styled endcans.

The Z1000 was as good to ride as it was to look at. The engine has plenty of power, and develops much of it at higher revs. This screaming nature makes for an exhilarating ride on winding backroads. On more sedate cruising rides, the little windshield helps deflect some of the windblast over your shoulders, and the riding position is relaxed and comfortable.

The Z1000 remained unchanged in Kawasaki's line-up until 2007. A combination of stiff competition in

Although it's quite a heavy bike, the Z1000 makes stunts like this easy for a skilled rider.

the market sector, and tighter emissions regulations meant the bike had to be revised. Kawasaki added some even more extreme components and styling. The exhaust system went totally over the top, flaring out its four silencers into enormous triangular sections. This was partly to accommodate the extra silencing and catalyzing components required to pass Euro III emissions rules. The front brakes were upgraded to radial-mount calipers, and all three brake discs were replaced with petal discs. The styling package remained essentially Z1000, but new accents on the engine covers, ZX-styled indicator panels and a new seat unit all sharpened its look even more.

But just to show that it wasn't just another headbanger option, Kawasaki offered the new Z1000 with an optional ABS antilock brake system, designed to aid stopping on slippery surfaces.

Kawasaki ZRX1200

Like the 1980s superbike from which the ZRX draws its inspiration, the modern ZRX1200 has an upright riding position, with widely set handlebars and a large, comfy dual seat.

This shows the ZRX's elderly engine design. Side-draught carburettors mean a long inlet tract, and a compromised intake valve design. Note the non-stacked gearbox layout – the crankshaft and gearshafts are all in one plane.

The unusual rear swingarm design is made from tubular aluminum, with eccentric chain adjusters. The twin rear shocks have 'piggyback' remote reservoirs, which hold some of the damping components.

A modified ZZ-R1100 1052cc (64cu in) engine was used on the first ZRX, the 1100. It was then increased in capacity to 1164cc (71cu in) for the ZRX1200.

Kawasaki offered the ZRX1200 with three fairing options – a more touring-biased frame-mounted half fairing on the 'S' model, a small headlight fairing on the 'R' and a ZRX1200 with no nosecone at all, and just a round headlight.

Kawasaki's ZRX1200 is perhaps the most authentic of all the modern 'muscle bikes' built by manufacturers keen to capitalize on their 1970s and 1980s heritage. It was that firm's Z1000R racebike, ridden by Eddie Lawson, that epitomized the hard-man racing that went on back then. Kawasaki was so pleased with Lawson's 1981 AMA championship win, that it built a replica of his race bike and offered it for sale. The KZ1000R Eddie Lawson Replica had the trademark 'Team Green' paintwork, as well as altered steering geometry, wider tires, a Kerker four-into-one performance exhaust and race suspension, among other modifications. This official Replica was rare and popular, so many standard Z1000 owners built their own replicas of the Replica.

By the mid-1990s, the retro-style of naked bikes like Kawasaki's own Zephyr range had become very popular, especially in the Japanese home market. So for 1997, Kawasaki built a bike which was clearly

Kawasaki ZRX1200

Top speed:	233km/h (145mph)
Engine type:	1164cc (71cu in), l/c inline-four, 16-valve, DOHC
Maximum power:	120bhp (88kW)@8500rpm
Frame type:	steel-tube double cradle
Tyre sizes:	front 120/70 17, rear 180/55 17
Final drive:	chain
Gearbox:	five-speed
Weight:	223kg (490lb)

Despite its classic design, the ZRX1200 is a fine-handling bike, with enough ground clearance, braking and suspension performance for fast road riding.

looking to play on this retro popularity, while incorporating the latest superbike technology. The bike was the ZRX1100, and it used an engine based on the supersports-touring ZZ-R1100 design. That 1052cc (64cu in) engine was de-tuned from the ZZ-R's 147bhp (108kW) to a more sedate 104bhp (76kW), thanks to smaller carbs, reduced compression and revised valve timing. It also dropped its sixth gear – the torquey new power delivery rendering the extra ratio moot.

This motor was fitted into a new steel-tube cradle frame, which looked just like the 1980s design, only with much more stiffness and much less weight. The rear swingarm was an authentically styled braced item, manufactured from aluminium tubing and operated a pair of similarly authentic-looking shock absorbers. These piggyback units and forks were softly sprung and damped as standard, but were adjustable, and could be altered. Bodywork was restricted to a small headlight fairing, which kept a little windblast off the rider, and looked just like Eddie's.

One thing that certainly did not look authentic was the front brakes. 'Steady Eddie' Lawson would have ripped your arm off at the elbow if you'd offered him these Tokico six-piston calipers in 1981, in place of the single-potters his bike had. To be honest, they didn't offer much more performance than a good set of four-piston calipers, but they did look more impressive.

The ZRX was a fun bike to ride, although it was heavy. More than 220kg (485lb) dry, it took a lot of muscling to make fast progress down a twisty back road, and together with the soft suspension and touring-specification rubber, it wasn't liable to trouble modern superbikes. In its class though, the ZRX felt commendably small and modern. Compared with

This photo shows the ZRX's elderly basic engine design. Side-draught carburetors mean a long inlet tract, and a compromised intake valve design. Also note the non-stacked gearbox layout.

heavier, air-cooled designs like Suzuki's Bandit 1200 or Yamaha's XJR1300, the ZRX was much livelier and more dynamic. For city cruising or even the daily commute, it made a classy-looking choice, but the tiny fairing made it a chore on highway journeys of any real distance.

Few complaints were made about the ZRX's engine, but it was the engine that Kawasaki updated in 2001. The ZRX1200 released that year basically took the 1100 and added a bigger 1164cc (71cu in) engine. Power was up by 16bhp (12kW), and torque was amplified by 11 Nm (8lbf ft) too.

Kawasaki also released two other versions of the ZRX. The ZRX1200 had no fairing, just a round headlight up front. The ZRX1200R had the traditional Lawson-style headlight fairing, and a new ZRX1200S had a more substantial half-fairing, which enabled it to perform a more practical touring role.

There was also a smaller, 400cc (24cu in) version of the ZRX specially built for Japan only, where smaller bikes were much more popular. This mini-ZRX used a modified ZXR400 engine, in a downsized chassis, and as much style and design as its bigger sibling.

KTM Super Duke

KTM's main business is off-road motorcycles, and these influences can be seen in the Super Duke. The steel tube trellis frame and V-twin engine are developments of the firm's Adventure 990 enduro machine.

KTM's radical fuel tank design looks great, but is a little impractical. Its 15l (4gal) capacity can run dry in less than 145km (90 miles), under hard riding.

KTM has a very close relationship with Dutch suspension firm WP, and uses the distinctive white-springed suspension units on all its bikes. The Super Duke's WP units are fully-adjustable race items.

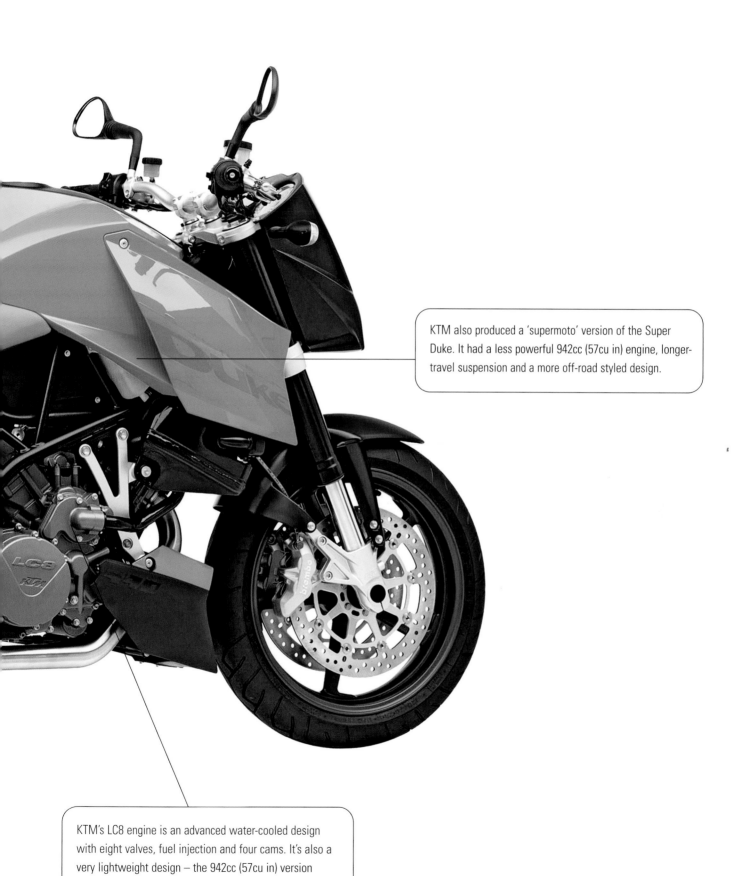

KTM also produced a 'supermoto' version of the Super Duke. It had a less powerful 942cc (57cu in) engine, longer-travel suspension and a more off-road styled design.

KTM's LC8 engine is an advanced water-cooled design with eight valves, fuel injection and four cams. It's also a very lightweight design – the 942cc (57cu in) version weighs just 58kg (128lb).

Although KTM seems like a fairly young company, it can, in fact, trace its roots back to the mid-1930s. The Austrian firm made its name and reputation in the off-road sports market, where its range of motocross and enduro machines won many titles. But in the mid-1990s, the firm began expanding into more road-biased machinery. Bikes like the single cylinder 609cc (37cu in) Duke brought offroad technology to the road in the form of a 'supermoto'. Supermotos were motocross bikes fitted with roadbike-sized wheels, grippy racing tyres and powerful roadbike brakes. Their torquey engines, light weight and long travel suspension made them highly usable on poorly surfaced roads. They became popular as a niche choice for performance fans wanting something a little different. Supermotos were generally 'home made', with fans developing the bikes themselves from offroad machinery, rather than buying prebuilt bikes from manufacturers.

Most supermotos used single-cylinder dirtbike engines, which couldn't reliably produce large

The LC8 990 is KTM's most powerful roadbike engine, and it's a modern, compact design. The small bellypan echoes the angular design of the rest of the Super Duke's bodywork.

KTM Super Duke

Top speed:	233km/h (145mph)
Engine type:	999cc (61cu in), l/c 75° V-twin, eight-valve, DOHC
Maximum power:	118bhp (87kW) @9000rpm
Frame type:	steel-tube trellis
Tyre sizes:	front 120/70 17, rear 180/55 17
Final drive:	chain
Gearbox:	six-speed
Weight:	184kg (406lb)

amounts of horsepower. But KTM was working on a twin-cylinder engine for its offroad business; a 942cc (57.5cu in) 75° V-twin. This engine first appeared in the KTM 950 Adventure, a large enduro/touring bike aimed at the market built up by BMW's R1100GS. The Adventure was an excellent bike, and its engine was both powerful and flexible.

So it was no surprise when KTM fitted the engine to an even more road-focussed machine, the Super Duke.

Although it's really a short-range city bike, KTM offers, among other accessories, a GPS navigation system for the Super Duke. Note the all-LCD dashboard.

The bike first appeared in 2004, and it made an immediate impact. The styling was typical KTM, with angular bodywork, unconventional lines, and the firm's trademark bright orange and black paint scheme. A pair of underseat silencers lend a clean edge to the styling of the back end, while the large radiator cowling and bellypan give an aggressive, hunched stance to the front end.

Under the styling was a very high-performance machine. That V-twin motor, which had been such a success in the Adventure, was expanded in capacity to 999cc (61cu in), and fitted with a new fuel injection system to replace the Adventure's carbs. It was a modern, advanced design, with compact cylinder heads, four valves per cylinder and DOHC. The power figure of 118bhp (87kW) is good, but not exceptional for the capacity, KTM engineers aiming at good midrange and delivery, not ultimate outright horsepower.

The engine is held in a chrome-molybdenum steel-tube trellis frame, which is very stiff, tough and light. KTM has a close relationship with WP suspension of Holland, and it is this firm that has supplied the fully adjustable front and rear suspension units that give very good damping control. The Brembo brakes could easily grace any top-specification superbike, and this chassis package gives the Super Duke amazingly composed handling and dynamism on the road. It's a light bike, weighing 184kg (406lb) semi-dry (with fluids and battery, but no fuel). Together with the taut frame and commanding riding position, this makes the Super Duke a very controllable bike.

That's not to say it doesn't have a nasty side. Like many of these high-performance streetfighters, it's not a bike for the newly-qualified rider, or faint-hearted. The engine has an abrupt edge to its acceleration, and the front wheel regularly pops up off the ground under hard acceleration in lower gears. Living with a Super Duke can be a chore too. The fuel tank is small at 15l (4gal), and the effective fuel range is well under 160km (100 miles) with hard riding, and there's little wind protection on longer rides.

For 2006, KTM released an even more extreme version of the Super Duke, the 950 Supermoto. This bike used a 96bhp (71kW) 942cc (57cu in) engine, in a more focussed chassis, with radial-mount front brake calipers and lowered final gearing.

Moto Morini Corsaro

Morini also produced a lower-specification version of its roadster, the 9½. This was intended to have a 950cc (58cu in) version of the Corsaro engine, but the 1200 was so successful that the firm used a slightly detuned version of it instead.

Unlike similar machines from small Italian manufacturers, Moto Morini used its own engine design instead of buying in an engine from elsewhere. The 1200 V-twin motor is built by the separate Morini Franco Motori firm, which is located next door to the Moto Morini factory in Bologna.

Morini's Corsaro uses an ultra short-stroke V-twin engine design, with vertically split crankcases, eight valves, fuel injection and water cooling. It produced a potent 140bhp (103kW) power output.

The small-scale production of the Corsaro meant many parts were essentially hand finished, including the two-tone painted nylon fuel tanks.

The Corsaro's handsome front end is dominated by its twin headlights, small flyscreen and wide handlebars.

Moto Morini is one of the oldest names in Italian motorcycle production, the original firm dating back to 1937. Despite its illustrious history, the company fizzled out in the 1980s, with lack in investment and dated technology spelling the end of the line for its sporty, lightweight series of twins.

But in the early part of the twenty-first century, a new firm, backed by an Italian electronics manufacturer, had resurrected the Moto Morini name, and showed a range of prototype machines. Based around a V-twin engine designed by Morini's former chief designer, Franco Lambertini, the bikes looked like typical high-performance Italian roadsters, with trellis frames, top-quality running gear and slick design.

By 2005 the firm had launched its first machine, the 1200 Corsaro. A striking, handsome design, the Corsaro (named after the corsair pirates from the Barbary coast) had the figures to back up its hunched, purposeful looks. The Bialbero Corsacorta (twin-cam

Naked bikes like the Corsaro make a point of showing off their most crucial components. So the aluminium swinging arm, powerful V-twin engine and classy front forks are all proudly on display.

Moto Morini Corsaro

Top speed:	265km/h (165mph)
Engine type:	1187cc (72cu in), l/c 87° V-twin, eight-valve, DOHC
Maximum power:	140bhp (103kW)@8500rpm
Frame type:	steel-tube trellis
Tyre sizes:	front 120/70 17, rear 180/55 17
Final drive:	chain
Gearbox:	six-speed
Weight:	200kg (440lb)

short-stroke) engine was reckoned to produce 140bhp (103kW), with very high levels of torque, from an extremely short stroke design. Short-stroke engines generally rev quite high, and produce a peaky power delivery, but the Corsaro's power curve was different. A compact, high-compression combustion chamber with a tight 'squish' band gave good efficiency, and

Despite its large capacity and huge potential performance, the Corsaro is a sleek, attractive machine in the flesh. Early pre-production machines suffered from poor ground clearance on corners.

helped create strong, progressive power all through the rev range. A Magneti Marelli fuel-injection set-up with large 54mm (2in) throttle bodies allows a potentially high peak-power figure, while its powerful ECU 'brain' offered the engine tuner fine control over fuelling, while reducing emissions. That's helped further by a catalytic converter in the huge 70mm (2.75in) exhaust pipes. These end in a massive pair of reverse cone 'megaphone' silencers, which dominate the rear end of the bike, like a pair of missile launchers.

The chassis components were of a pretty high standard too – Brembo brakes, Marzocchi forks and a Sachs rear monoshock, fitted to a steel-tube trellis frame, with a cast-aluminium rear swingarm. Excellent Pirelli Diablo sports tyres, mounted on cast-aluminium Brembo wheels, further underlined the sporting intentions of the Corsaro.

Those very intentions become clear the instant a rider pulls away on the Corsaro. The bike is dominated visually by its engine, and it's dominated dynamically by the engine's huge performance. Just off idle, on even very small throttle openings, massive waves of torque slingshot the Corsaro forward. The mighty acceleration easily lifts the front wheel off the ground, even in second and third gear, and needs a careful throttle hand, particularly on less grippy surfaces. The naked layout of the bike means you're soon feeling the drag of the wind on your shoulders, as the Bialbero engine propels you towards 160km/h (100mph).

The Morini's chassis can handle all this with no problem. The frame is stiff, and while the suspension lacks some of the sophistication of more expensive track-biased bikes, it still gives good wheel control. The Brembo brakes have stopping power to match the engine's go, and even the riding position helps the rider stay in charge, with wide bars and low-set pegs.

Like many small firms, Morini hit some initial problems with the Corsaro. Poor fuel-injection mapping and a production fault in exhaust marred early models, resulting in poor low-down starting and running, and early grounding from the header pipes. But these teething problems were soon resolved, allowing the Corsaro to offer a genuine alternative to the likes of Ducati's Monster range.

Moto Morini also offered a lower-specification Corsaro, the 9½. Named after the Morini's legendary 3½ twin from the 1970s, the 9½ was originally intended to have a smaller-capacity, 950cc (58cu in) version of the Bialbero engine. But Morini bosses later decided to use a detuned version of the 1187cc (72cu in) Corsaro 1200 engine instead. This engine produced 105bhp (77kW), 35bhp (26kW) less than the Corsaro, and was mounted in a lower-spec chassis.

Morini opted for a classically Italian solution for the Corsaro's frame. A welded steel tube trellis uses triangulation to give the stiffness required for good handling and stability, without excessive weight.

MV Agusta Brutale 910

MV Agusta produced several special edition Brutales – an 'America' finished in red, white and blue, an 'Oro' version with magnesium wheels and frame parts, and the 'Gladio' with special paint and wheels, as well as an 'Italia' version celebrating Italy's 2006 soccer World Cup win.

Instead of using the underseat four-into-four exhaust system from the donor F4 superbike, Agusta developed an all-new twin-silencer system, with high-mounted cans on the right.

The Agusta's footpegs and pedals have neat eccentric adjustment systems to allow a perfect fit. Brake and clutch levers are also adjustable.

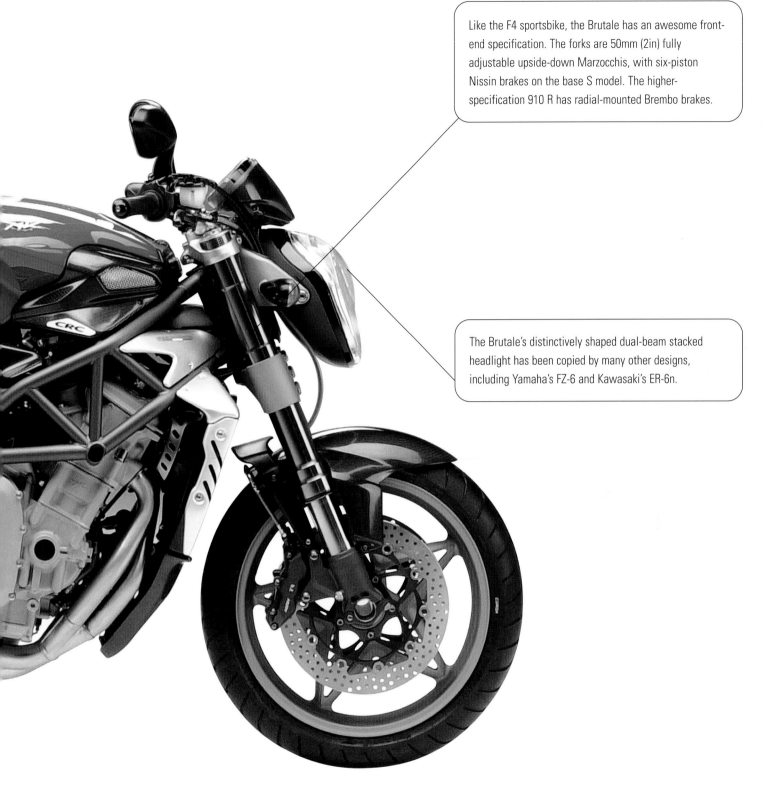

Like the F4 sportsbike, the Brutale has an awesome front-end specification. The forks are 50mm (2in) fully adjustable upside-down Marzocchis, with six-piston Nissin brakes on the base S model. The higher-specification 910 R has radial-mounted Brembo brakes.

The Brutale's distinctively shaped dual-beam stacked headlight has been copied by many other designs, including Yamaha's FZ-6 and Kawasaki's ER-6n.

In 1997, Italian motorcycling's most celebrated figure, Claudio Castiglioni revealed his new MV Agusta superbike. That bike, the F4S, was truly one of the most beautifully designed bikes ever, but it wasn't the only use Agusta had for its new four-cylinder engine. Just a year later, the firm revealed plans for a naked version of the F4 – dubbed Brutale.

Italian schedules being what they are, it wasn't until late 1999 that the F4 superbike arrived, and naked bike fans had to wait until 2003 to try out the Brutale. But it was worth it. The audacious styling of the Brutale is clear to see, with several design cues straight from the F4: the single-sided swingarm, steel-trellis frame and compact motor. But the Brutale had a novel twin-silencer exhaust system, an avant-garde dual-parabolic headlight, curvaceous fuel tank and angular seat unit. The first Brutale was, like the F4, an 'Oro' (Italian for 'gold') version. This meant a magnesium swingarm and forged magnesium wheels, both expensive, lightweight parts, as well as carbon-fiber body parts.

The Brutale has the same gorgeous swingarm as the F4 superbike. This 'Oro' bike has a cast magnesium part, with an ECU diagnostic plug incorporated and integrated carbon chainguard.

MV Agusta Brutale 910

Top speed:	265km/h (165mph)
Engine type:	908cc (55cu in), l/c inline-four, 16 radial valve, DOHC
Maximum power:	136bhp (100kW)@11,000rpm
Frame type:	steel-tube trellis/aluminium plates
Tyre sizes:	front 120/65 17, rear 190/50 17
Final drive:	chain
Gearbox:	six-speed
Weight:	185kg (408lb)

So the Brutale looked good – but how did it go? Like the first F4, the initial Brutale design used a 750cc (46cu in) engine, with a high 127bhp (93cu in) output. It had a somewhat revvy delivery though, and not totally suited to a naked bike, where relaxed, torquey engines are generally preferred. The fuel injection could be a little abrupt too, with a hint of jerky delivery appearing on occasion.

The 750 Brutale's short wheelbase makes lifting the front wheel easy, but the revvy engine made long wheelies hard to control. The 910 improved matters with more midrange.

The chassis was every bit as impressive as the styling. The front end in particular stood out to most testers, with the extra-thick 50mm (2in) Marzocchi forks and six-piston brake calipers combining extraordinary stiffness with amazing feel and control. The bike itself is extremely small for a 750, and this compact, nimble nature makes itself felt when riding, particularly on twisty back roads. The Agusta isn't particularly light, but most of that mass is centralized around the powerplant, further aiding the agile feel.

MV had long made clear its intentions to build a 1000cc (61cu in) version of the F4 superbike, but it

The sleek four-into-two exhaust system has the Agusta logo etched into the silencer. The high-mount cans also beautifully show off the rear wheel.

was less clear what would happen to the Brutale. The 750 could do with a little more stomp, but it didn't need the screaming 180bhp- (132kW)-plus of the F4 1000. So, Agusta's engineers chose a halfway house for the Brutale. It took the 76mm (3in) bore from the 1000, but used a different crankshaft with a 50.1mm (1.9in) stroke, 4.9mm (.19in) shorter than the F4 1000 motor. The result was a 908cc (55cu in) motor, and the results were very impressive. Torque was up and power had increased, and the new engine had a much stronger low- and mid-rpm performance.

There was little wrong with the chassis, so MV just got on with building and selling the 910S for 2005. The running gear was more than capable of handling the extra grunt from the motor, and the stellar handling, still-devastating styling and new, stronger engine made the Brutale 910S top dog for many naked fans.

A real critic may have pointed towards the Nissin six-piston calipers as being a little dated though, and for 2006, Agusta released the Brutale 910R. This bike featured uprated chassis gear, particularly some new radial-mount Brembo calipers, 10mm (.4in) larger front disks, forged aluminium wheels and revised Marzocchi RAC 50mm (2in) forks. The sharper brakes and lighter wheels refined the Brutale's handling to new heights, making it a real connoisseur's machine.

MV's president, Claudio Castiglioni is not a man without a sense of event. So when the Italian football team defeated France in the 2006 World Cup championship final, MV Agusta immediately announced the release of a special edition 'Italia' Brutale 910R. MV awarded one of the specially painted bikes to each team member, and produced a limited run of 100 bikes.

Suzuki Bandit 1200/1250

The Bandit has a tough nature, strong engine and cheap price. It was the bike of choice among stunt riders, who used the big Suzuki to perform wheelies, stoppies and burnouts.

For 2007, Suzuki produced an all-new water-cooled, fuel-injected 1250cc (76cu in) engine to replace the old 1200 motor. This was needed to meet tightening emissions regulations. Suzuki styled the new engine to look like the old one, however.

Like the engine, the Bandit's chassis is a straightforward, no-fuss design. A steel-tube double-cradle frame houses the motor, while conventional running gear front and rear gives ample performance.

The faired Bandit was perhaps one of the sports tourers with the best value, matching much more expensive machinery on comfort and ease of progress.

Although the faired Bandit is the best option for touring work, the naked version is still comfortable enough for riding with a passenger.

Motorcycle development lead times are so long that Suzuki couldn't have known how successful its 600 Bandit would be before beginning on the 1200 version. Only one year passed between the 600 appearing in 1995 and the launch of the 1200, and the smaller bike's success – both critical and sales – must have settled any executive nerves before the launch.

The bigger bike followed almost exactly the same pattern as the 600, although Suzuki took the opportunity to build an engine specifically for the 1200, rather than just fit one from another model. That engine was the mighty oil-cooled 16-valve four from the GSX1100F roadster, given an extra 1mm oversized bore, which increased capacity from 1127cc (69cu in) to 1157cc (71cu in). Different 36mm (1.5in) carburetors and altered cam timing cut the power output from the GSX's 125bhp (93kW) to 96bhp (71kW), but with a much more swollen midrange. The transmission only had five gears, but the broad spread of torque from the big engine meant it didn't need a sixth ratio.

The Bandit 1200's chassis was simple, yet capable. The engine was bolted into a steel-tube double-cradle frame that was stiff, light and cheap to build. It also gave the styling required, and showed off the engine really well. The suspension was unremarkable, but did the job. Front forks were conventional 43mm (1.75in) parts, adjustable for preload, and the rear monoshock had preload and rebound adjustment. Twin four-piston front brake calipers with 310mm (12in) disks worked well, and a neat box-section aluminium swingarm gave good handling while adding to the classic 1980s streetfighter feel of the design. The Bandit 1200 wasn't a particularly light bike, weighing in at 211kg (465lb) dry, but that was a reasonable mass for a naked roadster. When launched, it was fitted with Michelin Macadam sport-touring tyres.

As with the 600, Suzuki also built a half-faired version, the GSF1200S Bandit. The fairing was the only real difference. The handlebars and clocks were altered to suit, and it was only marginally heavier.

The Bandit 1200 had a slightly different character to

the 600. The smaller bike was seen as a good choice for novices and commuters, while also offering decent performance for more demanding riders. But the 1200 was a pretty serious motorcycle, with a potent engine and chassis package. The naked version quickly became the bike of choice for budding stunt riders – its short gearing, torquey engine and high bars made wheelies, stoppies and burnouts easy. And the lack of any plastic bodywork meant if a rider did drop the Bandit while practising, damage was usually limited.

While the naked bike became a hooligan's choice, the faired bike made an excellent budget sport tourer. The riding position was relaxed, the seat was comfy for two and the neat fairing gave enough wind protection for longer runs.

Both versions also attracted modifying fans. The pretty basic standard specification meant riders could personalize their machines with different exhausts and other tuning parts. And the cheap purchase price meant that there was cash left over for tuning.

The big Bandit remained largely unchanged until

Suzuki Bandit 1200	
Top speed:	225km/h (140mph)
Engine type:	1157cc (71cu in), a/c inline-four, 16-valve, DOHC
Maximum power:	100bhp (74.5kW) @8500rpm
Frame type:	steel-tube double-cradle
Tyre sizes:	front 120/70 17, rear 180/55 17
Final drive:	chain
Gearbox:	five-speed
Weight:	214kg (472lb)

late 2000, when it received an update in a similar vein to the 600. The frame was new, and the faired bike had a different nosecone and projector headlight. Small changes to the ignition on the engine improved power delivery, but it was essentially the same bike. Then, for 2006, Suzuki offered the Bandit S with a new sophisticated ABS antilock braking system.

Sadly for its fans, the Bandit couldn't continue in the same form for ever. For 2007, Euro III emissions regulations came into force, and the elderly air-cooled carburetted motor in the Bandit couldn't comply with them. So Suzuki developed an all-new 1250 engine, with liquid cooling, fuel injection and a range of other technical updates. The engineers kept the external styling of the engine similar to the old design though, with fake air-cooling fins and a silver finish.

The Bandit has always been a classic good looker – its large round chromed headlamp echoes the styling of 1970s superbikes. Faired clocks help guide the windblast over the rider.

Suzuki GSX1400

Its sheer size and bulk makes the GSX1400 appear an imposing bike at first. That's accentuated by its slabby fuel tank and wide handlebars.

The GSX's front end has fully adjustable 46mm (1.8in) conventional forks, and a pair of six-piston Tokico calipers with 320mm (12.5in) disks.

The GSX1400 was a premium model, and Suzuki gave it a much higher standard of finish than its 1200 Bandit roadster. Deep chrome plated the four-into-two exhaust and headlight, while the classic Suzuki blue/white paint scheme echoed the firm's GS1000 AMA superbike raced by Wes Cooley.

The GSX has a practical side – there's a large underseat storage area, the dashboard has a fuel gauge and clock, and the pillion seat is spacious and comfortable.

A beautifully crafted aluminum swingarm operates twin rear shocks, which are fully adjustable for damping and preload, and incorporate a 'piggyback' gas reservoir. Preload is adjusted by a simple hydraulic knob.

On the face of it, the GSX1400 seemed like a curious machine for Suzuki to launch. It already had the massively successful Bandit 1200 in its range, so why did it feel like it had to produce yet another heavyweight, four-cylinder, traditionally styled roadster? Indeed, when the 1400 appeared in 2001, the Bandit had just had a bit of a makeover, and its inexpensive, cheerful performance was as successful as ever. The GSX1400 was £450 ($750) more expensive in the UK, and didn't seem to offer much more performance over the Bandit.

The GSX's four-into two exhaust system is deeply chromed, and gives classy good looks. It does reduce ground clearance though, and hard cornering can scrape the cans on the road.

Suzuki GSX1400

Top speed:	241km/h (150mph)
Engine type:	1402cc (85.5cu in), a/c inline-four, 16-valve, DOHC
Maximum power:	106bhp (78kW) @6500rpm
Frame type:	steel-tube double cradle
Tyre sizes:	front 120/70 17, rear 190/50 17
Final drive:	chain
Gearbox:	six-speed
Weight:	228kg (502lb)

But the GSX1400 was aimed at a different niche within the naked musclebike fanbase. It was intended as a premium product, with much higher-specification chassis parts, and stronger design.

At the heart of the GSX was its massive engine. But it wasn't just a bigger version of the GSF1200 engine. It was developed from a different engine in the firm's oil-cooled four-cylinder line. Unlike the Bandit, the GSX motor had a six-speed gearbox, as well as a balancer shaft in the bottom end, to cut vibration. It also used a cutting edge dual-valve fuel injection system.

The SDTV throttle bodies measured just 34mm (1.3in), and these small inlets, coupled with the low 9.5:1 compression ratio and 'soft' low-lift camshafts meant the GSX1400 didn't make massive peak power. In fact, its 106 peak-power output was only about 10bhp (7kw) more than the lower-tech, smaller Bandit 1200. However, this figure was produced at an incredibly low engine speed of just 6500rpm. Engines this low revving are normally giant V-twin cruiser engines, and the GSX engine really performed more like an incredibly strong twin, than a high-tech four.

Suzuki also went for premium level components to kit out the chassis. The frame was an unremarkable steel-tube cradle design, but the rest of the chassis looked more like an early 1980s superbike racer. A super-sized aluminium box-section swingarm at the back holds a massive, 190-section rear tire, and operates a pair of shock units. These are high-quality, piggyback units, with full adjustability for preload and damping. The front forks have super-wide 46mm (1.8in) stanchions, and are also fully adjustable. Front brakes use a pair of six-piston calipers, similar to those found on the 2001 GSX-R1000.

All this lavish chassis equipment is closely matched to the design, which echoes the musclebike designs of the 1970s. That means a massive, slab-sided fuel tank, deeply padded seat, shapely tail unit with grab rail and a large round headlight. Finishing the whole look off is classic blue and white Suzuki paint (or mean black), and absolutely loads of chrome plating. The enormous four-into-two exhaust is chromed, as is the headlight and the clocks, while the engine covers and fins were polished alloy.

It's not until you sit on the GSX1400 that you realize just how large it is. The seat and fuel tank are extremely wide, the handlebars are a big stretch away, and the whole thing feels like it's been designed for some gigantic race of chrome fetishists. It utterly dominates the road as you ride along, and there are few bikes that look better reflected in a shop window on a sunny day.

Ridden at a gentle, yet committed pace, the GSX offers genuine rider fun on winding back roads, as well as looking great cruising around town.

The GSX's performance seems somewhat moot, but it does actually go very well. The engine has huge torque, but runs out of revs very quickly, and the chassis is short of ground clearance. The suspension and brakes have a lot of mass to deal with – the GSX weighs 228kg (503lb) dry – but like the engine, they have the capacity to deal with most situations. It's by no means a nimble twisty backroad blaster, and would be out of place on any kind of track, save a drag strip. But for city posing, weekend cruising and the occasional stoplight GP, the GSX1400 makes you very glad that Suzuki built it.

Triumph Speed Triple

Triumph promoted earlier versions of the Speed Triple with a one-make race series. This T509 Speed Triple Challenge series attracted many experienced racers, and ran in the UK in 1997.

Triumph offers a range of optional accessories for the Triple, including race exhausts, flyscreens and anodized bodywork fittings.

The Triple's 1050cc (64cu in) engine is the most powerful version, with 132bhp (97kW) and 77lbf ft of torque. The same unit is used in the firm's Sprint ST tourer and Tiger adventure sportsbike.

The Speed Triple has classic 'streetfighter' styling, with twin headlights, wide flat handlebars and stubby twin silencers. It also features Triumph's trademark single-sided swingarm. The shapely fuel tank is moulded in nylon.

The Triple's running gear is right up to sportsbike standards. Front brakes are radial-mount Nissin calipers with 320mm (12.5in) disks, suspension is fully adjustable, and its Bridgestone tires offer plenty of grip for track or fast road riding.

Triumph's 'Speed' range dates back as far as 1937, when the original Triumph firm produced a 500cc (30.5cu in) Speed Twin, a model name that continued in various forms until 1966.

But it was when building magnate John Bloor reinvigorated the Triumph brand, setting up a new factory in the early 1990s that the Speed range got serious. The first Speed Triple was launched in late 1993, using the modular concept that Triumph used to quickly develop a wide product range. The 1994 Triple used an 885cc (54cu in) three-cylinder engine in a steel-tube spine frame: essentially the same engine and chassis as the Daytona 900 sportsbike. The Daytona's bodywork was dropped in preference of a single round headlight, black painted fuel tank and seat unit, and clip-on low handlebars. The design harked back to the high-performance 'café racers' of the 1960s, and was totally in keeping with Triumph's heritage.

This first Triple stayed in production until 1996, but Triumph was beginning to move away from the modular production concept, and developing more specialized models. The result for 1997 was the T509 Speed Triple, a radical overhaul of the design, based on the T595 superbike launched at the same time. The T-series bikes had a new 885cc (54cu in) fuel-injected engine, an aluminium perimeter frame, and a distinctive single-sided swingarm. Triumph produced too a limited run of 750cc (46cu in) Speed Triples, using the old design, and engine from the 750 Trident.

Triumph Speed Triple	
Top speed:	256km/h (160mph)
Engine type:	1050cc (64cu in), l/c inline-triple, 12-valve, DOHC
Maximum power:	131bhp (96kW)@9250rpm
Frame type:	aluminium perimeter
Tyre sizes:	front 120/70 17, rear 180/55 17
Final drive:	chain
Gearbox:	six-speed
Weight:	189kg (416lb)

The T-series machines were popular, and the T509 had a good mix of style and performance. The front end had a bug-eyed twin headlight set-up, and that single-sided swingarm added a touch of exotica to the back. The chassis was up to then-current superbike standards, with a light, stiff frame, high-specification, fully adjustable forks and shock, and race-specification front brakes, with dual 320mm (12.5mm) disks and four-piston Nissin calipers. The bike was 13kg (29lb) lighter, and had 11bhp (8kW) more power from the revised 885cc (54cu in) engine.

Triumph's most aggressive design, the Speed Triple is short and stubby. This, together with the incredibly strong, smooth engine, makes it a great bike for stunts and sports riding.

The dual stubby, high-mount silencers look good, comply with stiff Euro III emissions rules and show off the single-sided rear to best effect. Pillion pegs offer vestigial passenger accommodation.

The T509 series continued for only 18 months before being updated with a newer 955cc (60.1cu in) engine, taken from the 955i sportsbike, in mid-1998. It was offered in a range of outrageous paint schemes, such as electric pink and fluorescent lime green, and gained a firm following among streetfighter fans worldwide.

2002 saw the introduction of the Speed Four, a version of the ill-fated TT600 sportsbike with naked styling borrowed from the Triple, which continued until 2004. But it was the Triple that was Triumph's real streetfighter success, especially after it got another engine upgrade from the Daytona 955i in 2001.

By 2005, Triumph was ready to release yet another Speed Triple. This time, the engine had gone up in capacity again to 1050cc (64cu in). The bigger engine was shared with the Sprint ST sports tourer for 2005 but, bizarrely, the Triple version actually had more power. Giving a naked bike 6bhp (5kW) more than its faired sibling seemed strange, but the first ride on the 1050 Triple soon convinced any doubters. The engine was an absolute gem, bursting with creamy-smooth grunt right off idle, and making a delicious sound through the new short-cut silencers. The fuel injection was perfect, and the Speed Triple, always a good stunt bike, became the perfect wheelie bike.

But there was more to the update than the engine. Fully adjustable 43mm (17in) upside-down front forks graced the front end, fitted with a pair of radial-mount four-piston Nissin brake calipers and 320mm (12.5in) disks. The single-sided swingarm was updated, and new five-spoke wheels, a short seat unit and revamped fuel tank all added to the new style. A narrower 180-section rear tyre made the Triple turn faster, and new digital clocks gave a wider range of rider information.

Triumph Rocket III

Engine tuners have offered outrageous upgrade packages for the Rocket. British firm TTS produced a supercharger kit which increased power to almost 250bhp (184kW), while US firm Turbo Connections offered a turbo kit with similar performance.

The components of the Rocket and its engine were so much larger and heavier than any other Triumph that the factory in England had to up-rate some of the handling equipment on its assembly line.

The 2294cc (140cu in) Rocket III was, and remains, the largest capacity series production motorcycle ever built. Its pistons are the same size as those on a Dodge Viper supercar, and each cylinder ingests 765cc (47cu in) of fuel/air mix on each power cycle.

There is a 'Classic' version of the Rocket, with forward footpegs, pullback bars and other cosmetic changes.

Front brakes are taken from the 955i superbike – a pair of 320mm (12.5in) disks with four-piston calipers. The rear brake is specially designed for the Rocket – a 316mm (12.4in) disk with a twin piston caliper.

Like any other journalists, the world's motorcycle press rely on hearsay. New models are preceded by mutterings from 'factory insiders', sometimes plausible, sometimes fantastic. But none have been more fantastic than the wild stories that emanated from the UK's Triumph factory in 2002–3. The legendary marque, the story went, was about to release the biggest production bike ever – a massive 2.3l (140 cu in) three-cylinder cruiser. Cynics sneered at the tales, while Triumph fans secretly hoped that the Hinckley-based firm was going to bowl the world over.

Amazingly enough, the stories were true, and the Rocket III was unleashed on a stunned public in August 2003. It was reckoned to be the fastest-accelerating bike available, capable of pulling over 1.2g acceleration, while remaining as easy to ride and control as any other large cruiser.

Breaking the 2l (122 cu in) barrier for the first time in a motorcycle, the Rocket's engine is a true behemoth. With a capacity larger than many full-sized cars, it is mounted in an unusual 'fore and aft' layout, with the crankshaft running parallel to the bike's centre line. The three massive 101.6mm (4in) bore cylinders are fed by a multipoint electronic fuel injection system

Triumph Rocket III	
Top speed:	241km/h (150mph)
Engine type:	2294cc (140cu in), l/c inline-triple, 12-valve, DOHC
Maximum power:	140bhp (103kW)@6000rpm
Frame type:	steel-tube twin spine
Tyre sizes:	front 150/80 17, rear 240/50 16
Final drive:	shaft
Gearbox:	five-speed
Weight:	320kg (704lb)

mounted on the rider's left-hand side, while the exhaust exits on the right-hand side. Each cylinder has four valves, two exhaust and two inlets, operated by twin overhead camshafts, and a wet, multiplate clutch drives a five-speed gearbox. Final drive is by maintenance-free shaft.

This mighty powerplant is housed in a chassis only really remarkable for its size. A steel-tube twin spine

For such a massive bike, the Rocket has minimalist instrumentation. The tacho shows the enormous engine's comparatively low redline. Top speed on later Rockets was restricted to 217km/h (135mph).

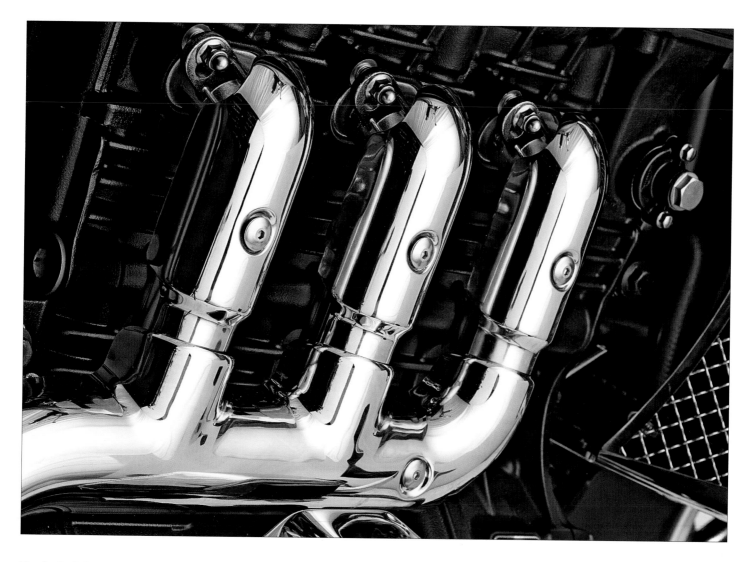

The Rocket's inline-three layout is clearly outlined by the exhaust system, which exits on the right. Chromed covers add more glitz to the stainless pipes underneath.

frame mounts the engine, a twin-shock rear swingarm and a pair of 43mm (1.7in) upside-down front forks. Aluminium five-spoke wheels wear super-wide rubber: a 150/70 17 cruiser style front tyre and a dragster-wide 240-section Metzeler on the rear, as well as powerful 320mm (12.5in) front disc brakes. The calipers are four-piston items, taken from the firm's 955i superbike, with a large twin piston caliper and 316mm (12.4mm) disk out back.

Triumph stuck with the tried-and-tested styling methods of the cruiser class: deep glossy-painted fuel tank, front fender and rear mudguard, deep chrome-plated exhaust silencers and a moody, black-finished powerplant. But there are a couple of modern touches to the design too: a pair of chromed headlights up front have twice the impact of a single light. And the kicked-out upside-down front forks (the first on a Triumph) give an intensely purposeful, sporting look to the front end.

But the Rocket's biggest surprise is how well it rides. It's not a light bike – 320kg (705lb) is almost the same as two Triumph 675 Daytona sportsbikes. But the Rocket carries that weight low down, and with a seat height suited to the stumpiest cruiser fan, wide bars and light controls, it's easily manhandled around at slow speeds. Remarkably, at high speed, the frame offers enough stiffness to prevent wallowing or wobbles, the suspension is comfy yet firmly damped to give sound wheel control, and the super-wide back tire always provides ample grip, despite the massive 200Nm (147lb ft) of torque surging through it. Even on the sort of twisty backroad that benefits small, taut sportsbikes, an experienced hand on a Rocket III will be a hard act to follow closely on a superbike.

But the Rocket was designed with more relaxed cruising in mind. And burbling through the city's mean streets, with the occasional stoplight GP race against all comers is perhaps its ideal territory. Although, equipped with a windshield and some panniers from Triumph's accessories list, the Rocket makes a great freeway tool for crawling up the Pacific Coast Highway, baiting any Harley riders you meet.

Yamaha FZ-1 Fazer

The FZ-series uses a cast aluminium frame and braced R1-type rear swingarm. This replaced the basic steel tube frame on the older Fazer.

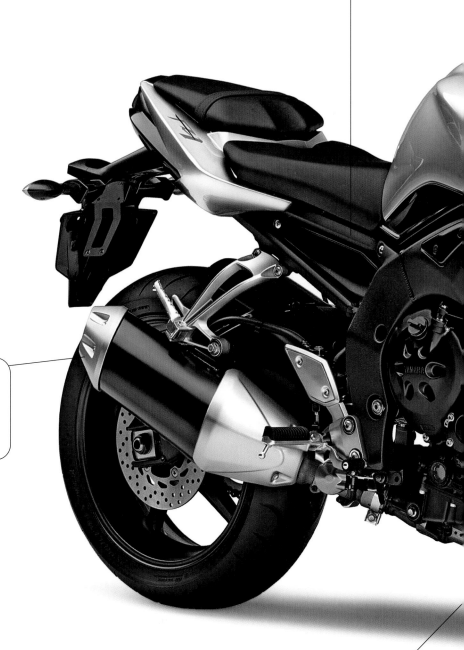

The four-into-one exhaust has a stubby silencer which incorporates a catalyst to cut emissions, as well as an electronically operated EXUP butterfly valve. This improves low-down power and reduces noise pollution.

Yamaha used its YZF-R1 superbike engine for both the original and FZ-1 Fazers. The first bike used a version of the 1998 carburetted R1 engine, while the 2006 FZ-1 used a later fuel-injected motor. Both were retuned for more midrange power.

The original Fazer 1000 was only available in a faired version, but Yamaha produced both a faired and a naked version of the FZ-1 second generation bike. The FZ-1 Fazer has a fairing, the FZ-1 is naked.

Yamaha offered an anti-lock braking system for the FZ-1 Fazer, to improve safety on slippery road surfaces.

It's one of the curious paradoxes of modern motorcycling that while the public and press are most excited about a firm's flagship sports models, many buyers prefer something a little less radical for everyday use. A more mature audience may find the prospect of a comfortable, less committed version of an ultimate sportsbike will be kinder on their aging bones and slowing reflexes.

With that in mind, Yamaha launched the first Fazer 1000 late in the year 2000. Aimed at replicating the success of the smaller Fazer 600, the new bike used a revised version of the company's R1 engine in a more relaxed roadster chassis.

Rather than just fit the engine direct from the R1, Yamaha engineers fitted smaller carburettors and a heavier crankshaft. Both these modifications improved the midrange performance of the 20-valve engine, at the cost of a small amount of peak power (down around 10bhp [7kW] from the R1) and responsiveness. They also made the engine easier to get along with, and the fuelling and power delivery were both flawless, making the Fazer 1000 a pleasure to ride.

This softer, yet still potent, engine was fitted into a new steel-tube cradle frame, with fully adjustable

The 2006 FZ-1 was equipped with top-notch sportsbike chassis components. Upside-down front forks were fully adjustable, and the brake calipers were borrowed from the firm's R-series bikes.

suspension front and rear. The forks and rear shock were softer than full sports parts, reflecting the Fazer's road bias, but still offered good damping and springing performance. One area where the Fazer was almost as

Yamaha FZ-1 Fazer

Top speed:	241km/h (150mph)
Engine type:	998cc (60 cu in), l/c inline-four, 20-valve, DOHC
Maximum power:	150bhp (111kW) @11,000rpm
Frame type:	cast aluminium diamond type
Tyre sizes:	front 120/70 17, rear 190/50 17
Final drive:	chain
Gearbox:	six-speed
Weight:	194kg (427lb)

good as its sporty sibling was the brakes: the same four-piston Sumitomo calipers and 298mm (12in) disks are fitted to both bikes. The Fazer was a touch heavier, and the softer forks and more touring-like tyres reduced ultimate braking performance slightly, but it still had the best brakes in its class. Handling overall was sound, although hard cornering did find the limits of the bike's ground clearance fairly quickly, and the soft suspension meant it did wallow a little in speedy corners. The Fazer 1000 was an incredibly practical machine though. Its strong engine meant fast touring was straightforward, the small half-fairing gave good protection from windblast and the riding position was comfortable all day long, even two-up. The only possible complaint against the big Fazer was its price. Yamaha had priced the Fazer as a premium machine in the UK, where it was nearly as expensive as the R1 was when launched. However, market forces caused Yamaha to cut the price for the following model years.

The most notable exception on the Fazer 1000 was, like the 600, the lack of an unfaired option. Yamaha rectified this for 2006, with an all-new version of the Fazer, available in two different types. The FZ-1 had no nosecone, while the FZ-1 Fazer had a new half-

On the 2006 bikes, Yamaha finished off the modern design with a massive low-mounted single exhaust silencer. Its 'stubby' design was intended to echo the systems used on the firm's MotoGP machines.

fairing. Both versions had a striking, large, stubby silencer mounted on the right-hand side.

These 2006 models used an engine based on the 2005 R1 design. It used fuel injection instead of the carburettors of the old bike, and was re-tuned to produce less power but more midrange. A lowered compression ratio and other changes cut peak output from 175bhp (129kW) to 150bhp (110kW). The bike's upside-down front forks and a rear monoshock were adjustable, and 320mm (12.5in) front brake disks, with new four-piston calipers, gave even better braking.

The new bike wasn't received with universal approval, however. Like several designs that moved from carburettors to fuel injection, the Fazer's power delivery had suffered. This rather mediocre fuelling, combined with a revvy motor, meant the 2006 bike had lost some of the usability of the older model. On the positive side, it had much more sporting ability, with the frame and suspension in particular being much more suited to harder riding.

Yamaha MT-01

The 'MT' range was extended in 2006 with the launch of the MT-03, a stylish single-cylinder 660cc (40cu in) machine aimed at novice riders.

Yamaha also fitted superbike brakes – radial-mount Sumitomo calipers from the R1. Upside-down forks and rear suspension unit are both fully adjustable.

Yamaha offered a massive range of MT-01 accessories, including Akrapovic exhausts, carbon/aluminium bodywork and performance upgrades. Owners could even purchase a stage-three tuning kit, with high-compression pistons, race camshafts and exhausts and a replacement engine ECU.

The MT-01's frame and swingarm are produced using Yamaha's CF cast process. This makes lighter, tougher components. The swingarm is very similar to that on the YZF R1 superbike.

Yamaha adapted the MT's engine from the Road Star cruiser. It simplified the transmission, saving size and mass, and fitted tougher internals to produce more power. It still used pushrod valve actuation though, limiting peak speed and power.

Only a brave manufacturer attempts to create a new class of bike. A motorcycle firm's road to financial ruin is paved with both good intentions, and wise-guy ideas. Telling a notoriously conservative motorcycling public that they've been getting it wrong with their bike choice all these years, and should now change to your latest new concept machine is at best risky.

All the major manufacturers have gone down this path over the years, and Yamaha is no exception. Such designs as its GTS1000 hub-centre steered sport tourer and the SZR660 single-cylinder sportsbike clearly passed some sort of marketing focus group, but failed to make much impact in the showroom. And the firm added another 'new concept' to its canon in 2005 with the MT-01.

The idea was 'Torque Sports', which aimed to provide sporting thrills by way of a low-revving, high-torque powerplant in an unconventional, but dynamic, sports chassis. The MT-01 was the resulting machine, and when it was unveiled in 2004, it looked absolutely stunning. A hunched, brutalist design, it was centered around a massive air-cooled V-twin engine with high-specification sports chassis components. The design

Although the MT-01 was rather heavy and low-powered, it had very composed handling. That's thanks to sophisticated sportsbike chassis components and careful design.

A large single clock incorporates a large tachometer, smaller LCD speedometer and warning lights.

Yamaha MT-01

Top speed:	224km/h (140mph)
Engine type:	1670cc (102cu in), a/c 48° V-twin, eight-valve, OHV
Maximum power:	90bhp (66kW)@4750rpm
Frame type:	cast aluminium twin beam
Tyre sizes:	front 120/70 17, rear 190/50 17
Final drive:	chain
Gearbox:	five-speed
Weight:	240kg (528lb)

had a high-quality, solid feel to it. A closer look revealed a massive pair of underseat silencers in titanium, a minimalist cast-aluminium frame, upside-down front forks with radial mount brake calipers, and a cast-aluminium swingarm. Most of the chassis parts looked as if they could have come straight off of a world superbike racer, and not just some sort of concept roadster.

The thing that jarred slightly was the engine. Although it was incredible to look at, the air-cooled V-twin didn't appear to have been designed for performance. In fact, it was a modified version of a cruiser engine, the 1670cc (102cu in) Road Star Warrior. It was a 'power cruiser' engine, making around 85bhp (62.5kW), but it still seemed strange to see such a lowly-tuned engine situated in such a capable chassis.

Looking at the press release confirmed the view that here was an exceptionally well appointed chassis, with an incredibly heavy, lowly-tuned, big-bore engine. Yamaha claimed to have saved 20kg (44lb) of weight from the engine, and it had a slew of high-tech ancillary equipment, including advanced fuel injection and an EXUP valve in the exhaust. The specifications included forged pistons, four-valve heads, ceramic-plated cylinder walls and two spark plugs per cylinder.

Yamaha got right behind the MT-01 concept, and pushed it hard, with a wide range of 'lifestyle' accessories, from clothing to watches, as well as a host of performance tuning parts for the bike itself. The firm also held a world press launch in South Africa. The reports from the launch were positive, although it became clear that this bike was in no way a replacement for the firm's legendary V-Max hot rod bike of the 1990s.

Riding the MT-01 is an unusual, but fun, experience. The chassis is superb, offering both stability in corners, and good agility. The brakes are excellent, the frame is stiff enough, and the adjustable suspension is both compliant and well damped. Having said that, two things let the chassis down. First is the mass, which at 240kg (530lb) is too heavy, another downside to the huge engine. Second, unfathomably, Yamaha placed Metzeler MeZ4 tires on the bike. The Z4 was a mid-1990s tire, intended for touring. Handicapping the chassis with such a tire made absolutely no sense, especially considering the MT-01's high price. The cost, together with the mediocre engine performance and indifferent practicality outweighed the bike's undoubted strengths, and it did not sell well in the UK. It was more popular in other European markets, but the 'Torque Sports' class seemed destined to be a niche market at best.

The massive V-twin engine makes an impressive centrepiece to the MT-01 design, although it does impose a significant weight penalty.

Open-class Superbikes:
large-capacity sportsbikes

Apart from an astronaut, a Formula One driver or a fighter pilot, it's hard to think of anyone who regularly experiences the acceleration achieved by a 21st-century open-class sportsbike such as Suzuki's GSX-R1000 K5. It weighs 166kg (366lb), its four-cylinder engine provides 133kW (178bhp), will hit 60mph (96km/h) in around three seconds, and is generally accepted to be one of the most outrageous motorcycles ever built.

Bikes with these performance figures have come about due to ever-improving materials technologies, computer-aided design techniques, and lessons learnt from the race track. The Superbike race class, at world and national level, changed its regulations to allow 1,000cc (61 cu in) four-cylinder designs from 2003 (fours were limited to 750cc [46 cu in] until then, competing with 1,000cc [61 cu in] twins). This change intensified the pace of development in the 1,000cc (61 cu in) four-cylinder class, as manufacturers competed to build a bike that could win on the track.

The hardest part of building a successful litre-class superbike is making its performance usable. It is actually fairly straightforward to make an engine that can put out almost 150kW (200bhp) per litre with current production technologies. Materials and component design means 250cc- (15 cu in)-sized pistons can be made to rev safely to around

A serene image – but BMW's K1200S is an incredibly potent piece of engineering. Its inline-four engine produces almost 127kW (170bhp), while its advanced chassis boasts a host of novel design innovations. The result is simply stunning.

12,000rpm, while making sufficient torque. And making a chassis light and stiff enough is also reasonably simple with off-the-shelf components. But putting them both together into a package that most riders, with reasonable experience, can safely manage and control is incredibly difficult. This 'black art' is down to such diverse elements as steering geometry, weight distribution, tyre choice and engine power delivery.

Less sensitive to chassis design, but still incredibly exhilarating, are the 'hypersports' bikes. These machines are slightly heavier than the pure race-replicas of the 1,000cc (61 cu in) class, and generally have larger engines. Bikes like Kawasaki's ZZR1400 have top-spec sporting components and extremely powerful engines. But they also have extra room for the rider, added wind protection, and are much more suited to longer trips. What they sacrifice in terms of track performance, they make up for with extra practicality and long-distance ability. They are also insanely fast – the ZZR1400 is restricted to 300km/h (186mph), but its 150kW (200bhp) engine output would allow a much higher de-restricted speed.

BMW K1200S

The large triple-bulb headlight unit gives superb illumination at night, and is shaped to help aerodynamic performance. The twin ram air intakes underneath improve high-speed power production.

BMW's brakes use 320mm (12.5in) front discs and four-piston calipers, with an optional ABS system, and steel brake lines. Together with the Duolever suspension, they give superb stopping performance.

The front suspension unit is hidden behind the fairing, and the wheel is solidly mounted into a cast-aluminium wheel-carrier unit. The system is based on the 1980s designs of UK engineer Norman Hossack.

BMW also produced a more touring-biased version of the K1200, the K1200GT. This had a larger fairing and standard-fit panniers, electric windshield and more relaxed riding position. The engine was slightly detuned, but still produced 152bhp (113kW).

The four-cylinder engine is BMW's most powerful unit ever, producing almost 170bhp (127kW), with strong, torquey delivery and smooth fuelling. It's an advanced design, with cutting-edge electronic control and numerous engineering innovations.

Despite its high power output and relatively high mass, the K1200S is BMW's most sporting bike. It's a match for many Japanese machines in terms of handling, and offers incredible all-round performance.

BMW always maintained that it built a range of high-performance sportsbikes. However, this claim should be placed before the qualification 'for a BMW'. The Munich firm had very definite ideas of its own regarding performance, and these rarely coincided with the rest of the market. The K1200RS of the late 1990s was an example. It was promoted as a sports tourer, and certainly had a lot of power from its laid-down 1172cc (72cu in) engine. But it weighed an incredible 265kg (585lb) and was very long, ruling out exciting performance, at least, as it was defined by most other manufacturers.

But BMW underwent a renaissance in the early years of the twenty-first century, which saw it focus more on performance. The R1200GS, R1200S and F800 were all launched with significantly reduced mass and increased performance over their predecessors.

The flagship of BMW's performance line, though, was the K1200S. It first appeared in mid-2004, although some problems with preproduction models led to a pause before production began properly for 2005. It was an incredibly high-tech machine, with novel solutions to many chassis and engine design questions. But like many ground-breaking machines, it was the bike's raw performance stats that impressed. A claimed 167bhp (124.5kW) made this by far the most powerful BMW bike ever made, and a glance at the claimed mass figures showed the engineers had grasped this nettle too. A dry weight of 226kg (498lb) was not much more than the Japanese competition in the hypersports category, particularly Suzuki's 215kg (474lb) Hayabusa.

Behind the figures was a genuinely innovative, high-performance design. Starting at the engine, you see a laid-down design, with the cylinders tilted forward,

allowing the aluminium frame rails to pass over, rather than around, the motor, cutting width. The cylinder head is very compact, thanks to a novel camshaft drive – only the exhaust camshaft is driven by a chain from the crankshaft, the inlet shaft is driven by a gear on the camshafts. The waterpump is also mounted in the cylinder head and also turned from the inlet camshaft.

This F1-derived head design is fed by an advanced fuel injection system. This includes a knock sensor to allow use of high-octane (98 RON) fuel. This gives the best power and economy, but if lower octane fuel is used, the sensor detects any pre-ignition, and retards ignition accordingly.

Like the engine, the chassis uses a series of interesting design solutions. The basis of the chassis is a stiff twin-beam frame that passes over the engine and mounts the front and rear suspension systems. The rear suspension is BMW's tried-and-tested Paralever system, which incorporates a shaft drive inside a single-sided swingarm. Cleverly designed linkages prevent unwanted suspension movement under acceleration and deceleration, and the arm is controlled by an adjustable monoshock unit.

The front suspension is unique to the K1200S (and R version, see page 150). This 'Duolever' set-up is a twin-wishbone system, with a cast-aluminium wheel carrier mounted on the wishbones, and a single shock absorber in the middle controlling movement. The carrier pivots around the steering stem, controlled by a scissors linkage from the handlebars. This allows sporty steering geometry, and compliant springing, while separating out the heavy braking forces.

BMW K1200S

Top speed:	289km/h (180mph)
Engine type:	1172cc (71cu in), l/c inline-four, 16-valve DOHC
Maximum power:	167bhp (124.5kW)@10,250rpm
Frame type:	aluminium twin spar
Tyre sizes:	front 120/70 17, rear 180/55 17
Final drive:	shaft
Gearbox:	six-speed
Weight:	226kg (498lb)

This clever front suspension is responsible for much of the bike's nimble performance. For its length and mass, it is highly agile, and this, with the excellent engine performance, makes it a superb, fast roadbike.

The rest of the bike lives up to the suspension and engine. Power brakes give phenomenal stopping power, and the bodywork protects the rider from wind blast. Standard equipment includes a trip computer and informative dashboard, excellent mirrors and brilliant headlights. Optional accessories can transform the S into a grand tourer, with hard luggage, sat-nav, heated handgrips and electronic suspension.

The screen and top fairing give deceptively high levels of wind and weather protection. Clever aerodynamic design means the rider sits in a bubble of still air up to and beyond 225km/h (140mph).

This computer-generated image shows how the Duolever suspension operates. The wheel carrier is mounted on two pivoting links that operate a single shock absorber. The handlebars turn the wheel by means of a neat scissor linkage.

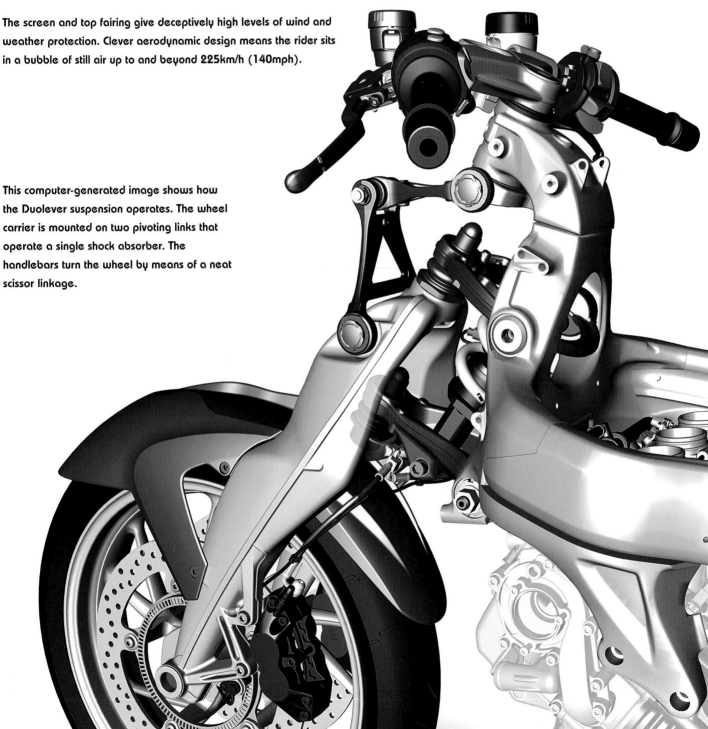

BMW R1200S (+R1100S)

The dashboard has twin analogue dials for speedo and tachometer, as well as an LCD display. This shows fuel remaining, range, time, gear position, along with other useful information.

There are twin spark plugs in each cylinder, to help burn the fuel in the large combustion chamber. The large inlet valves also feature sodium cooling, and the camshafts have an extra bearing each over the R1200GS engine to allow higher rev limits.

The stainless steel exhaust system incorporates a catalytic convertor to cut emissions, and has a dual-outlet underseat silencer. Header pipes are 2in (50mm) in diameter

BMW's R engine can use air cooling, thanks to its Boxer configuration, which places the cylinders well out into the airstream. An oil cooler mounted below the headlights provides extra cooling.

BMW offered optional sports parts: Öhlins suspension units front and rear, and a wider 150mm (6in) rear wheel that can hold a 190-section tyre. Other accessories included heated handgrips, a satellite navigation system, an alarm and soft luggage.

Before BMW changed its design direction, focussing more on performance from 2004 and onward, the R1100S was its most sporting model. First revealed in late 1998, it used the firm's 1085cc (66cu in) Boxer engine, which also powered the R1100GS, the R1100RT and the R1100RS. This flat-twin engine was the latest version of BMW's traditional twin, and offered decent performance, with 98bhp (73kW) and a torquey power delivery. Fuel injection meant reliable, predictable fuelling, each cylinder head had a high-mounted camshaft and four valves, operated by rocker arms. A six-speed transmission and the usual BMW shaft drive provided fuss-free final drive. The engine was mounted in a version of the R-series chassis, with extra sporting bias. The front suspension was BMW's Telelever system, which used a pair of telescopic sliders mounted to a wishbone linkage that operated a monoshock suspension unit. Rear suspension was BMW's paralever, with a single-sided swingarm, monoshock unit and anti-torque reaction linkage.

This engine/chassis package was dressed in some rather racy (for BMW) bodywork. A small half fairing gave both wind protection and added aerodynamic efficiency, while the back end displayed a most un-BMW-like set of sexy underseat silencers.

The R1100S provided an alternative option to Japanese sports tourers like the VFR800 or Triumph's Sprint for the next seven years. The handling was surprisingly good, helped by the Telelever front end, which allowed fierce braking without upsetting the balance into a corner. The brakes themselves were strong, and for a 208kg (459lb) bike, it was pretty dynamic. What power the engine did have was very useable, if not over-endowed with torque. BMW also offered an SS version with a steering damper, and sports suspension package.

Wide mirrors give an excellent view, and a clear, dashboard conveys rider information quickly. BMW's switchgear is unusual compared with Japanese machinery, and includes a switch to turn off the ABS system.

Seven years is a long time in motorcycle design, and by 2006, the R1100S was well overdue for an update. This, combined with the new focus on performance from BMW senior management meant that a serious, wheels-up revamp was required. And that's exactly what appeared, in the shape of the R1200S, launched in late 2005. The basic stats on the R1200 update are pretty impressive. The dry weight had fallen by 18kg (40lb) to 190kg (420lb), and the power from the engine had increased by 24bhp (18kW) to 122bhp (90kW).

Starting with the engine, BMW took the new 1170cc (72cu in) engine used in the R1200GS, RT and LT, and tuned it further. New cylinder heads had a stiffer camshaft housing with an extra bearing, stronger springs and rocker arms, all allowing a higher rev ceiling of 8800rpm, higher than any other Boxer engine. Compression ratio was raised to 12.5:1. A new fuel injection system used a knock sensor to allow the use of either 98 or 95 octane fuel – the higher octane fuel providing better power and reduced consumption.

The chassis was all-new, but essentially the same design. The Paralever rear suspension system is much lighter than before, and the Telelever front suspension has new geometry. New brakes have switchable ABS, which can be turned off for use on track where extreme braking can confuse the system.

BMW had also improved the R1200S's equipment levels. New CAN electronics provided extra functionality and fault diagnosis to the dashboard, a built-in immobilizer prevents theft, and a wide range of BMW accessories are available to further customize the bike to each customer.

The R1200S's improved performance was obvious when ridden. The engine delivered exciting power, and the chassis dealt easily with the new performance.

BMW R1200S

Top speed:	257km/h (160mph)
Engine type:	1170cc (72cu in), a/c flat-twin, 8-valve, SOHC
Maximum power:	122bhp (90kW)@8250rpm
Frame type:	aluminium/steel composite
Tyre sizes:	front 120/70 17, rear 180/55 17
Final drive:	BMW Paralever shaft
Gearbox:	six-speed
Weight:	190kg (419lb)

This dramatic shot of an R1200S tearing around a mountain corner clearly shows the indicators built into the mirrors, and the vents below the headlight which feed air to an engine oil cooler.

Stripped down, the minimal frame and unusual front suspension of the R1200S is clear. Careful design is used to cut weight throughout the bike compared with the R1100S.

Honda NR750

Even nearly a decade and a half after it first appeared, the NR750 is an incredible-looking machine. Many of its design features have since appeared on other production bikes, from Honda and other firms.

Despite its amazing specification, the NR750 only offered average performance, with a 125bhp (93kW) power output and 223kg (491lb) dry mass. Honda's own CBR900RR FireBlade of 1993 was nearly 40kg (88lb) lighter, with similar power.

All the deep red bodywork was hand-finished carbon fibre, and the windshield was coated with titanium.

The two small exhaust pipes under the pillion seat give little indication of the complexity of the full system. Each cylinder has two exhaust outlets, so the full system goes from eight pipes to four, then two, then one, then back to two at the exit.

Even mundane parts like the sidestand were made special on the NR. An articulated cover folded in and out of the fairing automatically when the sidestand was extended and retracted.

For a company such as Honda, engineering is all. The Japanese firm has long been run by engineers, and the firm's founder, Soichiro Honda, was the epitome of the committed, passionate 'dreamer with oily hands'.

As a result, Honda has always placed immense importance on its engineering, and it shows in projects like the ASIMO robot or the Hondajet business jet. However, Honda has also pursued unusual engineering solutions in its motorbikes.

The NR750 was built in order to try to overcome the natural advantages of a two-stroke engine. Honda's corporate attitude to two-stroke engines was ambivalent at best, and where it could avoid building them, it did. Sadly, in most race classes, the superior power-to-weight ratio of two-strokes made them essential. In the premium 500cc (30.5cu in) GP class, engines were limited to four cylinders – and there was no way a conventional four-cylinder four-stroke engine could make as much power as a two-stroke.

So Honda approached the problem from a different angle. An eight-cylinder design could perhaps make sufficient power, so the firm planned an engine with oval – not round – pistons. Each oval 'cylinder' would be almost like two normal round cylinders in terms of space for valves and potential for making horsepower. Indeed, the design called for two spark plugs, two con rods and eight valves in each cylinder.

The NR500 race-bike project was a glorious failure, dogged by bad luck and terrible unreliability. But Honda had learned enough about the technology to build a roadbike with oval pistons. It was something that really could only be done by Honda, which seemed reason enough to do it.

The NR750 appeared at the prestigious Suzuka Eight Hour race in 1991, ridden by race marshals. Its design looks pretty futuristic even 15 years later, but at the time, it was unimaginably exotic. Every part of the NR's design, from the single-sided swinging arm and underseat exhausts, to the twin headlights and mirror-mounted indicators seemed novel, although many cues have been picked up by production bikes since.

The engineering was just as exotic. Apart from the Byzantine complexity of the engine, with its 32 valves, eight conrods, eight sparkplugs and four oval pistons, there was an eight-barrel/eight-injector fuel injection system, an '8 into 4 into 2 into 1 into 2' exhaust, and a digital LCD dashboard. The wheels were magnesium, the bodywork was carbon fibre, the forks were an upside-down design (Honda's first on a roadbike) and windscreen was tinted with titanium. The key was specially made from nickel silver and carbon fibre.

The price of the NR was as extreme as its specification. When launched, it cost £38,000 ($62,700) in the UK, making it a collector's item and toy for the super-rich. But what wasn't so extreme, disappointingly, was its performance. Although the design had the potential for much more power, Honda decided to cap the peak power at 125bhp (86kW) @14,000rpm. Together with a torque figure of 50.5lb ft (68.5Nm) @11,500rpm, these were very good figures for an early-90s 750cc (46cu in) road bike. But since the NR also weighed a hefty 222kg (489lb), the result was a bike that gave only middling performance. The power was beautifully produced, the engine bewitchingly smooth and the chassis handled gloriously, but the NR750's performance was nowhere near as mind-bending as its design.

This was further underlined by the firm's CBR900RR FireBlade released the following year, which weighed just 185kg (408lb) while making 118bhp (88kW) and

Honda NR750

Top speed:	257km/h (160mph)
Engine type:	748cc (46cu in), l/c 90° V-four, 32-valve, DOHC, oval piston
Maximum power:	125bhp (93kW)@14,000rpm
Frame type:	aluminium twin spar
Tyre sizes:	front 130/70 16, rear 180/55 17
Final drive:	chain
Gearbox:	six-speed
Weight:	223kg (492lb)

Despite its technical innovation, the NR was quite a heavy machine. Its stiff chassis and superlative suspension components made this less important, but the handling tended to be stable rather than dynamic.

offering much more radical sporting performance.

But that wasn't the point. The NR wasn't about sales figures or even about the ultimate in motorcycling performance. It wasn't even about racing. Other bikes in Honda's range could do all these things better. Instead, the NR750 was a titanium, carbon and scarlet expression of Honda's ultimate engineering prowess. There's simply been nothing like it before, or since.

A carbon-fibre dashboard included a radical 'heads-up' speedometer display which projected the speed readout onto the inside of the titanium-coated windshield. The large white-faced tachometer is located, racebike-style, right in the middle of the rider's viewpoint.

Honda RC45 (+RC30)

Two small inlets feed air to the engine through a pair of tank scoops.

The upside-down forks on the RC45 were a first for Honda on a large-capacity roadbike. The RC45 also used a then-fashionable 40cm (16in) front wheel, which Honda claimed improved handling. However, this did limit tyre choice initially.

The RC45 initially enjoyed limited World Superbike success. An American racer, John Kocinski, won the world title in 1997, despite problems with the handling. The last RC45 racebikes used a dual-sided swingarm in an attempt to try and improve the chassis.

Honda's PGM-FI system was still considered a novelty in 1993, especially on racebikes, where carburation changes often have to be made in set-up. Therefore the Honda race kit included a box with dials to alter fuelling in different parts of the rev range.

The RC45 had a close-ratio race gearbox, which meant that the first gear was incredibly tall. In standard roadbike trim, the bike could touch 145km/h (90mph) in first gear.

A 431-mm (17-inch) rear wheel wears a 190-section tyre. The single-sided swingarm design allows fast wheel changes in endurance races, but was swapped for a double-sided arm in WSB to improve handling.

Honda has never been a company to go for the usual solutions – particularly in its motorcycles. And while most other Japanese superbikes of the 1980s used simple, inline-four engines, Honda decided instead to use a V-four layout instead. V-fours have many advantages in a bike design. For example, they are narrower than an inline-four, with a shorter, stiffer crankshaft, they offer a more concentrated mass package and are more compact than a straight four. On the downside, they are more expensive to build, requiring two cylinder heads and four camshafts to be produced. Engine cooling is more complicated on the rear cylinders, and inlet and exhaust systems are harder to accommodate efficiently.

The first V-four Hondas were beset with design and production flaws. These cost Honda dear, not least in terms of reputation. But by the late 1980s, the firm's VFR750 and VFR750R (RC30) had restored this, with their superb reliability and strong power. And in the case of the RC30, there was massive racing success, especially in endurance, and the Isle of Man TT races.

By 1993, however, the RC30 was due to be replaced. This legendarily successful race-replica presented a tall order to surpass, but when Honda released the first details of its replacement, it looked like the firm had easily superseded the old bike. The RVF750, or RC45, took its name from Honda's equally legendary endurance racebikes, and it oozed exotic race design and materials from every vent in its full race fairing.

The heart of the design was still a V-four engine, but an all-new layout. A more oversquare design, with a 72x46mm (3x2in) bore and stroke, allowed it to rev higher than the old bike, while Honda's PGM-FI fuel injection system promised total, precise control of fuelling, essential for race teams using highly tuned engines. The standard roadbike's peak power figure of around 120bhp (89kW) was good for a 750, but

because the real point of the RC45 was to homologate race versions for Superbike racing, it was only a start. Fitting Honda Racing Corporation (HRC) race-kit parts and extensive tuning work produced nearer 165bhp (123kW) @14,000rpm from the motor.

Like the engine, the chassis was designed for the crucible of World and national Superbike championships, so while the suspension and brake components were of a very high quality, most were destined to be replaced with even more exotic racing parts. Nevertheless, the RC45 has race-specification upside-down front forks, a fully adjustable Showa rear shock, lightweight alloy wheels and Nissin brakes.

Despite the might of Honda's race department though, the RC45 struggled for success in World Superbike racing. With Ducati's 916 dominating, the RC45 didn't win a race until 1996. Even when it won the WSB championship in 1997, under John Kocinski, it still wasn't replicating the success of the RC30, and by 1999, the RC45 was replaced by a 1000cc (61cu in) V-twin, the VTR1000 SP-1. There had long been complaints about the capacity limits in world superbike – twins were allowed a 1000cc (61cu in) capacity, fours were restricted to just 750cc (46cu in).

The RC45 instruments had an easily-removed speedo to allow for competition use. Race kit parts often replaced the dashboard on more serious race bikes.

Honda RC45 (+RC30)

Top speed:	257km/h (160mph)
Engine type:	749cc (46cu in), l/c 90° V-four, 16-valve, DOHC
Maximum power:	118bhp (88kW)@12,000rpm
Frame type:	aluminium twin spar
Tyre sizes:	front 130/70 16, rear 190/50 17
Final drive:	chain
Gearbox:	six-speed
Weight:	189kg (417lb)

Many people considered that this capacity limit worked better for twins, so Honda decided to switch from the four-cylinder 750.

The road-riding experience of an RC45 is a very rare treat. The bike was produced in limited numbers, and was extremely expensive – the launch price in the UK was almost £18,000 (nearly $30,000). But plenty of well-heeled Honda fans bought RC45s for the road.

Although the very high first gear is a handicap, the RC's engine performs beautifully on the road. Designed for race use, it allows a maximum speed of 145km/h (90mph) in first gear, making it tricky to pull away smoothly from rest. The fuel injection gives smooth running from tickover to the redline, and the trademark strong torque of the V-four engine fires the RC out of corners like a slingshot.

Race-ready suspension, stable handling and smooth, torquey power delivery makes the RC45 a real connoisseur's choice for cornering. Note excellent ground clearance, even with standard footpegs.

The four-into-one exhaust is designed to produce strong peak power. The muffler is mounted on the left to increase the visual impact of the single-sided swingarm, while maximizing access to the rear wheel.

Honda CBR1000RR Fireblade (+ CBR900RR Fireblade)

The CBR1000RR used an advanced electronically controlled steering damper, which increases damping effect at higher speeds.

Early CBR900s used a 40.6cm (16in) front wheel with a 130/70 section tyre. Starting in 1999, this changed to a conventional 43cm (17in) part with a 120/70 section tyre.

The FireBlade was the first bike to exploit the advantages of lightweight components. The first CBR900R weighed 185kg (408lb), and the 2007 CBR1000RR weighed 179kg (395lb). The lightest was the 2003 900, weighing just 168kg (370lb).

A CBR1000RR ridden by Ryuichi Kiyonari won the 2006 British Superbike championship. The bike also won the prestigious Suzuka Eight Hour race in 2004, 2005 and 2006.

Both the 900 and 1000 versions used straightforward inline-four engines, with 16 valves, twin cams and water cooling. Fuel injection appeared on the year 2000 model. Power increased from 118bhp (88kW) on the first 900 to 170bhp (127kW) on the 2007 CBR1000RR.

If you had to count the most important modern motorcycles on the fingers of one hand, you'd have to dedicate one digit to the FireBlade. Like the Kawasaki GPZ900R, Honda's own CB750 and the Yamaha R1, the original FireBlade was a true shifter of paradigms, changing forever what expectations of a sports motorcycle should be.

First seen in 1992, the CBR900RR represented a radical departure from the bikes that had gone before. Rather than disappearing off on the quest for ever more power (with associated extra mass) that had afflicted the opposition, Honda instead focussed on cutting weight and increasing control. This 'Total Control' concept, put forward by the FireBlade's designer, Tadao Baba, was intended to allow the rider to use all the performance available. Reducing weight was a good thing in two ways. First, it gave even more acceleration and dynamism for a given level of horsepower. Second, it made the job of the suspension and brake systems easier, giving better handling, stopping and steering.

Apart from the low mass and small dimensions, the CBR900RR wasn't so far off bikes like Yamaha's FZR1000R Exup. They both had a four-cylinder engine, making around 120bhp (89kW), in an

Visible here are the radiator to cool the high-output engine, the exhaust header pipes and the cast aluminum engine mount points. The silver cylinder behind the exhaust is a water-cooled oil cooler.

aluminium beam frame, with monoshock suspension, full fairing and four-piston front brakes. The bike produced by Honda didn't even have the fashionable upside-down forks such as those worn by the Yamaha.

Honda CBR1000RR Fireblade (+ CBR900RR Fireblade)

Top speed:	282km/h (175mph)
Engine type:	998cc (61cu in), l/c inline-four, 16-valve, DOHC
Maximum power:	170bhp (127kW)@11,250rpm
Frame type:	aluminium twin spar
Tyre sizes:	front 120/70 17, rear 190/50 17
Final drive:	chain
Gearbox:	six-speed
Weight:	179kg (395lb)

But no one had appreciated what a difference the lighter mass could make. At 185kg (408lb), the CBR was 24kg (53lb) lighter than the FZR, and its wheelbase was 55mm (2in) shorter. And the FZR was by far the best of the opposition.

The Honda was unchallenged for five years, until Yamaha's R1 appeared in late 1997. In that time, the Honda had been refined every couple of years, with a larger capacity 919cc (56cu in) engine (up from 893cc/54.5cu in), more power and less weight. Honda also brought the brakes and suspension up to date, and so the 1997 CBR was an accomplished, smooth machine, some way off its more focussed, 'headbanger' ancestor.

The R1's success knocked the CBR out of top place, and while the next few CBR900 updates kept improving the bike, it couldn't match the R1 for performance. The FireBlade gained fuel injection, a 929cc (57cu in) capacity boost, and upside-down forks for the year 2000, and a capacity increase to 954cc (58cu in) in 2002. But it wasn't until the introduction in 2003 of the CBR1000RR Fireblade (note the capital 'B' had disappeared) that Honda had a bike capable of attacking the very latest superbikes. An all-new machine, the CBR1000 followed the same principles of the previous year's CBR600RR to produce a much

The Honda Electronic Steering Damper gives different steering control depending on road speed. The HISS ignition system prevents casual theft – only the correct microchip-equipped key will start the bike.

more radical, track-focussed machine. It resembled the firm's RC211V MotoGP machine, with a sharp, pointed nosecone, underseat silencer unit and a Unit Pro-Link rear swingarm. The engine was more compact and more powerful than before, with strong power delivery, Dual-injector fuel injection and more than 165bhp (123kW) was generated from its 998cc (61cu in) capacity. The chassis was based around a new cast-aluminum frame, with that GP-style rear suspension unit and 43mm (1.75in) USD forks. Front brakes were radial-mount four-piston calipers, and the bike had a novel electronic steering damper. This HESD (Honda Electronic Steering Damper) design, mounted behind the steering head, had a hydraulic camper circuit to reduce steering instability. But an electronic solenoid valve inside the unit altered the amount of damping force, based on a signal from the ECU. At slow speeds, the damping effect was backed off. As the bike sped up, the damper firmed up to add stability.

While the CBR1000 was placed in the same league as the R1 and GSX-R1000, it lacked their performance.

Honda CBR1100XX Super Blackbird (+X-eleven)

The CBR1100XX shares its name with a high-tech
American spyplane, the Lockheed SR-71 Blackbird. Like its
namesake, the Honda is extremely fast, thanks to
advanced aerodynamics. The plane is somewhat faster,
though. Its speed record is 3528km/h (2193mph),
compared with the 261km/h (175mph) of the bike.

On the fuel-injected CBR1100, the two small chin vents
under the headlights feed air to the sealed-ram airbox.
However, on early carburetted bikes, these vents led to
an oil cooler.

A relaxed riding position, comfortable seat and large fairing make the CBR1100 a superb fast touring bike. The comprehensive dashboard, good mirrors and excellent headlight add to its practicality.

Honda fitted its CBS linked brakes to the Blackbird. These operate both front and rear brake systems, whenever either the hand or foot levers are operated.

The Blackbird engine was derived from the 1996 CBR900RR FireBlade design, and shares its inline-four 16-valve layout. Peak power is 152bhp (113kW).

This stripped down photo shows the Blackbird's large airbox, compact engine and twin spar frame. The oil cooler under the instrument panel shows this is an early carburetted bike.

Honda was doing pretty well in the mid-1990s. It had the best supersports machine (the CBR900RR FireBlade), as well as the best 600 (the CBR600) and the best sports tourer, the VFR750. But, not content to rest on its laurels, the firm launched the CBR1100XX Super Blackbird in 1997.

Honda's target was the Kawasaki ZZ-R1100, a rather elderly design, but still the fastest, most comfortable sports tourer available. The Kawasaki generated around 147bhp (110kW), and weighed in at 228kg (503lb), so the Honda's figures of 162bhp (122kW) and 223kg (492lb) easily surpassed the ZZ-R.

The Blackbird was based around a new engine, derived from the FireBlade. With a capacity of 1137cc (69cu in) from a bore and stroke of 79x58mm (3x2.25in), the inline-four 16-valve engine had a pair of balancer shafts fitted to the bottom end, to reduce vibration and allow the engine to be solidly mounted in the frame. This made the frame stiffer and resulted in a significant mass saving. The engine breathed through a set of carburettors and a four-into-one-into-two exhaust system. The transmission used a six-speed gearbox and chain final drive.

That engine was fitted to an aluminium twin-beam frame, with conventional 43mm (1.75in) front forks, a monoshock rear suspension system and full fairing. Honda also fitted its Dual-CBS combined braking system, which had first appeared on the CBR1000F. This set-up used a system of hoses and valves to link together a set of three three-piston sliding calipers, two at the front, one at the rear. When the rider pulls the handlebar brake lever, the two outer pistons on

the front calipers, and the centre piston on the rear are operated. When the foot pedal is pressed, the centre pistons on the front calipers and the two outer pistons on the back caliper are operated. This gives controlled, progressive braking, whichever lever is operated.

This first Blackbird was an incredible package, and its strong engine and excellent handling trounced the ZZ-R. But it wasn't perfect. An intrusive flat-spot in the low-down power delivery marred an otherwise flawless performance. Several aftermarket fixes were available, but Honda itself resolved the matter for

Honda CBR1100XX Super Blackbird (+X-eleven)

Top speed:	280km/h (175mph)
Engine type:	1137cc (69cu in), l/c inline-four, 16-valve, DOHC
Maximum power:	152bhp (113kW)@9500rpm
Frame type:	aluminium twin spar
Tyre sizes:	front 120/70 17, rear 180/55 17
Final drive:	chain
Gearbox:	six-speed
Weight:	224kg (493lb)

1999. A ram-air system and fuel injection were the only high-performance systems missing from the original design, so Honda fitted them now, using the original bike's oil-cooler vents as intakes. The oil cooler was moved down below the steering head, freeing up space below the headlight for air intakes.

A PGM-FI fuel injection system based on that used on the RC45 and VFR totally eliminated the flat-spot, while improving economy, reducing emissions and even allowing a fuel tank that was 2l (.5gal), thanks to the redesigned airbox. Using a single injector per

A large dual seat and decent grab rail makes life easier for Blackbird passengers. Large silver strapping points are provided for attaching soft luggage.

Tucked in, holding on, throttle fully opened. The Blackbird's high power output and superior aerodynamics mean this rider will quickly see 280km/h (175mph) on the speedometer.

cylinder and 42mm (1.75in) throttle bodies, it was one of the first FI systems Honda used. It performed brilliantly, giving superb fuelling at all engine speeds.

This second-generation Blackbird remained unchanged, apart from minor cosmetic alterations, right up to 2007. Although it was pushed down the performance scale, first by Suzuki's Hayabusa in 1999, then Kawasaki's ZZR1200, ZX-12R and ZZR1400, as well as the BMW K1200S, the Blackbird remained a strong seller for Honda. Its classy design, excellent build quality and 'gentleman's express' character guaranteed that it held a strong place in the affection of a certain type of Honda fan, regardless of developments taking place elsewhere.

Honda experimented with the Blackbird once, releasing a naked version in 2000. This bike, called the X-Eleven, had rather curious styling, and with its 134bhp (99kW) de-tuned Blackbird engine, was essentially pointless. Its frame was designed with 'tuned flex' built in to it, to give it a more exciting feel, but the machine wasn't a success, and Honda discontinued it after only two years.

Kawasaki ZX-7R (+ZXR750)

One of the strongest features of the ZX-7R is its styling. The front-end biased look, with a large fairing hunched over the front wheel and minimalist tail section gives it an authentic endurance racer feeling. A huge 190-section rear tyre adds even more menace to the 750 Ninja.

The massive air intakes in the front fairing lead through the twin beam aluminium frame to a sealed ram-airbox under the tank.

Track-specification upside-down forks and six-piston front brake calipers combine with the forward weight bias to give a very stable, planted front end. Front-tyre feel under braking is excellent.

Performance-wise, Kawasaki allowed the ZX-7R to wither over its lifetime. There were no serious updates, leaving its 122bhp (90kW) and 203kg (447lb) vital statistics looking rather dated by 1999.

Kawasaki also produced a race-homologation version, which had flat-slide race carburettors, a single-seat unit, more adjustable race suspension, and adjustable frame geometry.

Kawasaki's engines have always been strong, and the ZX-7R was no exception. But its late 1980s design roots can be seen in the upright cylinders and lengthy crankcases.

The twin ram-air intakes feed directly through the frame rails and into the sealed airbox. It's essential to have a large airbox to produce strong power on modern, high-revving motorcycles.

The 1980s were very good for Kawasaki. It began the decade with comparative dinosaurs like the GPz1100 and 750 Turbo – old, air-cooled designs that nevertheless offered good performance and decent handling. But with the 1984 GPZ900R and 1985 GPZ600R, it launched the first two superbikes of the modern era. The GPZ water-cooled range morphed into the GPX600 and 750 in 1988, and it was this GPX750 that formed the basis of the ZXR750, Kawasaki's first 750cc (46cu in) race replica.

Like the GPZ range, the GPX was more of a road bike. But when its engine was transplanted into the ZXR750, it was transformed into a pure competition machine. The ZXR took much of its chassis design and styling from the firm's incredible ZXR-7 endurance racebikes. When it appeared in 1989, it was the most extreme-looking bike Kawasaki ever built. Much of its specification seems common now, but then, an aluminium-beam frame, aluminium swingarm and outrageous air ducts leading to the engine were all very special indeed. The engine produced around 105bhp (77kW), and at 205kg (550lb), it was a sound package, and a strong performer in 750-class racing.

The ZXR developed over the next eight years, receiving chassis and engine updates to keep it competitive in the class against Suzuki's GSX-R750 and then Yamaha's YZF750. Upside-down forks appeared on the 1991 J1 model, although Kawasaki actually cut power to 100bhp (73kW) to comply with a projected (but never enacted) European power limit. Later models increased in power again, and the twin

'Hoover Hose' air ducts from the fairing to the top of the fuel tank were replaced in 1992 by a single ram-air intake to the left side of the headlight.

For 1996 though, Kawasaki released an all-new update of its 750, dubbed the ZX-7R. This bike quickly gained a cult following, who fell in love with its brutal, hunched looks, serious race heritage and no-nonsense reputation. A new fairing had a pair of ram-air intakes either side of the twin headlights, and dropped down low towards the front mudguard. A two-piece race seat sat on the sleek tail unit, and the four-into-one exhaust ended in a massive silencer. The suspension was high-specification, with new 43mm (1.7in) upside-down front forks and an adjustable rear shock. The front brakes were dual six-piston Tokico

Kawasaki ZX-7R (+ZXR750)

Top speed:	266km/h (165mph)
Engine type:	748cc (45.6cu in), l/c inline-four, 16-valve, DOHC
Maximum power:	122bhp (90kW)@11,400rpm
Frame type:	twin spar aluminium
Tyre sizes:	front 120/70 17, rear 190/50 17
Final drive:	chain
Gearbox:	six-speed
Weight:	203kg (448lb)

calipers with 320mm (12.5in) disks, and the rear tyre was the widest of any production bike, a mighty 190-section Dunlop.

The ZX-7R motor was a new short-stroke design, and was much more powerful than the previous designs. Though it was less than the GSX-R750, 122bhp (90kW) was a reasonable power output.

The ZX-7R's biggest downside, though, was its mass. It weighed in at 24kg (53lb) more than the Suzuki, and this slowed down the ZX-7's performance, as well as dulling its handling. Even with that weight handicap, the front end in particular was impressive, with real accuracy and precision. The ZX was super-stable too, helped by the solid chassis and forward weight bias.

Unusually for a Japanese sportsbike, the ZX-7R received no updates during its lifetime. Kawasaki seemed to forget all about it, and while it was a strong seller right up until it was dropped in 2004, it was a real anachronism by then. Almost no other bike was still using carburettors, or a manual fuel tap, and the performance was by then far behind even the 600cc (36.6cu in) class. None of this bothered the 750 Ninja's legion of fans though, and its disappearance was mourned by many.

The 750 Ninja was accompanied by a homologation version, from the 1991 ZXR750R to the ZX-7RR of 1996. These models varied from year to year, but were limited edition versions fitted with parts essential for race teams to use. These parts included better suspension, close-ratio gearboxes, flat-slide race carburettors, aluminium fuel tanks, adjustable frame geometry and a single seat.

Despite its rather poor statistics on paper, the ZX-7R was a fast, capable road bike. This, together with 'mean' styling and excellent reliability, turned the ZX-7R into a popular bike with a cult following.

Kawasaki ZX-10R (+ZX-9R)

Compared with the ZX-9R, Kawasaki's ZX-10R was much lighter, more powerful, and had much more track ability. The radical changes put Kawasaki's flagship sportsbike on a par with competition from Suzuki, Yamaha and Honda.

The first ZX-10R had a side-mounted oval silencer on its four-into-one exhaust system. But from 2006 the bike changed to a dual underseat silencer setup.

The inline-four cylinder 16-valve water-cooled engine produces an impressive 182bhp (134kW) peak power output – the highest in its class.

Kawasaki fitted a top-specification Ohlins steering damper to the ZX-10R in 2006, in an attempt to calm down the steering under acceleration. Front forks also have a DLC (diamond-like carbon) coating to reduce friction and improve feel.

The central ram-air intake duct between the headlights feeds through the frame steering head into a sealed airbox containing the fuel-injection bodies. These use a twin-valve set-up to improve drivability.

The first ZX-10 Kawasaki built was, in many ways, ahead of its time. It replaced the GPZ1000RX in 1988, had a 1000cc (61cu in) engine and an aluminium frame. Too heavy for good handling, it was replaced after three years by the ZZ-R1100, which carried Kawasaki's flag in the 'big bike' class through the early 1990s. Once Honda's FireBlade showed the benefits of a lightweight sportsbike though, Kawasaki realized it had to try a bit harder than softly sprung, heavy sports tourers. The result was the ZX-9R, which ran from 1994, for a decade, with varying success.

The 900cc Ninja never really challenged the top dogs of the class though, and so for 2004, Kawasaki released a new ZX-10R. This was a serious, full-on assault on the likes of Suzuki's GSX-R1000 and Yamaha's R1, and it succeeded in putting Kawasaki's 1000cc (61cu in) sportsters back on the map.

The 10R was an all-new design, and it was based on Kawasaki's firm foundations of engineering excellence. The firm had learned many lessons from its revised

Some riders have criticized the ZX-10R's LCD tachometer display as hard to read. However, the instrument panel is a neat, compact design. Note the immobilizer key to prevent theft.

Kawasaki ZX-10R (+ZX-9R)

Top speed:	298km/h (185mph)
Engine type:	998cc (61cu in), l/c inline-four, 16-valve, DOHC
Maximum power:	182bhp (134kW)@11,700rpm (with ram-air assistance)
Frame type:	twin spar aluminium
Tyre sizes:	front 120/70 17, rear 190/55 17
Final drive:	chain
Gearbox:	six-speed
Weight:	175kg (386lb)

ZX-636R of 2003, and the 10R shared several design cues with its excellent smaller sister. The sharp, dual-headlight nosecone with a central ram-air intake 'nostril', upside-down forks with radial-mount brakes and 'petal' type brake disks, and the side-mounted silencer all echoed the ZX-6R.

The bigger bike had its own design touches though. The aluminium beam frame had deeper walls, and it

The massive frame castings and low-mounted engine can clearly be seen in this stripdown photograph. The space above the engine is taken up by the large airbox and fuel tank.

arched up and over the top of the engine instead of around it, in a bid to keep the bike more narrow. The engine itself was a new design, with titanium exhaust valves for high-rpm performance, dual-valve fuel injection and a butterfly exhaust-gas control valve inside the all-titanium exhaust system. It produced a claimed 182bhp (134kW), a phenomenal amount of power for a 170kg (375lb) dry-weight machine.

Riding the ZX-10R was an intimidating experience. All the large-capacity sportsbikes produce enormous power, but the ZX-10R's lightweight package had such a focussed track bias, it felt even more extreme. It's this focus that counted against the ZX-10R. If you were on track, or in full-on attack mode on the road, the cramped riding position, sharp steering, razor brakes and super-fast throttle response were all perfect. But for the rest of the time, a more rounded machine from one of the competitor firms made more sense.

Kawasaki realized that, making a 170kg (375lb), 180bhp (132kW) sportsbike wasn't so hard, but making such a bike that's easy and fun for a typical rider to cope with is much harder. With this in mind, the firm revised the 10R for 2006. A new exhaust system had

dual underseat silencers, and various modifications all aimed at making the ZX-10R smoother and more controllable. An Ohlins steering damper helped calm down the steering under acceleration, and new Dunlop Qualifier tires improved grip and handling too. The bike was actually 5kg (11lb) heavier than before, with catalysts, required by tighter emissions rules. Other changes included a new 3-D, 'floating' speedometer display, and taller-profile rear tire.

The changes did lead to an improved bike. The handling was better than before, and the 2006 ZX-10R had a wider range of capability than before.

Unfortunately, the cosmetic aspect of the redesign was widely criticized – the new smaller headlights were too far apart, and the massive underseat silencer cans looked like a tacked-on afterthought. Some advanced riders felt the unusual 190/55-section rear tyre had badly affected the bike's steering too, and the ZX-10R still just missed the mark.

Of course, Honda and Yamaha had updated their bikes for 2006 too. The Fireblade in particular had much improved performance, and Suzuki's GSX-R1000 remained the best choice for most riders.

Kawasaki ZZR1400

For 2007/8, Kawasaki produced a Grand Touring version of the ZZ-R1400, the 1400GTR. This had a much bigger fairing, with built-in luggage, a variable valve timing system and a complex shaft final-drive system.

Despite its enormous size and performance, the ZZR is much lighter than previous Kawasaki big-bore machines. At 215kg (474lb), it's the same weight as Suzuki's GSX1300R Hayabusa.

Emissions and noise regulations mean the standard ZZR's exhaust is enormously long and heavy. Many riders fit aftermarket race parts, which give much more power, while giving a significant mass reduction.

The dashboard has a large LCD panel that gives extensive information to the rider on fuel consumption, range left, time, trip meters, gear position and other diagnostic information.

A total of six lights mounted in the nosecone provide superb illumination at night. The tail lights are lightweight, maintenance-free LED units.

If there's one bike firm that has always been associated with power and speed, it's Kawasaki. From the firm's 210km/h (130mph) Z1 superbike, built in the 1970s, through the 240km/h (150mph) GPZ900 of 1984 and the 290km/h (180mph) ZZ-R1100 of 1990, Kawasaki's bikes have always been top for sheer grunt.

Partly that's down to the firm's corporate culture – Kawasaki Motors' parent company, Kawasaki Heavy Industries (KHI) spends most of its time building ships, railroad systems, airplanes and space rockets.

But during Kawasaki's somewhat low period in the late 1990s, it seemed to lose its way. The ZZ-R1100 was superseded in the 'top-speed stakes' first by Honda's Super Blackbird, then Suzuki's Hayabusa comprehensively trounced them both. Kawasaki hit back with the sporty ZX-12R in 2000, but although it was lighter and slightly more powerful than the Suzuki, its revvier engine and sporting focus had the effect of making it less of an all-round machine. In the

Kawasaki ZZR1400

Top speed:	300km/h (186mph) (factory limited)
Engine type:	1352cc (82.5cu in), l/c inline-four, 16-valve
Maximum power:	190bhp (140kW)@9500rpm (198bhp/145.6kw with ram-air), DOHC
Frame type:	monocoque aluminium
Tyre sizes:	front 120/70 17, rear 190/50 17
Final drive:	chain
Gearbox:	six-speed
Weight:	215kg (474lb)

The latest in a long line of incredibly fast hypersports bikes from Kawasaki, the ZZR1400 is a real powerhouse that delivers hammerblow acceleration when the throttle is opened.

Mean and moody...the ZZR's six headlights flank an enormous ram-air intake snout that sucks in the vast quantities of cool, fresh air that the engine needs to make its near-150kW (200bhp).

The ZZR's dash mixes classic and modern – white-faced analogue dials for speed and revs combined with a large, central LCD screen that can scroll through a host of detailed information.

year 2002 a ZZ-R1200 was introduced to replace the ZZ-R1100, with a similar touring bias.

Kawasaki seriously revamped much of its range in the first half decade of the twenty-first century, and the ZZR1400 was a killer punch in the hypersports class. First shown at the 2005 Paris show, it hit the road in early 2006, and went straight to the top of an outrageous class. For the first time ever, a production motorcycle engine was claiming 200ps (197bhp/147kW), albeit with ram-air assistance at speed. There is nothing particularly special about this engine – it's a development of the ZX-12R engine, with 1mm (.03in) larger bores and a 5.6mm (.22in) longer stroke. It's the same width as the 1200 engine, and has Keihin fuel injection, with dual-valve 44mm (1.7in) throttle bodies. A 32-bit ECU controls the fuelling, and the ram-air intake passes through the steering head to channel cool, high-pressure air into the engine's airbox. Kawasaki also added a pair of balancer shafts to the engine to smooth out vibrations, improving refinement and allowing a rigid frame mounting. This adds stiffness to the frame and reduces its weight.

The frame itself is, like the ZX-12R, an unusual monocoque design. Aluminium sheets are welded together to form a box-like structure that passes back from the steering head and back over the top of the engine down to the swinging arm pivot. The rear suspension uses a rather insubstantial-looking cast-aluminum swingarm with an adjustable monoshock unit, while the front suspension uses 43mm (1.7in)

upside-down forks, also fully adjustable. Brakes are radial-mount four-piston calipers up front.

One of the biggest challenges facing manufacturers is emissions legislation. Noise and harmful gases have to be kept below government limits, and these limits require ever more complex exhausts. On the ZZR1400, this means a massive four-into-two set-up that incorporates catalytic converter elements to clean up the gasses and two huge silencers to reduce noise.

The ZZR1400 is aimed at the sport touring market, so it has pretty high equipment levels. The dashboard includes a large LCD display panel, which displays a range of trip computer functions, including fuel consumption, range remaining, ambient temperature and trip mileages. The mirrors give a great view of the road behind, and a large well designed seat makes the ZZR very comfortable for long trips.

However, it's the ZZR's riding experience that's truly phenomenal. It's a fairly manageable load at low speeds, despite its imposing dimensions. But with 200 bhp (147kW) peak power and maximum torque of 154Nm (113.5lb ft), it's the engine that dominates the proceedings. At low speeds, it's actually fairly docile, as if Kawasaki has purposefully retarded the performance at low revs/low speeds. But as soon as the revs pass the 5000rpm mark, the world very quickly turns into a blur. This is truly an incredibly fast motorcycle. And with a chassis package well up to the power, this ZZR put Kawasaki smack bang at the top of the class again.

Suzuki GSX-R750

At first glance, it's hard to tell the 2006 model GSX-R600 and GSX-R750 apart. That's because they're pretty much identical, apart from engine capacity and paint schemes. The GSX-R750 also has a special coating on the fork inners – the 600's are plain chrome.

The most striking styling change is the exhaust, which has been transformed into a large under-engine muffler, with a small 'stubby' side-exit pipe.

The 2006 model saw an all-new engine fitted, which had a balance shaft for the first time. It was also smaller and lighter than previous engine designs, and made 148bhp (109kW), while meeting Euro II emissions rules.

The dashboard has a combined analogue tachometer with LCD speedo display and a new gear position indicator.

Although the GSX-R750 hasn't been suitable for any major race classes since superbike rules allowed 1000cc (61cu in) fours, Suzuki runs its own GSX-R Cup one-make series.

Sometimes a machine is so important to a manufacturer, so crucial to its heritage and history, that it's impossible to imagine the firm ever ceasing production. And there's no bike that fits this description more closely than the GSX-R750. Originally launched in 1987, when the 750cc class was one of the most important in the market, the GSX-R has outlived all its competitors, until it's now pretty much in a class of its own – the only 750cc (46cu in) four-cylinder supersports bike still produced.

Back in the 1980s, 750s were popular because 1000cc (61cu in) machines were very big and heavy, and offered relatively ungainly handling. Meanwhile, 600cc (36.6cu in) machines were underpowered, putting out around 85bhp (62.5kW), and often had budget chassis components. Add in the importance of the 750cc (46cu in) racing classes in superbike racing, and it's easy to see why all the Japanese manufacturers offered a 750.

But through the 1990s, the litre class handling improved and weight dropped, while 600s got much faster and started featuring top-specification chassis parts. Squeezed from both sides, the 750 became less popular, and when superbike racing finally dropped them in 2003, in preference to 1000cc (61cu in) fours,

The GSX-R750 is a compact, neat bike, but the riding position is still quite comfortable. It's easy to tuck in behind the windshield for high-speed riding.

the future looked bleak. Honda in 1999 (RC45), Yamaha in 2000 (R7) and Kawasaki in 2004 (ZX-7R), all dropped their 750cc (46cu in) sportsbikes.

But Suzuki seemed totally unconcerned by all this. The early GSX-R750s used oil-cooled engines in

Suzuki GSX-R750

Top speed:	282km/h (175mph)
Engine type:	749cc (46cu in), l/c inline-four, 16-valve, DOHC
Maximum power:	148bhp (109kW)@12,500rpm
Frame type:	aluminium twin-spar
Tyre sizes:	front 120/70 17, rear 180/55 17
Final drive:	chain
Gearbox:	six-speed
Weight:	163kg (359lb)

aluminium perimeter frames. By the end of the twentieth century, the GSX-R750 was a well developed bike with almost enough power to take on the 1000cc (61cu in) class. The layout was a water-cooled inline-four engine in a twin-beam aluminium frame, with full plastic race fairing and high-quality brakes and suspension. That motor was a 16-valve DOHC design, with a dual-valve fuel injection system (first seen on this bike) and it made a very healthy 139bhp (102kW). The chassis featured 43mm (1.7in) upside-down front forks, and a single rear shock, both fully adjustable Showa parts, and dual 320mm (12.5in) front brake disks, with four-piston Tokico calipers. It had an incredibly low dry weight of just 166kg (366lb), 13kg (29lb) less than the previous version.

This K0 GSX-R750 debuted a host of design methods and technologies that would appear on later GSX-R600 and GSX-R1000 models. And when Suzuki unveiled the next version of the 750 in 2003, it had another set of performance-boosting engine and chassis changes. The K4 model had borrowed styling cues from the previous year's GSX-R1000, including the narrow 'stacked' headlight, which allowed the ram-air intakes to be closer to the bike's centreline. More angular bodywork sharpened the styling and improved

Suzuki stuck with tried and tested designs for the GSX-R750's front end. Showa upside-down forks are fully adjustable, and the Tokico radial-mount calipers are powerful and progressive.

aerodynamics, and an LED tail light cut mass, and added reliability and safety. Engine internals were modified to produce more power, and detail changes to frame and running gear, including radial-mount front brakes, further enhanced the GSX-R's performance and handling. It had also lost 3kg (6.6lb) and gained 9bhp (6.6kW) – impressive changes.

Another new GSX-R750 arrived in 2006. This was another major revamp, in a similar vein to that year's GSX-R600. Emissions rules were requiring increasingly large and heavy exhausts, so Suzuki redesigned the engine and frame to make space for the exhaust inside the belly pan. This keeps the mass low and central, improving handling. The required engine and chassis changes meant every part of the GSX-R750 was new for 2006, and although the weight and power figures didn't change very much, it was a far better bike. The handling was even more sublime, especially on track, and although the engine was slightly more revvy in its delivery, it was smoother, more refined, and ultimately slightly more satisfying.

Suzuki GSX-R1000 (+GSX-R1100)

In 2005 the GSX-R1000 took the first four-cylinder World Superbike title for seven years for Suzuki when Australian Troy Corser easily won on his Alstare Corona machine. The GSX-R has also won AMA and BSB titles.

Early GSX-R1000s used a conventional cylindrical side-mounted silencer, while the K5 model switched to a 'stubby' triangular can. Increasingly tight sound and emissions standards forced the manufacturers to switch to a twin silencer system in 2007.

Trademark GSX-R front fairing includes a stacked vertical headlight and a pair of large ram air-intake ports. These collect cool high-pressure air from the front of the bike, and channel it into the engine's air box.

Brakes on early GSX-Rs used six-piston calipers, but offered only average performance. Later, radial-mounted four-piston calipers improved on this.

The GSX-R's fuel injection system uses two injectors per cylinder. This gives better fuelling than one injector, and helps the GSX-R's incredibly smooth power delivery.

Of all the Japanese superbike ranges, the GSX-R is perhaps the most evocative, and certainly the longest running. Stretching over two decades from the first 1985 GSX-R750 to the 2007 GSX-R1000K7, those four letters and single hyphen have always stood for ultimate performance and commitment to track riding.

The first open-class GSX-R was the 1986 GSX-R1100G, which produced 125bhp (93kW) from a 1052cc (64cu in) oil-cooled 16-valve engine, and weighed 197kg (434lb). It had a radical aluminium-perimeter frame, race-replica suspension and brakes, and a large, slab-sided fairing and fuel tank. It was much sportier than any of its competitors, and the GSX-R1100 range continued its development right through the next decade. That development was mostly forward, although the design did enter a few dead ends, where untested chassis changes affected handling badly, and the weight and power of the bike both crept steadily upward. The final WT version in

There's nothing radical or unusual about the GSX-R1000 in this stripdown shot, just careful design. The dual-valve throttle bodies can clearly be seen, as can the aluminium frame and rear subframe.

Suzuki GSX-R1000 (+GSX-R1100)

Top speed:	299km/h (186mph) [restricted]
Engine type:	999cc (61cu in), l/c inline-four, 16-valve, DOHC
Maximum power:	175bhp (130.5kW) @9800rpm
Frame type:	aluminium twin-spar
Tyre sizes:	front 120/70 17, rear 190/50 17
Final drive:	chain
Gearbox:	six-speed
Weight:	166kg (366lb)

1996 was achieving more than 130bhp (97kW), but now weighed above 230kg (507lb).

Honda's CBR900RR FireBlade and Yamaha's R1 had shown the benefits of reducing mass from a sportsbike design as much as possible. Therefore Suzuki took a break from the open class for a while, allowing its GSX-R750 to hold the fort.

But it returned with a bang in 2001, with a new GSX-R1000. This was an all-new model, though based on the GSX-R750 platform, and it offered class-leading performance figures. In the event, it swept the open-class board in every major press test of the 2001 litre-class superbikes.

The GSX-R1000 was fairly conventional in design. Like the 750, it had a four-cylinder liquid-cooled 16-valve engine, with dual-valve fuel injection and ram-air intakes. A high 161bhp (120kW) claimed power output. The chassis was similar in concept to the 750, with a twin-spar aluminium frame, upside-down front forks and six-piston front brake calipers. What was exceptional was both the light weight of the whole bike (just 170kg/375lb) and the strength of the engine. The motor had very high peak-power output, but also managed to have a very strong, torquey low- and mid-range delivery. The handling was more than up to the task too, with nimble steering, stable handling and amazing ability both on and off the track.

The digital clocks combine a classic analogue tachometer with an LCD readout for speed. The gear position indicator and white gearshift light help the rider keep track of gear changes.

Some criticisms were levelled at the brakes, but the GSX-R ruled the litre class for the next three years, thanks to an update in 2002.

Yamaha's R1 got close to the Suzuki in 2004, but the GSX-R hit back in 2005, with another major overhaul. The K5 model weighed just 166kg (366lb) dry, while a bigger 999cc (61cu in) engine had a 175bhp (130.5kW) power output. Two injectors were carefully placed for perfect fuelling – one was located upstream nearer the intake tract, while the second was pointed straight at the secondary butterfly valve. The fuel stream splashed onto the valve face, further breaking up and mixing the fuel spray into the airflow.

It was the sheer rideability of the K5 that amazed people. Here was a bike with the power of a world-class superbike of a few years previously, that could easily be ridden around town.

For 2007, Suzuki released yet another GSX-R1000, this one with a twin exhaust system, to cut emissions. It had a three-position handlebar switch, which let the rider choose from three engine maps: one for full power; one for normal riding with less power; and one for wet riding, which reduces the power accordingly.

Suzuki GSX1300R Hayabusa

To deal with the high power output, the GSX's swingarm is a massive braced-aluminium design, with large castings welded to extruded sections.

At the rear, a bulbous pillion seat cover helps reattach the airflow to the back of the bike, cutting drag.

To deal with the high power output, the GSX's swingarm, and a four-into-two exhaust system, have enough volume to effectively cut noise while allowing strong power production. The swingarm also adds structural strength to the rear subframe.

The Hayabusa's strong engine made it extremely popular among drag racers and extreme power tuners: turbocharged versions can make over 500bhp (368kW). It has also been used in several kit-car applications.

The Hayabusa's bodywork is incredibly aerodynamic. The bulbous dual headlight is vertically stacked to make it narrower, and give more space for power-boosting ram-air intakes. Even the indicators are shaped to channel more air into the intakes.

The title of 'world's fastest bike' is perhaps one of the most pointless – yet most closely contested by the manufacturers. Open-class motorcycles have long been capable of enormous speeds. Back in 1984, Kawasaki's GPZ900R managed 240km/h (150mph), and that firm's ZZ-R1100 took on the top speed mantle in 1991, with a derestricted top speed approaching 290km/h (180mph). Honda pipped the ZZ-R1100 for top spot when its CBR1100XX Super Blackbird appeared in 1997 and added a few mph to the ZZ-R's peak velocity.

Suzuki had clearly been eyeing this prize for some time. When its GSX1300R Hayabusa was launched in 1998, it was unquestionably the fastest, most powerful bike around. A chassis and engine based on the familiar GSX-R range and a set of extremely aerodynamic bodywork panels were the basics, while a 175bhp (129kW) power output and a 354km/h (220mph) speedometer dial showed how serious Suzuki was about making this bike go very fast. Even the name echoed this desire – Hayabusa is the name of the Japanese peregrine falcon, which can reportedly

Once the sleek bodywork has been removed, it's easier to see the sportsbike heritage of the Hayabusa. Its aluminium beam frame and inline-four engine are derived from Suzuki's GSX-R750.

reach 300km/h (186mph) in a dive. The suggestion that Hayabusas also prey on Blackbirds may have been a joke put about by mischievous Suzuki PR people.

Whatever the naming pranks, the Hayabusa was a far better machine than the Honda. It had much more straightline performance, and its larger-capacity engine made for a more relaxing, gruntier, power delivery. The layout was unremarkable – an inline-four 16-valve DOHC design based on the GSX-R750, with fuel injection, water cooling and a six-speed gearbox. An advanced ram-air system fed cool,

Although the Hayabusa is a fairly big, heavy bike, careful design kept mass as low as possible. Modern electronics, including the analogue dashboard displayed, helped achieve this goal.

Suzuki GSX1300R Hayabusa

Top speed:	299km/h (186mph)
Engine type:	1298cc (79cu in), l/c inline-four, 16-valve, DOHC
Maximum power:	175bhp (129kW) @9800rpm
Frame type:	aluminium twin-spar
Tyre sizes:	front 120/70 17, rear 190/50 17
Final drive:	chain
Gearbox:	six-speed
Weight:	215kg (474lb)

pressurized air from two large scoops either side of the headlight into a sealed airbox. This increased power as the bike travelled faster.

Apart from the bulbous, aerodynamic bodywork, the chassis had no real stand-out features. The specification included an aluminium beam frame, upside-down front forks, adjustable suspension and a massive aluminium swingarm. Dry mass was 215kg (474lb) – not sportsbike light, but 9kg (20lb) less than a Blackbird. Braking was taken care of by dual six-piston calipers out front, which were fashionable at the time.

The GSX's ground clearance was good, and the standard Bridgestone BT56 tires gave excellent grip, though the Hayabusa's mass, speed and power can render a rear tyre scrap in under 1609km (1000 miles), if the throttle is used fully. On track, the massive engine performance makes up for any slackness through the corners, and the Hayabusa is a formidable opponent for any sportsbike on a fast track.

Bizarrely for such a committed powerhouse, the Hayabusa is also very easy to live with. Add some soft

The curvaceous nosecone and windscreen lift the airflow over the rider, and the bulbous tail section helps re-attach the flow, cutting the turbulence and increasing the top speed.

luggage and an iPod, and you can cross continents in almost as much comfort as on a committed tourer. Even the fuel range is good, the 21l (5.5gal) tank permitting over 290km (180 miles) between fillups with a careful throttling.

It's a sure sign of a good design that not many changes are made. And this 'if it ain't broke' theory applies to the GSX1300. Suzuki didn't change anything on the bike from 1999–2006, apart from fitting a 300km/h (186mph) speed limiter for 2001. This was part of a 'gentleman's agreement' between the major manufacturers to pre-empt government intervention to limit motorcycle performance. This has rendered the top speed fight even less relevant, and as bikes like the Suzuki GSX-R1000 have become as powerful as the Hayabusa, even they can reach a similar top speed to the GSX1300.

Yamaha YZF-R1 (+Thunderace)

Yamaha has established a very specific look for the R1 – a pair of 'fox-eye' headlights with a sharply raked windshield. Ram-air intakes appeared to feed a sealed airbox in 2004.

Yamaha uses a variety of techniques to add stability and usability to the R1. The engine is designed to be short front-to-back, so a longer swingarm can be used. And long-travel front forks keep the front wheel on the ground under hard acceleration.

Yamaha's MotoGP M1 machine has a similar inline-four layout to the R1. Yamaha claimed to use inputs from the race division while developing its 2007 machine.

The R1, like its 1000cc (61cu in) predecessors, used a 20-valve inline-four engine. It dropped the unusual design of five valves per cylinder for the 2007 model.

The aluminium frame and swingarm are made using a novel 'controlled fill' casting process that makes lighter, stiffer components.

The title 'king of the open class' is one that Yamaha has held a few times in recent years. Its first champ in the class was the FZR1000R EXUP of 1989 and onward. It offered a great blend of power and handling, and was the top litre sportsbike until Honda's FireBlade in 1992. Yamaha attempted to top the 'Blade with the Thunderace in 1996, which used a tuned 145bhp (107kW) EXUP engine in a sporting chassis. Mostly due to excess mass, the attempt failed.

Yamaha engineers had been watching Honda closely, and it didn't make the same mistake again. The first YZF-R1, released in late 1997, used all-new design principles to bring a new level of lightness and compactness to the litre class. Every part of the R1 was new: the super-compact engine, aluminium frame and sharp, angular bodywork. That engine used a 'stacked' gearbox layout, with the clutch and transmission located high up behind the block to make a shorter unit (the first time this had been seen on a bike). This also allowed a longer swingarm, which enhanced stability, despite the extremely short 1395mm (55in) wheelbase. The front forks were also designed with extra-long travel, to keep the front wheel on the ground for longer under acceleration. Wide, grippy sports tyres gave a tenacious hold on the road, and powerful Sumitomo brakes gave immense stopping power, particularly with the R1's low overall mass.

Yamaha fitted the R1 with an all-new LCD/analogue dashboard when it was first launched. Later models incorporated a gearshift light, gear position indicator and other refinements.

The engine was strong, both at the bottom end of the rev range, and high up near its red line. In addition, the stiff aluminium frame, well damped suspension and powerful brakes helped riders use more of this power – although the R1 could snap back at the unwary.

This 1998 model R1 knocked Honda's FireBlade clean off top spot, and the Yamaha stayed there for

Yamaha YZF-R1 (+Thunderace)

Top speed:	297km/h (185mph)
Engine type:	998cc (61cu in), l/c inline-four, 20-valve, DOHC
Maximum power:	175bhp (129kW)@12,500rpm
Frame type:	cast-aluminium twin-spar
Tyre sizes:	front 120/70 17, rear 190/50 17
Final drive:	chain
Gearbox:	six-speed
Weight:	173kg (381lb)

Yamaha paid attention to saving weight on every part possible, from the engine and frame, to ancillaries such as the instrument panel and fairing brackets.

three years. An update in 2000 gave it a slightly stiffer frame, and some cosmetic updates, though the rather wild nature of the R1 remained unchanged. The year 2001 saw the launch of Suzuki's GSX-R1000, and the first serious challenge to the R1. The Suzuki had an even stronger engine in a superb chassis, and just nosed ahead of the R1 in sheer performance terms. Yamaha hit back for 2002 with a lighter, more powerful fuel-injected R1, which boasted 152bhp (112kW), weighed 174kg (383lb), and had a suction-pump type of fuel injection system. The chassis was also heavily revised, with new 43mm (1.7in) forks, a stiffer frame and asymmetrical swingarm.

The black-finished silencer identify this R1 as a first generation model. Some riders consider this the 'purest' version, thanks to its raw, exciting handling and engine performance.

The next generation R1 arrived in 2004. Instantly identified by its underseat exhaust system, this bike had an all-new engine, with a larger bore and shorter stroke, and another new fuel injection system, this time with an ECU-controlled secondary throttle valve. It was 4kg (9lb) lighter than the old engine, and made an extra 20bhp (15kW), up to a claimed 172bhp (126.5kW). The chassis was built around another all-new frame design, with new upside-down forks and fashionable new radial-mount brake calipers.

For 2005, another minor update saw a few more peak horsepower for the R1, and the launch of a special 'SP' version, which had lightweight forged Marchesini racing wheels and Ohlins suspension units.

Yet another all-new design appeared for 2007. Yamaha went back to the drawing board to produce a radically different machine. The 2007 R1 dropped the firm's long-running 20-valve design, and moved to a 16-valve cylinder head. The engine also featured variable-inlet geometry and fly-by-wire throttle control. An electric motor moved the inlet trumpets into two different positions according to rpm, optimizing power production at all speeds. The result was 189bhp (139kW), an immense figure for a 1000cc (61cu in) engine.

The 2007 chassis was also new, and used six-piston radial brake calipers – a first on any bike.

Grand Tourers:
mile-munching superbikes

The criteria for a good Grand Touring bike varies depending on the end user. At one end of the spectrum is the pure luxury touring machine, such as Harley-Davidson's Electraglide or Honda's Gold Wing. At the other end of the touring range is the sports-touring bike, for example Triumph's Sprint ST or Ducati's ST3. And in the middle are the heavy tourers and 'Adventure Sport' machines that offer the best of both worlds.

Luxury tourers like the Harley, Gold Wing or BMW's K1200LT are first and foremost about comfort for rider and pillion, as well as luggage carrying capacity. Gigantic protective fairings, electrically heated handlebar grips and seats and onboard entertainment systems are considered essential, as are large built-in luggage cases. And extras such as satellite navigation systems, intercoms and even drinks holders aren't unusual aftermarket fitments.

While these machines have powerful, large-capacity engines and capable chassis, they're too heavy and have insufficient ground clearance to offer much in the way of sporting performance.

At the other end of the scale, Sports touring bikes like the Honda VFR800 combine decent sports potential with a full, protective fairing, comfortable passenger accommodation and the facility to carry hard luggage systems mounted on the rear. But once the long hard journey to a far-flung, sun-drenched destination is complete, the dedicated sporting tourer can remove the luggage cases, leave his or her pillion by the side of the pool, and head for the twisty mountain roads, or even the local racetrack, to enjoy the bike's sound handling and powerful performance.

The middle way for touring fans is to choose a heavy tourer that offers nearly all the luxury of the super heavyweight luxury tourers, yet in a more manageable, dynamic package. BMW has long been a strong contender in this market, and its R1200RT is the latest in a long line. There are strong Japanese options too – Yamaha's FJR1300 has performance to match many a large-bore superbike on fast roads, while Honda's Pan European has a cult following of mileage junkies who admire the Pan's sturdy design and build quality.

Finally, there is a class of bikes called 'Adventure Sport' machines which combine a degree of off-road performance and styling with a large-capacity engine and touring ability. By far the best of these bikes is BMW's R1200GS and its predecessors, Equipped with hard luggage and some choice aftermarket accessories, a GS makes a superb long-distance tool.

Sportsbike specialist Ducati may not seem like the ideal touring marque, but its ST3S is a strong sports tourer. A bespoke V-twin engine in a softer version of the firm's superbike chassis leans towards the performance end of the spectrum, but is still eminently practical.

BMW K1200LT

It's the equipment list of the K1200LT that makes it stand out. Standard and optional equipment includes a CD player, radio, heated handgrips, heated seat, satellite-navigation systems, reverse gear, automatic hydraulic centrestand, intercom and cruise control, to name just a few.

BMW's Telelever front and Paralever rear suspension systems help the K1200LT handle much like a normal heavy tourer. BMW's EVO ABS brakes add extra safety when riding on slippery surfaces.

The cockpit and handlebar controls are almost bewilderingly complex: there are around 18 switches on the bars alone, three LCD displays and a pair of large analogue dials for speed and tachometer.

The built-in luggage top box and panniers offer more storage space than some exotic sports cars.

Unusually for a large tourer, BMW fitted 'normal' sportsbike-sized tyres to the LT – a 120/70 17 front and 160/70 17 rear. Standard tyres are Dunlops, which give good grip and mileage.

For a large part of its production run, Honda's Gold Wing was pretty much in a class of one, in terms of ultra-heavyweight luxury tourers. But in 1999, BMW, a name virtually synonymous with touring bikes, unveiled its entry into this class, the K1200LT. LT means Luxury Touring, and it's an apt model suffix. BMW's press department insisted on comparing the new K12 with the firm's seven-series luxury automobiles, and the huge tourer certainly offered a massive list of optional accessories.

The LT is more of a 'conventional' motorcycle than the Gold Wing, and it certainly has a less audacious design. The four-cylinder engine is taken from the first K1200 range, itself developed from the elderly K1100 design, and is unconventional only in its laid-down configuration. It's a 16-valve, DOHC design, with BMW's Motronic MA engine-management system and a five-speed gearbox, with shaft final drive.

The cylinders are arranged so the pistons move across the axis of the bike, with the crankshaft on the right, running parallel to the direction of travel, and the cylinder head on the rider's left. This somewhat illogical layout places very tight restrictions on intake and exhaust-system design, as well as requiring a narrow bore to prevent the engine from being too long. This engine should not be confused with the K1200S

BMW K1200LT	
Top speed:	210km/h (131mph)
Engine type:	1172cc (72cu in), l/c inline-four, 16-valve DOHC
Maximum power:	116bhp (86kW) @8000rpm
Frame type:	aluminuim-bridge type
Tyre sizes:	front 120/70 17, rear 160/70 17
Final drive:	shaft
Gearbox:	five-speed (plus reversing aid)
Weight:	353kg (778lb)

transverse engine of 2005, which was a much more advanced, high-performance design.

The first LT had a 97bhp (73kW) engine, while later versions boasted a considerable boost in performance to 116bhp (86kW). This engine is incorporated into a chassis that bears a fairly close relationship to the rest

An incredibly powerful headlight and auxiliary front light system give supreme illumination. An optional high-intensity discharge headlight system mimics those found on some luxury cars.

The LT's dashboard is a seductive blend of classic analogue dials for engine and road speed, with a high-tech LCD panel for supplementary rider info and also a map reading light.

of BMW's range – the front suspension is the firm's Telelever system, which uses a wishbone arrangement to mount a single suspension unit, the wheel being mounted on a pair of sliding 'forks', which have no suspension function. Rear suspension is a shaft-drive Paralever setup, also typical of BMW. Powerful four-piston brake calipers front and rear include an ABS function, and the suspension is adjustable for preload to suit different loads of luggage and passenger.

But it's the LT's bodywork and equipment that really stand out. An enormous windshield and fairing gives all-enveloping protection from the elements, and the screen itself is electrically adjustable up and down to suit conditions. There's cavernous built-in luggage capacity, with centrally locked panniers and a huge top box, with more than enough space for a week's luggage for two. The adjustable-height double seat is broad and well padded, with supports for rider and pillion, as well as optional electric heating elements. A radio/CD sound system is standard, with an optional CD changer. Satellite navigation, cruise control, xenon

headlight, alarm, floor lighting and a taller windshield are also on the options list.

Handling the LT is, as with the Gold Wing, less daunting than it first appears. The laid-down engine keeps the mass low down, and there's an electric reversing aid that uses the starter motor to help slow-speed manoeuvring. The main stand is also an electro-hydraulically assisted design, avoiding the strain required to put the bike on a manual stand.

Once you're moving and on the road properly, the LT is much like any other large tourer. The touring suspension and sheer mass of the bike means there is a certain vagueness about the handling that would be unacceptable on a more sporty bike. The engine is strong low down, and with its broad, well spaced gear ratios, makes for a relaxing, powerful cruising package.

But those brakes are powerful, and the sport-touring tires give good grip. Ground clearance is decent for a tourer, and the LT is certainly capable of keeping up with a briskly-ridden sport-tourer on the right sort of fast, sweeping roads.

Of course, the LT is best used as BMW intended. It was meant to be a Grand Tourer that crosses continents at high speed, carrying its rider and pillion in unrivalled comfort and style.

BMW R1200GS

BMW offered some extreme versions of the GS. The Adventure had a larger 33l (9gal) fuel tank, extensive crash protectors and large aluminium panniers, while the HP2 had conventional forks and much reduced weight.

Optional equipment includes hard and soft luggage, cast or wire-spoked wheels, heated handgrips and satellite navigation aids.

Although styled in a style similar to an off-road enduro machine, the GS' size, weight and power mean it's best left for off-road experts. Most riders will get the best from the GS on the road, where its good handling and usable engine make it an excellent, practical all-rounder.

The R1200GS was the first bike to use the next-generation 1200 Boxer. It gave 15 per cent more power and was 12 per cent lighter. Innovations like advanced engine management, balancer shaft, helical gearbox and twin-spark ignition also improved refinement and usability.

The flat-twin oil/air-cooled Boxer engine is BMW's signature design, and although it looks somewhat unwieldy, it's a solid, reliable performer.

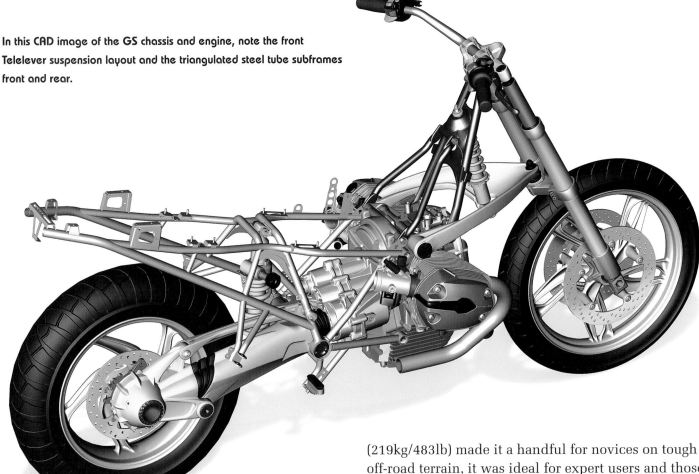

In this CAD image of the GS chassis and engine, note the front Telelever suspension layout and the triangulated steel tube subframes front and rear.

Motorcycling is one of the most acronym-laden pursuits, with many seemingly meaningless yet highly significant groups of letters. And the suffix 'GS' is one of the most succinct. It has a literal meaning, standing for Gelande/Strasse, (German for off-road/road), but to a generation of riders, it simply means BMW's highly capable offroad-styled enduro range.

The first GS was a genuine offroad machine, while the R80 G/S of 1980 was an altered version of the R-series roadbikes, with longer-travel suspension, and a two-valve air-cooled boxer engine. Through the 1980s and 1990s, the GS range evolved into an accomplished roadbike, via various 800, 850, 1000 and 1100cc (49, 52, 61 and 67cu in) versions. The GS range was constantly developing alongside the various extreme enduro events, especially the various Paris-Dakar rally events, which BMW won four times in the 1980s.

So by the beginning of the twenty-first century, the flagship GS was the R1150GS, with an eight-valve fuel-injected engine in a competent chassis that was capable of coping with off-road riding, and excellent touring capabilities. While its high all-up weight

(219kg/483lb) made it a handful for novices on tough off-road terrain, it was ideal for expert users and those looking for mild off-road ability. It had the ground clearance, longer-travel suspension and wire-spoked wheels necessary for off-road use, and ample power and torque from the big flat-twin engine.

For the vast majority of GS owners, a gravel parking lot was as close as they got to offroad riding. But the bike was such a capable and flexible all-rounder, this was no real loss. For long-distance touring, even two up and heavily laden, the GS was superb, so

BMW R1200GS

Top speed:	210km/h (130mph)
Engine type:	1170cc (71cu in), a/c flat-twin, eight-valve SOHC
Maximum power:	98bhp (73kW)@7000rpm
Frame type:	aluminium/steel tube composite
Tyre sizes:	front 110/80 19, rear 150/70 17
Final drive:	shaft
Gearbox:	six-speed
Weight:	199kg (439lb)

commuting and weekend road-riding for sheer leisure were well within its remit. Part of the GS's flexibility was down to its good handling, thanks to the Telelever front suspension system, which separated braking and suspension forces. The low centre of gravity of the flat-twin motor also helped, as did the smooth, predictable power delivery from the fuel-injected engine. Build quality and reliability were excellent, and a wide range of BMW accessories included luggage, heated handgrips and even satellite-navigation devices.

For 2003 though, BMW's new design principles of lower mass and higher performance first appeared in the metal of the new R1200GS. Almost 30kg (66lb) lighter than the 1150, this next-generation GS retained all the practicality of the older bike, while adding a large chunk of extra engine performance and losing large quantities of unnecessary mass. Every part of the chassis was revamped, including the Telelever front suspension, and its next-generation Paralever rear suspension system was ten per cent lighter than

Although it looks rather basic, the GS instrument panel is a sophisticated, CAN device, with a full range of rider information readouts and diagnostic functions.

before. BMW's 'Evo' brake system has an integral ABS system, which can be de-activated for off-road riding. Its new cast-aluminium wheels are more suited to road use, although there's an option of wire-spoked wheels for off-road riding.

The engine produced 18 per cent more power and torque, while fuel consumption went down by eight per cent. Almost every part of the motor was updated, with a longer stroke increasing the capacity over the 1150, new pistons, crankshaft and crankcases. The engine also has a new balancer shaft to cancel out the secondary vibrations inherent in a Boxer engine, and the entire unit was 3kg (7lb) lighter than the 1150.

A new six-speed gearbox used helical gears for strength and lightness, and an all-new engine-management system optimized fuelling and ignition to give the best possible power and economy at all engine speeds. Modern Controller Area Network (CAN) electronics simplified wiring and allowed a more 'clever' electrical system, which permits a smart dashboard with a range of trip computer readouts. Combined with an adjustable windshield, 20l (5gal) fuel tank and a seat with an adjustable height, the result is a supremely practical machine.

BMW R1200RT

The R1200RT fills the 'heavy tourer' role for BMW. It is aimed at mileage fans who don't need the luxury or want the sheer bulk of the firm's K1200LT super heavyweight.

The RT is well equipped as standard. It has an electrically adjustable screen, adjustable seat and handlebars, as well as hard luggage and a comprehensive dashboard.

The Boxer engine uses a 'high-cam' design. The camshafts sit next to the cylinder, instead of in the head, operating the valves via rocker arms. This reduces the size of the heads and thus engine width, which is essential for good ground clearance.

Optional equipment includes a CD/radio system, GPS satellite navigation, cruise control, heated seats and handgrips, and electronic suspension adjustment.

BMW's trademark Telelever front and Paralever rear suspension systems give the 229kg (505lb) heavyweight tourer excellent handling for its size and class. Integrated ABS adds a margin of safety on uncertain road surfaces.

The tall windscreen is electrically adjustable by a handlebar switch. This allows the rider to tailor the wind protection according to road speed, weather conditions and rider preference.

Before its performance-biased renaissance took hold in the first few years of the twenty-first century, BMW seemed to excel at producing touring bikes. It had two basic ranges of machines (the Boxer twin 'R' series and the laid-down four-cylinder 'K' series) and built a range of machines around these two engine designs. The twin cylinder range dates back to BMW's earliest years, and it's perhaps the most flexible, available in various capacities and chassis layouts.

In the early 1990s, BMW released an all-new Boxer range, with fuel injection, four-valve heads and air/oil cooling. It came in 1085 and 848cc (66 and 51cu in) capacities. The first bike to use the new 90bhp (67kW) powerplant was the R1100RS sports tourer in 1993, followed by the R1100RT full tourer in 1995. The RT had a full fairing, with integrated panniers, ABS, tall windshield, large, comfy dual seat and a host of other touring-biased equipment. It was a large bike, weighing in at 282kg (622lb), but its chassis went a long way towards dealing with the weight. BMW used its latest front and rear suspension systems (Telelever and Paralever), which also coped well with the weight of the RT. Braking was strong and progressive, helped by the inherent anti-dive properties of the Telelever system, and BMW's handling design was more than sufficient for most touring riders.

The RT fitted into the BMW range between the R1100RS sports tourer, and the larger K1100LT, and was a strong performer for BMW. It remained essentially unchanged from 1995 to 2002, when BMW released an 1150 version. This had the bigger 1130cc (69cu in) engine from the R1150GS, tuned for more power, and the RT now had 95bhp (71kW), up from 90bhp (67kW). The brakes were revised, with BMW's new EVO assisted system and ABS, and the back wheel changed to a size of 43cm (17in).

But the RT underwent its real change in 2005, when the R1200RT appeared. This bike, like the R1200GS and R1200S, had received the latest generation 1170cc (71cu in) version of the venerable flat-twin Boxer engine, and almost every part of the bike was new. Starting with the engine, power had gone up to 110bhp (82kW) from 95bhp (71kW), thanks to the larger capacity, new pistons, heads and fuel injection system. A new balancer shaft in the bottom end of the engine reduced vibration, and a new six-speed gearbox was mated to the latest-specification Paralever shaft drive. The chassis retained the typical R-series layout, with a steel-tube space frame, Telelever front end and Paralever rear. The suspension systems were revised to make them lighter and stiffer, and BMW also offered an optional Electronic Suspension Adjustment (ESA) system. This allowed the rider to alter the damping and spring-preload settings on the front and rear suspension units via a pushbutton control on the handlebars. The BMW EVO brake system was enhanced with the integrated ABS function, and new lighter alloy wheels wore sport-touring tyres.

BMW R1200RT

Top speed:	225km/h (140mph)
Engine type:	1170cc (71cu in), a/c flat-twin, eight-valve SOHC
Maximum power:	110bhp (82kW)@7500rpm
Frame type:	aluminium- or steel-tube composite
Tyre sizes:	front 120/70 17, rear 180/55 17
Final drive:	shaft
Gearbox:	six-speed
Weight:	229kg (505lb)

The RT's equipment levels were high as standard. The dashboard had a host of display functions, thanks to the smart CAN wiring system. An immobilizer ensured the bike only started with the correct key, and an electrically adjustable windshield, adjustable seat and built-in hard pannier cases all made touring life easier. BMW's optional equipment list was longer than ever, and offered luxuries like an electrically heated seat and handgrips, satellite navigation, radio/CD system, cruise control and hard luggage top cases.

Like the original RT, the R1200RT was a delight on the open road. It had lost 20kg (44lb) over the previous model, and this, along with its extra performance, enhanced its acceleration and handling. The improved suspension systems gave even better control and stability, yet the RT was incredibly nimble for its size.

Two-up continent-crossing trips are where the R1200RT excels. It will carry rider, passenger and luggage at high speed and in luxurious comfort, for thousands of miles with ease.

This RT has the full range of optional extras: satellite navigation, audio system and electric heaters, as well as the extensive standard cockpit equipment.

Ducati ST3

The fairing is typically Ducati, with broad red flanks, large single headlight, and colour-matched mirrors. It is a little more enveloping than usual though, adding the wind protection required on a sport-touring bike. Handlebars and levers are adjustable.

The ST3's V-twin engine is unique to that bike. It has an unusual cylinder head, with three valves per cylinder; two inlets and one exhaust, operated desmodromically.

Ducati kept the chassis specification on the sporty side of sport-touring. The upside-down Showa forks and Sachs rear shock are adjustable, Brembo brakes are sportsbike-spec, and the cast aluminium wheels wear wide, sticky sports tyres.

Hard luggage panniers were occasionally offered as standard fit in some markets. The silencers are height-adjustable – they have a low position to fit the panniers, and a high position to give extra ground clearance when the panniers are removed.

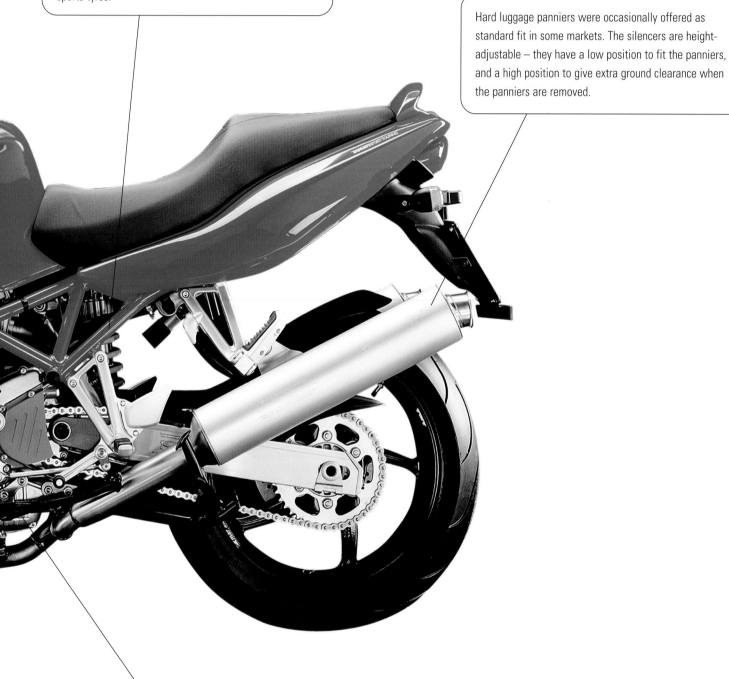

Ducati fitted its usual Magneti Marelli fuel injection system to the ST3. It gives good economy, strong power, and excellent rideability.

While Ducati is (rightly) best known for its sports bikes, and its success in high-level racing, the Bologna firm has also worked hard developing sport touring (ST) models. The first member of the modern ST family, the ST2, appeared in 1996, and the line developed through the ST4 before Ducati settled on the ST3 as its ultimate sport touring machine.

The ST2 used a 944cc (57.6cu in) version of the elderly two-valve 907i engine, in a chassis not dissimilar to that of Ducati's 916 superbike. A steel tube trellis frame, with Brembo brakes and Showa suspension, was equipped with a protective full fairing, spacious dual seat, and factory-option hard luggage panniers. It was a good bike, although it was rather short on long distance touring ability, and the engine was a touch underpowered. Ducati resolved this with the 1998 ST4, essentially a refined ST2, but with a four-valve DOHC desmo engine taken from the firm's legendary 916 superbike. The ST4S of 2000 used

Ducati ST3	
Top speed:	241km/h (150mph)
Engine type:	992cc (60.5cu in), l/c 90° V-twin, six-valve desmo, SOHC
Maximum power:	107bhp (79.7kW) @8,750rpm
Frame type:	steel tube trellis
Tyre sizes:	front 120/70 17, rear 180/55 17
Final drive:	chain
Gearbox:	six-speed
Weight:	204kg (449lb) [with fluids]

Although the ST3 errs towards the sporty end of the sports tourer spectrum, it's still a capable, comfortable, long distance machine – even with a passenger and luggage.

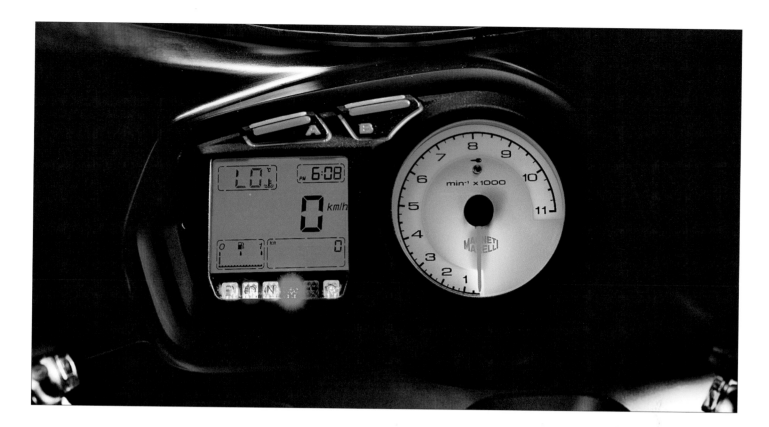

Ducati uses modern electronics on its superbikes, so the digital dash offers a range of diagnostic and rider readouts. Note the antitheft LED – only the correct chip-equipped key can start the bike.

a 996 superbike engine, but both the ST2 and 4 ranges were discontinued in 2003, in favour of the new ST3. This bike had an all-new, specially developed V-twin engine, with an unusual three-valves per cylinder layout. This layout, with two inlet valves and one exhaust valve in each cylinder head, splits the difference between the two-valve and four-valve designs of the ST2/4 range in terms of power delivery. Two-valve designs tend to give better bottom end power, whereas four-valve heads are better for peak power. The ST3 engine has the best of both worlds, giving a strong, torquey delivery for relaxed cruising, as well as a burst of top-end power for exciting sports performance.

Like the engine, the chassis of the ST3 is typically Ducati. The firm's trademark steel tube trellis frame is on show behind the red fairing panels, and there's a pair of preload-adjustable Showa front forks up front, with a fully-adjustable Sachs shock at the back. These parts, together with the Brembo four-piston brakes, wouldn't be out of place on a full-bore sportsbike, and with full adjustability front and rear, the ST3 can be setup to suit most owners' riding style. Michelin sports tyres and three-spoke aluminium wheels further underline the sporting capabilities of the ST3.

But the ST3 is a strong distance performer too. The fuel tank holds 21l (5.5gal.), which gives a range easily in excess of 240km (150 miles), the broad seat offers rider and a pillion reasonable accommodation, and the windscreen and fairing give good wind and weather

protection. The dashboard incorporates a useful LCD information screen with fuel gauge, clock, fuel consumption, range remaining and other readouts, and factory option side and top panniers add useful luggage space, with satellite navigation also available.

On the road, the ST3 offers very satisfying performance. The engine is very strong and willing at all revs, and feels stronger than Honda's VFR800 (although it's not as effortless as Triumph's Sprint ST). The handling is light and agile, all the while the comfortable riding position, high bars and low footpegs helps the rider arrive at her destination refreshed, and on time.

For the 2006 model year, Ducati released an even higher-spec ST3, the ST3s ABS. As the name suggests, this model incorporates an advanced Brembo anti-lock braking setup. Unlike some setups, this system is biased towards sports performance, and can be turned off – useful if the bike is used on track where normal ABS systems can cut in unexpectedly.

Ducati also upgraded the ST3 chassis for the S ABS model. The front forks are fully adjustable, and the rear shock is changed for a race-specification Ohlins item. Together with lightweight Marchesini five-spoke wheels, the result is a noticeably sharper, better-suspended handling package.

Ducati Multistrada

A steel-tube trellis frame, aluminium swingarm and sportsbike suspension mean the Multistrada handles much better than most bikes in its class. It's at its best on twisty mountain roads.

The Multistrada's rear end is much more stylish than its front – a single-sided swingarm and dual underseat silencers give a neat, modern look.

The first Multistrada used Ducati's 1000DS engine – an air-cooled V-twin with two valves per cylinder. The firm later released a 620cc (38cu in) entry-level version, and a new 1100cc (67cu in) motor replaced the 1000 in 2006.

The Multistrada can be equipped with satellite navigation, hard luggage and taller screens to make it into a more serious touring machine. Other accessories focus on performance, with engine upgrades and other tuning modifications available from the factory.

The 'S' version of the Multistrada had higher specification adjustable suspension from Ohlins front and rear, and light carbon-fibre body parts.

It's difficult for relatively small firms like Ducati to expand its range of motorcycles. But Ducati had identified an important sector in the market that it felt it had to address, in its own inimitable fashion. The 'adventure sport' market pioneered by BMW's GS range is incredibly popular worldwide, and the idea of an enduro-styled machine, with a road-biased chassis seemed to make sense for Ducati. Bikes like the R1200GS and Triumph's Tiger are massive sales successes, especially in Europe, where riders find they make great touring bikes, with the ability to soak up mild dirt-road riding, and can then go on adventures off the beaten track.

Ducati's controversial design chief, Pierre Terblanche had the task of designing this bike. And when the first concept bike was revealed in 2001, it was as contentious as his 999 superbike designs. The new bike was, to most eyes, ugly in the way a Ducati had never been before. Its tall stance, curiously bulged fairing and twin high-mount silencers jarred a public eye used to the 916, as did the 'face' made by the oddly shaped headlight and air scoops.

Two years later though, Ducati released the first Multistrada, as the bike was called. The 'Multistrada', meaning all roads, was a bike to be used everywhere, from gravel firebreak roads to high-speed freeways.

Ducati is too small to develop an all-new engine and chassis just for this, but its air-cooled 1000DS engine,

Ducati Multistrada

Top speed:	224km/h (140mph)
Engine type:	992cc (60.5cu in), a/c 90°V-twin, four-valve, SOHC desmo
Maximum power:	92bhp (68kW)@8000rpm
Frame type:	steel-tube trellis
Tyre sizes:	front 120/70 17, rear 180/55 17
Final drive:	chain
Gearbox:	six-speed
Weight:	196kg (432lb)

used in the 1000SS sportsbike and Monster 1000 seemed just right for the job. The air-cooled desmodromic V-twin is a mature, well developed design, and it has good low-down power characteristics, as well as being fairly light and compact. Ducati's trademark steel-tube trellis frame is a flexible design, and was easily adapted to the new design. To add an extra dash of style, Terblanche had

Like all modern Ducatis, the Multistrada used an advanced CANBUS electronic system. The dashboard combined comprehensive rider information and diagnostics with a classic white-faced tachometer.

A twisty mountain road on a sunny Sunday afternoon – the perfect location for the Multistrada. Although it's almost as good in town and on longer trips too.

added a single-sided rear swingarm, not dissimilar to the one fitted to the 916 range.

For the top-range Multistrada 1000S DS, Ducati chose high-specification suspension units from Ohlins, while the base 1000 had Showa units. Brembo brakes and cast aluminium wheels with special Pirelli tires completed the chassis specification.

Ducati launched the first Multistrada 1000 on Sardinia, and the first impressions were excellent. The looks of the Multistrada were still widely criticized, but everyone agreed it was an outstanding bike to ride. Most importantly, its stated intention of working on every type of road was realized. It raced up twisty mountain roads and coped with city riding. And that weird top fairing gave good wind protection at high speeds.

Best of all, the Multistrada was fun to ride. It had easy handling, and a strong torquey engine, without having an excess of power. Brakes were strong, the tires grippy, and the Ohlins suspension on the S version added even more competent handling.

Ducati extended the Multistrada range downward in 2005 with a 620cc (38cu in) entry level version, using the Monster 620 engine. A double-sided swingarm, cheaper suspension and a single front brake disk on the budget 'Dark' version cut the price, while retaining the unique character of the Multistrada. And for 2007, the 1000DS got upgraded to an 1100, with a new bigger bore engine. Capacity went up to 1078cc (66cu in) from 992cc (60.5cu in), power increased by 3bhp (2.2kW). Torque was also increased by 10Nm (8lb ft).

But the major problem most people still had with the Multistrada was its styling. This was a real shame, because under the right circumstances, it was an excellent machine.

Harley-Davidson Ultra Classic Electra Glide

The chassis is rather basic – a steel-tube cradle frame, with a rubber-mounted engine, conventional front forks and triple disc brakes. The rear suspension is air-adjustable, and the tires are narrow, 40cm (16in) touring types.

For 2007, Harley fitted the Ultra with its new Twin Cam 96 powerplant. The 1584cc (97cu in) air-cooled V-twin engine has two valves per cylinder, fuel injection and is mated to a new six-speed transmission.

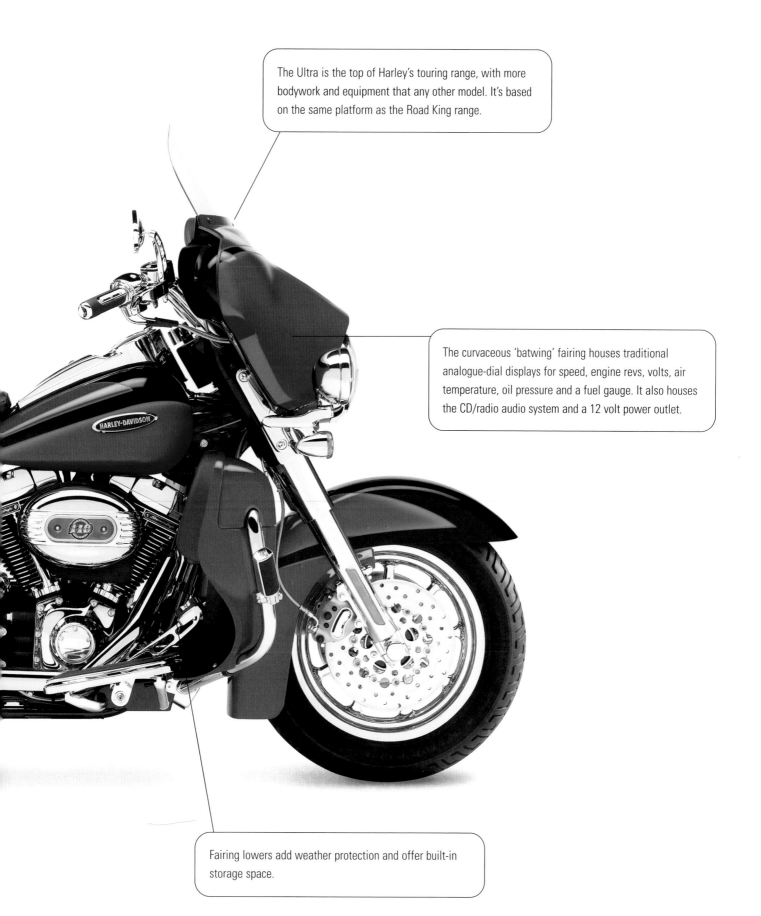

The Ultra is the top of Harley's touring range, with more bodywork and equipment that any other model. It's based on the same platform as the Road King range.

The curvaceous 'batwing' fairing houses traditional analogue-dial displays for speed, engine revs, volts, air temperature, oil pressure and a fuel gauge. It also houses the CD/radio audio system and a 12 volt power outlet.

Fairing lowers add weather protection and offer built-in storage space.

HARLEY-DAVIDSON

The Electra Glide is one of Harley-Davidson's most famous models, and therefore probably one of the best known motorcycle names. It dates back to 1965, when Harley installed an electric starter to its Duo Glide, and has been around in various guises ever since.

This Ultra Classic is Harley's biggest and most comfortable model, and is clearly aimed at fans of long-distance cruising along Route 66, Pacific Coast Highway 1 or any of the other classic US routes immortalized in road movies and beat poems. Like every Harley, the Ultra Classic approaches its job in its own unique way. In theory, it's competing with the likes of Honda's Gold Wing. In practice, it's carving out its own niche, where heritage, style and character are as important, if not more so, than conventional ideas of performance and practicality.

This 2007 model has all of Harley's very latest engineering built in, although to look at the fifties-styled bodywork and chrome-plated cycle parts, you could very easily mistake it for something from a museum of American kitsch from the middle of the twentieth century. Despite that, the 2007 Ultra is powered by the current pinnacle of H-D air-cooled powerplant design, the Twin Cam 96. This engine, launched for the '07 model year, is based on the earlier Twin Cam 88, but with capacity up from 1450 to

This top-of-the-line touring Harley is extremely well equipped for distance riding, especially with a passenger, but is biased towards lower-speed American use, than high-speed European roads.

1584cc (88 to 97cu in). The basic layout is unchanged though. It has a 45° air-cooled V-twin engine, with two pushrod-operated valves per cylinder, and two camshafts mounted in the crankcases.

The engine ancillaries had also been updated: the Electronic Sequential Port Fuel Injection (ESPFI)

Harley-Davidson Ultra Classic Electra Glide

Top speed:	177km/h (110mph)
Engine type:	1584cc (97cu in), a/c 60° V-twin, four-valve, OHV
Maximum power:	n/a
Frame type:	steel-tube cradle
Tyre sizes:	front 90/90 16, rear 85/85 16
Final drive:	belt
Gearbox:	six-speed
Weight:	372kg (820lb)

system gives improved fuelling and reduced emissions. Meanwhile a new Active Intake and Exhaust system uses valves mounted in the inlet tract and exhaust system to reduce noise and emissions, while boosting torque. At low engine speeds, the valves are closed to reduce noise around town, but when speeds increase, as on the open road, the valves are opened by an electronic control unit increasing power and allowing more noise. Finally, the engine is mated to a new, six-speed separate transmission unit, the Cruise Drive, which has one more gear than previously, and a lower top-gear ratio, reducing engine revs at highway cruising speeds.

Like the engine, the chassis is essentially an old design. A steel-tube cradle frame holds the rubber-mounted engine and transmission, with conventional front forks and air-adjustable rear suspension units. Dual disk brakes at the front and a single disk out back have 292mm (11.5in) rotors and four-piston calipers, and the wheels are cast aluminum.

The virtual armchair accommodation for the Ultra's pillion is clearly seen here, as are the timeless lines of the exhausts, footboards and chrome detail rails.

The steady, stately progress resulting from the ponderous chassis and unstressed engine is at least carried out in style and comfort. An enormous dual seat is well padded and sculpted for the benefit of both pillion and rider, both of whom are protected by a large 'bat-wing' fork-mounted fairing and vented lower fairings. Large, adjustable footboards, a passenger back/armrest and touring handlebars give extra comfort, and the built-in hard luggage cases offer ample luggage capacity. There's an electronic cruise-control system to ease the pain on long trips, and a four-speaker Harman/Kardon audio system.

Taken on its own terms, the Ultra Classic offers a unique riding experience. On a sunny day, with nothing but a quiet, scenic, straight road ahead, and no real hurry, the Harley tourer is perfect. But it isn't for everyone. This particular superbike is aimed at the huge home market, where Harley is strongest. Outside the US, Harley-Davidsons make less sense, especially on the twisty, crowded roads of Europe. Add in the very high cost of a Harley-Davidson, and it becomes absolutely clear why many riders outside the US find that other choices make more sense for them.

Classic styling shows in the Ultra's massive front fender, auxiliary driving lights and masses of chrome plate. Shrouded forks and dual disc brakes are well suited to cruiser touring.

Honda VFR800 VTEC

The aluminium twin-spar frame is light and stiff, and uses the engine as an additional structural member. The single-sided rear swingarm pivots on the engine cases rather than directly on the frame itself.

Dual underseat silencers have four outputs, and make pannier fitment easier, while also improving ground clearance. They do restrict underseat storage space, however.

The VFR is powered by a compact, powerful V-four engine. Honda's PGM-FI fuel injection system gives smooth, predictable power delivery, and a VTEC variable-valve system optimizes power at low and high engine speeds.

The engine's cooling radiators are mounted on the side of the bike, saving space at the front of the engine and allowing a shorter wheelbase.

The VFR uses Honda's CBS linked brake system, which integrates the front and rear brake systems. An ABS version is equipped with an anti-lock brake set-up.

Honda's VFR has been one of its most successful models in the two decades since it was launched, and virtually dominated its area of the market. First touted as Honda's entry in the 750cc (46cu in) supersport class, the character of the VFR was altered over the years, and it morphed from a sharp superbike into a capable all-rounder, and then into a fine sports tourer.

The original sportsbike, the VFR750F, was derived from the ill-fated VF750 range. The VF engine (a 90° V-four, water-cooled, 16-valve design) caused concern about its reliability almost from launch, with camchain and camshaft failures wrecking Honda's reputation. Installing a gear-driven camshaft system on the VFR engine solved the reliability issues for good, however.

Known as the Interceptor in the US (where it was also available as a tax-beating 700cc [43cu in]) and the VFR750F elsewhere, the 1986 VFR was an instant success, especially in racing. Virtually standard VFRs were beating full-factory superbikes from other firms, notably in the Transatlantic Trophy race at Donington, under UK racer Ron Haslam. As a result, the VFR750 virtually sold itself, it became so popular.

That first design clearly stemmed from the 1980s. It had narrow wheels, with a 40.6cm (16in) front and 46cm (18in) rear, fork anti-dive devices and smooth,

A tourer like the VFR has to be capable of high-performance sports riding, as well as practical enough for two-up touring. The Honda is a polished performer, and is extremely capable in both roles.

bulbous bodywork. The first VFR upgrade in 1988 showed how modern superbikes were developing: both wheels were changed to wider, 43cm (17in) parts, and thicker, stiffer forks were fitted without an anti-dive mechanism. These chassis models began the process of moving the VFR into the modern superbike age, but the next change in 1989 really defined the

Honda VFR800 VTEC

Top speed:	249km/h (155mph)
Engine type:	782cc (48cu in), l/c 90° V-four, 16-valve, DOHC
Maximum power:	107bhp (108kW)@10,500rpm
Frame type:	aluminium twin spar
Tyre sizes:	front 120/70 17, rear 180/55 17
Final drive:	chain
Gearbox:	six-speed
Weight:	218kg (481lb)

bike. This VFR750 FL model was the first with a single-sided swingarm. It also had a series of engine changes, received a new fairing, new radial tyres and different exhaust layout. Yet even this heavy update only lasted for a couple of years. For 1992, the VFR750 was further refined, with an all-new look that echoed the exotic NR750, which had debuted that year.

The VFR's chassis and engine were continually refined until 1998. By then the bike was very well built, supremely reliable, had ample smooth power, and provided plenty of comfort for touring.

But just before the century ended, Honda re-engineered the whole bike. A new engine, based on the RC45 supersports design, had a bigger capacity of 781cc (48cu in), so the bike was called a VFR800. The firm also installed its PGM-FI fuel injection system. The frame was entirely new, with a design that pivots the swingarm on the engine casings. The radiator was changed from a single front-mounted part to a pair of side-mounted radiators. This made the bike narrower, and careful design also improved its aerodynamics.

Honda's CBS linked brake system was used on this bike, and integrated both front and rear brake systems.

By this stage, the VFR had pretty much given up on the supersports race. Competitor 750s like the Suzuki GSX-R750 and Kawasaki's ZX-7R were much more sporting. However, Honda was happy with the VFR's more practical, touring bias. As were customers: the VFR enjoyed incredible sales success.

The next change in the VFR came in 2002, when Honda fitted its VTEC variable-valve system. This used a computer-controlled hydraulic circuit to 'switch' two of the four valves in each cylinder on and off. At low rpm, a two-valve layout gives better power and torque, while at higher rpm, all four valves give the best breathing and extra power. This switchover happens around 7000rpm, and makes a discernible difference in the power and sound of the bike.

Honda's handsome design and build quality shows in the twin dual-output silencers and integrated rear light units. Passenger grab handles and luggage hooks underline the VFR's usefulness.

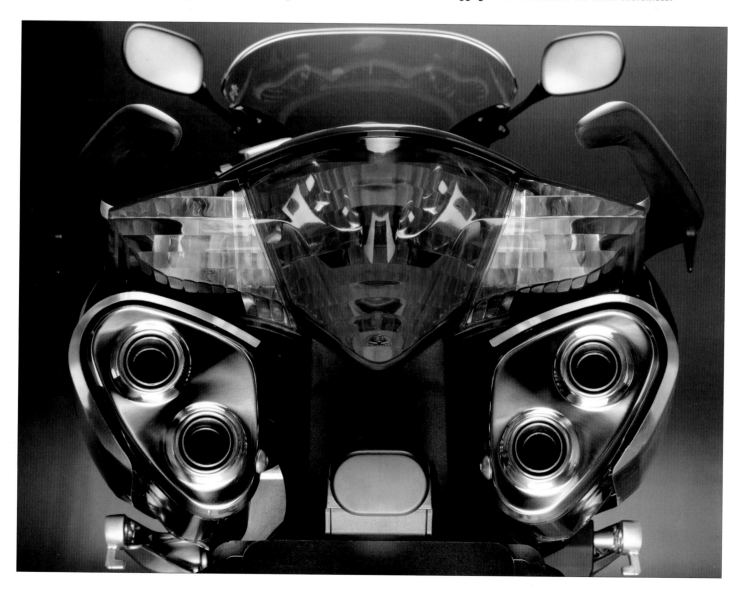

Honda STX1300 Pan European (+1100)

The Pan European uses an unusual transverse V-four layout, with the cylinders poking out either side of the fairing. This compact design makes sense for a shaft drive machine – the crankshaft is in the same plane as the final drive, simplifying the transmission.

Integrated panniers are standard fittings, and an optional top box further increases luggage capacity.

An enormous fairing envelops the rider and passenger in a weatherproof cocoon. An adjustable windshield can be lowered for a cooling breeze, or raised for ultimate blast protection.

The Pan's frame incorporates a pair of 'bump dampers' either side of the engine. These steel bars, covered with replaceable plastic guards, absorb the impact of low-speed crashes, protecting the engine from damage.

On the deluxe version the Pan's electric screen moves up and down. This lets the rider fine-tune the windblast, increasing the breeze on warm days or raising the screen in case of rain.

Honda is a firm with many proud landmarks and ground-breaking models in its motorcycling history. But even among this illustrious firm's list of flagship models, a few bikes stand out for their longevity, quality of design and sheer fitness for purpose. The CBR900RR FireBlade is one, as is the CBR600. And the Pan European is most definitely another. First released in 1989 as a high-performance heavy tourer, it immediately impressed with its mix of strong engine, surefooted handling and high comfort levels. An all-new design, it was built around an unusual transverse-mounted 1084cc 90° V-four engine, which had a five speed gearbox and shaft final drive. The motor is bolted into a steel tube perimeter frame, mostly hidden behind an all-enveloping plastic fairing. Suspension units were conventional – a 41mm (1.6in) front fork and a rear monoshock, adjustable for spring preload and rebound damping – as was the braking setup; a pair of front discs with dual-piston sliding calipers and a single rear disc.

The Pan's specification was unremarkable, yet it performed amazingly. Once moving, its high all-up weight seemed to disappear, and it could be ridden in a spirited fashion belying its outwardly sedate appearance. The engine was brilliant, combining tractor-like levels of low-down grunt with a lively top end, and the chassis was eminently capable of absorbing whatever was thrown at it. All this was matched to an incredibly comfortable riding position for the rider and passenger, and an enormous tank range. The 28l (7.4gal) fuel tank could be persuaded to last more than 400km (250 miles) before stopping.

The first major update for the Pan was the introduction of an ABS-equipped version in 1992, which also featured a traction-control system (TCS). This used the ABS sensors to cut engine power if the rear wheel lost traction under acceleration. Three years later, it received 43mm (1.7in) forks and new radial tires to improve handling, while the brakes were upgraded to Honda's new CBS linked system. This set-up linked the front and rear brakes together, so operating the front lever also partially applied the rear brake, and vice versa.

But it was in 2002 that the Pan European got its first major revamp. The STX1300 launched that year had an all new aluminium-framed chassis, totally redesigned 1261cc (77cu in) engine and sharper, more modern bodywork. The dry mass was down by 6kg (13lb), and power was up by 25bhp (18kW).

The engine changes included an increase in bore and stroke, new aluminium-coated cylinders, tougher, lighter pistons, PGM-FI fuel injection, a cambelt instead of a chain, dual balancer shafts, and moving the alternator to between the engine's vee. This lighter, smoother, smaller engine was solidly mounted in the beam frame, adding to its stiffness and helping reduce mass.

The running gear was also modernized and upgraded. Front forks grew to 45mm (1.77in) cartridge types, and the rear swingarm was altered from steel

Honda STX1300 Pan European (+1100)

Top speed:	240km/h (150mph)
Engine type:	1261cc (77cu in), l/c 90° V-four, 16-valve, DOHC
Maximum power:	125bhp (92kW)@8000rpm
Frame type:	extruded/cast aluminium diamond
Tyre sizes:	front 120/70 17, rear 170/60 17
Final drive:	shaft
Gearbox:	five-speed
Weight:	287kg (633lb)

The mark of a true super tourer is the provision of a sound system. In this case it's an optional extra, with radio and CD audio provision. Note also the electric screen control.

tube to cast aluminium, with a new suspension unit. A wider rear tire size and modern Bridgestone tires improved grip, stability and mileage.

Standard and factory-option equipment levels moved up a notch too. The dashboard included an LCD display with ambient temperature, fuel gauge and clock. The seat was adjustable to three positions, and on the deluxe version, the windshield is electrically adjustable. Fuel capacity was increased by 1l (¼gal),

and optional accessories included a CD/radio sound system, heated grips, luggage trunk and soft pannier inner bags.

The new STX1300, while being a quantum leap ahead of the old 1100 model, was still recognizably a Pan. And on the road, it's every bit as usable and comfortable as the old bike, while offering performance that will easily equal any sports tourers. In fact, a well ridden Pan-European is able to match some full-on sportsbikes on a fast road ride. This may prove to be a sobering thought for any rider being followed by one of the numerous police-specification Pan European superbikes.

Honda GL1800 Gold Wing (+GL1500)

Optional equipment includes an integrated GPS navigation system, chromed bodywork parts, a pannier cooler and many other comfort and styling parts.

Honda developed a very stiff, light aluminium frame and swingarm for the GL1800, which replaced the steel tube frame on the GL1500. This gave much improved handling, especially at higher speeds.

The Gold Wing's flat-six engine keeps much of the bike's mass down low. It's also a very smooth engine, with near-perfect balance. A single camshaft on each cylinder bank and two valves per cylinder keep the engine more compact.

An enormous windshield and fairing keep the rider and pillion in a cocoon of still air, even when travelling at high speeds. The windshield is manually adjustable for height, while hot-air vents and electrically heated grips and seat offer perfect comfort in the worst weather.

A combined ABS/CBS system links front and rear braking systems together, with an advanced antilock function adding safety on slippery roads.

The Wing's cockpit and dash are more like a small aeroplane than a motorcycle. Most controls are for the sound system, but there are also heated grips and seat, suspension, cruise and trip computer controls.

One look at Honda's legendary Gold Wing is all you need to see what it's been built for. This gargantuan, mammoth exercise in extremes was set out to be the last word in motorcycle touring comfort. It is more like a two-wheeled luxury automobile than a motorcycle, Honda's GL1800 Gold Wing is the sumptuous choice for mileage addicts with a sense of style.

The Wing has a long heritage – the first version was the GL1000 of 1974, which, while it was marketed as a tourer, had none of the luxuries of later models. This first GL had a flat-four 999cc (61cu in) liquid-cooled engine, which later developed into 1100 and 1200 versions. By 1988, with competitor machines snapping at the Wing's heels, Honda stunned everyone with a new, flat-six, 1520cc (93cu in) engine in an all new chassis. In 2001, the 1832cc (112cu in) version arrived.

The GL engine is built for smoothness and relaxed progress rather than outright power, but it still puts out a creditable 117bhp (86kW). The SOHC cylinder heads are compact (important for ground clearance), while Honda's PGM-FI fuel injection system gives good drivability. A five-speed gearbox and shaft drive transmits the power to the rear tyre, and incorporates a clever reverse gear. This uses the engine's starter motor to slowly push the bike back – a boon when manoeuvring at slow speeds on sloping surfaces.

The GL1500 was produced from 1988 to 2001, and was the first bike to feature a flat-six cylinder engine.

The Wing's chassis began as a basic steel-tube cradle type, but has evolved over the years into the current aluminium twin-spar version. This gives excellent stiffness while cutting weight, as does the aluminium swingarm. Suspension preload can be adjusted electronically from the rider's seat, while the front and rear disc brake systems are linked, and incorporate an antilock system as well.

But it's the Gold Wing's rider accommodation that really impresses. The giant front fairing keeps the wind and weather off rider and passenger, while heated grips and seat keep you warm in winter. The windshield is adjustable for different rider heights or riding styles, while a comprehensive dashboard shows every parameter the rider needs, including the displays for the onboard CD player (with six-disc changer and an MP3 player input), RDS radio and trip computer. There's a full cruise control system to maintain vehicle speeds up to 160km/h (100mph) without rider input, built-in intercom system for pillion communication, and even a pair of speakers in the back seat for the passenger. Its luggage capacity – two large side panniers, a top box and four small fairing pockets – exceeds some small sportscars.

Not content with this list of luxury equipment, Honda even fitted the 2006 Gold Wing with the world's first motorcycle airbag system. This used a large airbag mounted in front of the rider, which offered some impact protection in case of a head-on crash (a common incident for motorcycles).

Honda GL1800 Gold Wing (+GL1500)

Top speed:	225km/h (140mph)
Engine type:	1832cc (112cu in), l/c flat six, 12-valve, SOHC
Maximum power:	117bhp (86kW) @5500rpm
Frame type:	aluminium twin spar
Tyre sizes:	front 130/70 18, rear 180/60 16
Final drive:	shaft
Gearbox:	five-speed (plus reversing aid)
Weight:	363kg (799lb)

Riding the GL1800 for the first time is a sobering experience, as the sheer amount of metal and plastic confuses your two-wheeled senses. But like many heavyweight machines, the Wing holds its mass low down, and this, together with the short seat height, wide bars and strong low-down engine performance soon puts the rider at ease.

Clearly Honda intended this bike for long-distance highway touring, and here it excels, with only the average fuel range spoiling the comfy picture. The fuel tank holds a reasonable 25l (6.6gal), but hard riding can see the fuel gauge showing red in 240km (150 miles). However, if you wish to take the Gold Wing onto more exciting roads, it copes admirably. The stiff chassis just manages to tame the forces generated by the high all-up mass while the tyres and brakes supply ample grip and stopping power.

Honda also offered cruiser versions of the GL range, the GL1500 Valkyrie, and the GL1800 Rune. These used modified Gold Wing engines in custom cruiser-styled chassis, and attracted a keen cult following in North America and Europe.

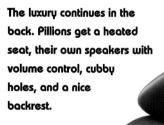

The luxury continues in the back. Pillions get a heated seat, their own speakers with volume control, cubby holes, and a nice backrest.

Triumph Sprint ST 1050

The Sprint's fairing is very protective, and with an optional taller screen, gives excellent weather protection. The riding position is relaxed and upright – perfect for touring.

Turn signals are integrated into the mirrors for a smoother look. Triple headlights echo the triple theme throughout the bike, from the dashboard to the silencer outlets.

Hard luggage panniers were initially offered as an option, but became standard fitments in 2007. An antilock braking system was also an option, as well as GPS navigation, screens, soft luggage and heated grips.

Triumph kept its trademark single-sided swingarm on the Sprint ST, despite its inherent weight penalty. The design makes rear wheel changes easier, but is essentially a styling choice.

Low footpegs can drag under hard track riding, but apart from that, the Sprint's chassis package offers excellent sporting performance. Stiffening up the adjustable suspension units is a simple mod to further improve circuit performance.

Triumph's bikes have always had excellent brakes. The Sprint ST's dual discs with four-piston calipers are taken from the firm's sportsbike range.

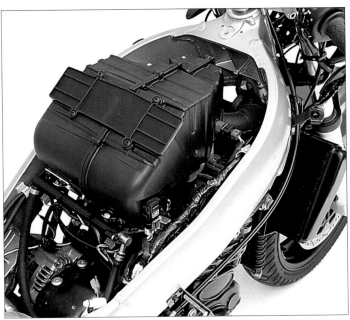

Under the nylon fuel tank, the large airbox helps the three-cylinder engine make strong power. The aluminium twin spar frame is stiff, light and gives stable handling.

In the future, motorcycling historians will perhaps look back on the early years of the twenty-first century as the time when the modern Triumph company really started to produce world-beating motorbikes. The Hinckley-based plant revived the legendary Triumph marque in the early 1990s, financed by property tycoon John Bloor, and began building dependable bikes. Early designs were adequate performers, with engineering based on Japanese principles, and the firm continued to improve its range throughout the first decade of production. And as Triumph moved into the new century, the firm was working on the next generation of machines, including the Rocket III, Daytona 675 Triple and the new Sprint 1050.

The Sprint marque goes back to the first days of the new Triumph company: the first Sprint was a half-faired version of the 1991 Trident 900, using the firm's original 885cc (54cu in) triple engine in a steel-tube spine-type frame. The second-generation Sprint ST used a variant of the firm's T595 superbike engine in an aluminium frame with full fairing, and this bike boasted very strong performance, sufficient to rival Honda's VFR800, the then class leader. That engine, a liquid-cooled 12-valve DOHC triple, was Triumph's first nonmodular design, and it was a very high performance package. Triumph also offered a budget version – the half-faired Sprint RS.

By the time the third-generation Sprint 1050 arrived in 2005, its three-cylinder engine had been extensively overhauled and refined. The capacity increase to

1050cc (64cu in) over the previous model's 955cc (58cu in) was achieved by lengthening the engine stroke by 6.4mm to 71.4mm (.25in to 2.8in), the bore remaining at 79mm (3in). A host of other changes to the motor resulted in a truly world-class powerplant, with a superbly strong, torquey delivery, and smooth, instant power. A new, smoother gearbox helps the rider get the most from the new engine, and a revised fuel injection system provided flawless fuelling. The same engine is fitted to the Speed Triple, although with a slightly different tune giving 5bhp (4kW) more peak power and extra torque.

For the 1050 Sprint, Triumph stuck with essentially the same basic chassis as before; an aluminum beam

Triumph Sprint ST 1050

Top speed:	250km/h (155mph)
Engine type:	1050cc (64cu in), l/c inline-triple, 12-valve, DOHC
Maximum power:	123bhp (90.5kW)@9250rpm
Frame type:	aluminium twin spar
Tyre sizes:	front 120/70 17, rear 180/55 17
Final drive:	chain
Gearbox:	six-speed
Weight:	210kg (462lb)

Although it's billed as a sports tourer, the Sprint ST isn't short of excitement. Later models offered even stronger performance, with additional practicality too.

frame that gives good stiffness without excessive weight and a single-sided rear swingarm. This is almost entirely an aesthetic choice: a double-sided swingarm is less expensive to produce and lighter. But Triumph owners like the single-sided rear end, and it does make rear wheel maintenance easier.

The weight issue is an important one, and perhaps the only criticism of the Sprint. At 210kg (462lb), it's 3kg (6.6lb) heavier than the old model, and while handling isn't affected, manhandling the Sprint at very low speeds can be a chore.

The rest of the chassis provides stable, predictable handling and good touring comfort. The brakes are borrowed from the 955 Daytona superbike, and offer strong stopping power, although the extra mass of the Sprint means they have to work harder than on some

competitor machines. Equipment levels are high – the excellent LCD dashboard incorporates a number of trip computer functions, including tank remaining range, average and maximum speeds and fuel consumption, as well as the usual time and trip displays. The mirrors give a good view of the road behind, and the built-in indicators are a neat touch.

Triumph worked hard to develop its own distinct styling, and the Sprint is a clear example of this. An unambiguous 'triple' theme runs through the whole bike, from the three-beam headlight unit to the triplicate dials on the dashboard, and the '000' exhaust exit ports on the underseat silencer. Subtle it's not, but it definitely stands out.

Triumph also offers a range of accessories for the Sprint, from a GPS satellite navigation system to heated handlebar grips. Added to the very strong basic engine and chassis package, these options can turn the Sprint ST into a superlative personalized machine: perhaps the best sports tourer available in the world.

Yamaha FJR1300

Yamaha utilized many of the design principles it explored in the YZF-R1 superbike while designing the FJR1300. Its light aluminum frame, powerful inline-four engine and racing-specification brakes took the FJR to a new level of touring performance.

Yamaha used an advanced fuel injection system on the engine, which also featured a five-speed gearbox, and shaft final drive. A semi-automatic version was also built for 2006, with push-button gearchange.

The FJR1300's DOHC water-cooled 1298cc (79cu in) engine is an expanded version of the R1 engine. Unlike the 1000cc (61cu in) design, though, it uses four valves per cylinder. It also has a pair of balancer shafts to reduce vibration.

The FJR has an electrically operated adjustable screen, and a large clear dashboard. It does lack some of the equipment offered by other touring bikes though, like an audio system, cruise control or trip computer.

The same Sumitomo brakes as used on Yamaha's R-series sportsbikes give strong, progressive stopping. Yamaha also offered a version with ABS.

Although Yamaha is one of the largest motorcycle manufacturers, sitting not far behind the number one, Honda, it has in the past had a somewhat limited product range. While there were plenty of sporty bikes in the Yamaha range, the firm had little to offer the sport-touring fan, especially in the late 1990s, after its elderly FJ1200 was finally pensioned off in 1996. Its ill-fated GTS1000 produced between 1993 and 1996 was a sales flop, and the XJ900 Diversion was far too old to compete with bikes like BMW's Boxer range or Honda's Pan European. So in 2001, the firm presented the all-new FJR1300, a big-bore touring machine intended to take on the ST1100 Pan European, with design and engineering principles borrowed from the firm's hugely successful 'R' series of sportsbikes.

The FJR engine had an all-new design, although it did echo the design of the R1 engine. A stacked gearbox design made it more compact and saved weight, while an advanced 16-valve cylinder-head design, electronic fuel injection and a four-into-two exhaust system helps it produce an impressive 143bhp (105kW) peak power, as well as a considerable 99lbf ft (134 Nm) of torque at just 7000rpm. The engine uses ceramic-coated cylinders to cut friction and weight, and also has a pair of balancer shafts to cut high-

Yamaha FJR1300

Top speed:	241km/h (150mph)
Engine type:	1298cc (79cu in), l/c inline-four, 16-valve, DOHC
Maximum power:	143.5bhp (105.5kW)@8500rpm
Frame type:	aluminium diamond
Tire sizes:	front 120/70 17, rear 180/55 17
Final drive:	shaft
Gearbox:	five-speed
Weight:	582lb (264kg)

frequency vibration, although the engine can still be somewhat buzzy at times.

This strong, smooth power is transmitted to the wide, grippy rear sports tyre by a five-speed gearbox and a virtually maintenance-free shaft final drive.

Though pretty comprehensive, this early FJR1300's dashboard lacks some of the more detailed rider information offered by competitors – like fuel range remaining, ambient temperature or gear position.

While some touring bikes offered more standard equipment, the FJR1300 was one of the most effective ways to transport two people and luggage in comfort over continental distances – fast.

The FJR's chassis also takes cues from sportsbike design, most notably with its aluminium beam frame. This saves weight over steel-tube designs, helping the FJR attain its 264kg (582lb) dry weight, which is light for its class. The brakes, meanwhile, are virtually a direct lift from the R1, and provide superb, strong stopping power. An optional ABS system gives extra peace of mind when stopping on slippery surfaces. The suspension is built for comfort instead of speed, but with the adjustable damping and preload set in the high position, the FJR provides reassuringly taut handling, helped by its sports-sized 43cm (17in) wheels and wide, sport-touring tyres.

On the road, the original FJR offered a more sporting, less touring ride than the Pan European. Its equipment levels are lower – panniers are an optional item, not integrated (although later models had panniers as standard), the dashboard gives less information, riding position and wind protection is less detailed – but it had an appreciable performance advantage. However, that power and mass gap was narrowed by Honda's improved STX1300 Pan European the following year.

In 2005 the FJR was given an all-new dashboard and revised bodywork that gave more wind protection. Yamaha also presented a new FJR1300 with a computer-controlled semi-automatic transmission set-up. The system, dubbed Yamaha Chip-Controlled Shift (YCC-S) does away with the left-hand clutch lever, instead allowing the rider to change gear via a switch on the bars, or merely by operating the standard gear foot lever. An on-board ECU operates the clutch via an electronic solenoid, moves the gear-change lever via another solenoid, and then engages the clutch again. At slow speeds, the ECU modulates the clutch appropriately, and safety lockouts prevent the rider from engaging first gear from neutral if the engine revs are too high. The ECU also stops gear changes that would over-rev the engine, or make the engine turn too slowly. Undoubtedly, the system is ingenious, but some riders complain that it removes too much control during some tricky, slow-speed actions, such as U-turns on steep hills.

But as a modern, fast tourer, the FJR makes an excellent choice. The latest version has awesome power and ace handling, the 25l (6.6gal) fuel tank gives a good range, and the electrically operated windshield lets riders tune the airflow over themselves easily, depending on circumstances.

GLOSSARY

ABS
Antilock braking system. Uses computer controlled sensors and pressure valves to release hydraulic brake pressure when a wheel is about to lock, preventing skidding and loss of control.

Aluminium twin spar
Design of frame with two aluminium beams between the steering and swingarm pivots. These have traditionally been extruded parts, welded to cast steering and swingarm pivot points, but recent designs have used all-cast designs.

Backbone frame
A frame design which uses a large single tube from the swingarm pivot to the steering head pivot, hanging the engine below it. Also known as spine frame.

Bevel drive
Mechanical arrangement to turn a shaft drive through 90º. Used on some camshaft drives as well as shaft final drive systems.

BHP
Brake horsepower. A measure of power, equivalent to 550ft-lb per second or 745.7 watts.

Camchain
Chain fitted inside an engine which turns the camshaft via a sprocket on the crankshaft. Can be located in the middle of the engine, between the inner cylinders, or more commonly on one end of the engine.

Camshaft
Rotating shaft with cam profiles machined on it, which push engine valves open and closed as it turns.

Carburettor
A mechanical device designed to introduce atomized fuel into the airflow in the engine.

CBS
Combined braking system. Used by Honda to link front and rear braking circuits via hydraulic hoses and valves.

Compression damping
A system for absorbing suspension movement on the compression (upward) stroke of a wheel.

Compression ratio
The ratio of the volume of an engine cylinder at bottom dead centre to the volume at top dead centre.

CV Carburettors
Constant Velocity carburettors use a vacuum diaphragm to control airflow into the engine.

Desmodromic
Valve operating system which uses two cams to positively close as well as open each engine valve. Used by Ducati in its V-twin engine designs.

DOHC
Double overhead camshaft. Engine layout with two overhead cams, one for inlet valves, one for exhaust valves.

Double cradle frame
Frame design which uses two rails running down from the steering head in front of the engine and back to the swingarm pivot. Normally used in steel tube designs.

EFI
Electronic fuel injection. Computerized system which uses electronic solenoid valves in a high-pressure fuel rail, controlled by an ECU, to deliver precisely metered, accurately timed fuel to the engine.

ECU
Electronic control unit. The 'brain' of an EFI system, which uses sensors (temperature, engine position, throttle opening) to determine how much fuel to inject into the engine, and when.

EXUP
Exhaust Ultimate Powervalve. Yamaha's system for controlling pressure pulses within a four-stroke exhaust to improve midrange power.

Fairing
Plastic or composite bodywork panels attached to the motorcycle. Provides accommodation for rider, instruments and ancillaries, as well as aiding aerodynamic performance and giving weather protection.

Floating disc

Brake disc which is attached to its carrier by loose dowels. This allows the disc to expand and contract as it heats up in operation without cracking.

Fly-by-wire

A system used in advanced fuel injection systems that disconnects the rider twistgrip input from the throttle valves. The twistgrip operates a sensor that sends a signal to the ECU. The ECU then works out the appropriate throttle position for maximum power, and opens the throttle, usually via an electric motor.

Four-piston caliper

Brake caliper design which uses two hydraulic pistons either side of the brake disc to clamp the brake pad onto the disc.

Ft-lb

Foot-pounds force. A measure of torque, or turning force. One ft-lb is equivalent to 1.356 newton metres

High/low-speed damping adjustment

Type of adjustment found on high-performance suspension units. Allows the high-speed damping used to deal with bumps to be adjusted separately from the low-speed damping that deals with weight transfer under acceleration or braking.

Inline-four

Most common form of sportsbike engine. Has four cylinders arranged in a line.

Master cylinder

Hydraulic control cylinder which is operated by hand or foot lever. Uses a piston to pressurize hydraulic fluid and operate hydraulic pistons in brake calipers.

Monoshock

Suspension system which uses one shock absorber to control (normally) a rear swingarm. Can use a rising rate linkage, which increases shock movement as the wheel moves, or a linear linkage.

OHC

Overhead cam. Type of engine layout where the camshaft is located above the combustion chamber.

OHV

Overhead valve. Engine layout with the valves above the combustion chamber operated by long pushrods linking them to a camshaft next to the crankshaft.

Parallel twin

Engine layout with two cylinders arranged side-by-side across the frame.

Radial master cylinder

Front brake (or clutch) master cylinder which has the pump mounted radially to the handlebar. This gives a more direct link to the hand lever.

Radial-mount calipers

Brake caliper design which uses mounting bolts arranged radially to the wheel's axis. This allows a lighter, more mechanically-sound mounting than the traditional type, which uses bolts in a 'shear' arrangement.

Radial tyres

Modern tyre construction type which uses radial construction threads running from one side of the tyre to the other. Allows a lighter, cooler-running tyre carcass.

Rake

Measure of steering geometry. This is the angle between the steering axis (the point around which the steering rotates) and the vertical as viewed from the side.

Ram-airbox

A sealed airbox with intakes positioned at the front of the motorcycle. As road speed increases, wind blast pressurizes the airbox slightly, giving a power increase

Rebound damping

A system for absorbing suspension movement on the rebound (downward) stroke of a wheel. Normally uses oil forced through small holes.

Ride height adjustment

Method of adjusting the position of a suspension unit in relation to the chassis, which moves the chassis up or down relative to the ground.

Slide carburettor

Slide carburettors use a simple piston valve connected to the throttle to control airflow into the engine.

SOHC

Single overhead camshaft. Engine layout with one camshaft for inlet and exhaust valves.

Slipper clutch

Type of clutch that improves stability under hard braking. When the rider changes down gears quickly, the rear wheel can lock, causing 'hop' and instability. Under these conditions, the slipper clutch releases slightly, disconnecting the rear wheel from the engine and preventing it from locking up.

Spring preload

Means of adjusting the static load on a suspension spring. Uses a threaded or cammed collar.

Swingarm

Pivoting fork which allows a (usually) rear wheel to move up and down over bumps. Controlled by one or two suspension units.

Tachometer

Instrument to display engine speed.

Traction control

A safety system to prevent rear wheel slip under acceleration. When sensors detect the rear wheel spinning faster than the front, the engine's power output is cut.

Trail

A measurement of steering geometry. Trail is the distance between the point where the front wheel touches the ground, and the point where a line drawn along the steering axis touches the ground. A larger trail figure generally means a more stable bike.

Upside-down fork

Type of telescopic suspension fork where the inner chromed stanchion tube attaches to the front wheel, and the outer slider tube is mounted at the top, attached to the steering yokes.

V-four

Engine layout with two pairs of cylinders arranged at an angle to each other in a 'V' or 'L' shape, commonly 90º.

V-twin

Engine layout with two cylinders arranged at an angle to each other in a V-shape.

Wheelbase

Measurement of length between the points where the front and rear wheels touch the ground.

Yokes

Pair of clamps that attach the telescopic forks to the steering axle which passes through the steering head on the frame. Known as triple trees in the United States.

INDEX

PICTURE CREDITS

All pictures courtesy of Alan Dowds except:

Action Library: 10, 14, 24–25, 44, 62–65, 72, 127, 173, 181, 185, 194–197

Art-Tech/Aerospace: 16–23, 32-34, 35(t), 36–37, 82–83, 100–103, 112–115, 120–123, 128–130, 224–225, 228–231, 236–243, 264–267, 306–309

Roland Brown: 27, 98, 104–107, 110, 116-9, 134–135, 140, 142–143, 146–149, 154–157, 170–172, 178–180, 182–184, 186–189

The author would like to thank the Press and PR departments of all the manufacturers featured in this book for their help in providing technical information and images.